DESERTS

DESERTS
MIRACLE OF LIFE

Jim Flegg

Facts On File

Facts on File, Inc.
460 Park Avenue South, New York
NY 10016.

Library of Congress Cataloging in
Publication Data available on request from
Facts on File.

ISBN 0-8160-2902-4

Facts on File books are available at special discounts when
purchased in bulk quantities for businesses, associations,
institutions or sales promotions. Please call our Special
Sales Department in New York at 212/683-2244
(dial 800/322-8755 except in NY).

10 9 8 7 6 5 4 3 2 1

Typeset by MS Filmsetting Ltd, Frome, Somerset
Printed and bound in Hong Kong

To Caroline
with love

PICTURE CREDITS

Patricia L. Baker: page 6.
Kathryn S. A. Booth: page 36.
British Petroleum: page 154.
Darius Bunch: pages 1, 2–3, 8, 16–17, 23, 38–9, 138.
Jim Flegg: pages 19, 20–1, 27, 35, 43, 53, 55, 56, 66, 70, 71, 72, 79, 85, 89, 97, 118–19, 128, 129 (both), 136 (inset), 136–7, 148.
Robert Harding Picture Library: pages 64–5.
Chris Mattison: pages 82, 100, 102, 104, 105, 106, 108, 121, 124, 133 (lower), 135.
Bruce Mullins: pages 3 (inset), 12, 32, 50–1, 122, 151.
David Nicolle: pages 24–5, 142–3, 144–5.
Premaphotos Wildlife/K. G. Preston-Mafham: pages 10–11, 13, 14, 28, 30–1, 40, 45, 46, 49, 61, 74–5, 83, 107, 110 (both), 115, 117, 125, 126, 127, 130, 131, 132, 133 (upper), 134.
Wildlight/Carolyn Johns: page 147.
Wildlight/Mark Lang: pages 156–7.
Wildlight/Philip Quirk: pages 58–9.

CONTENTS

A Bactrian camel on the limitless Mongolian desert plains.

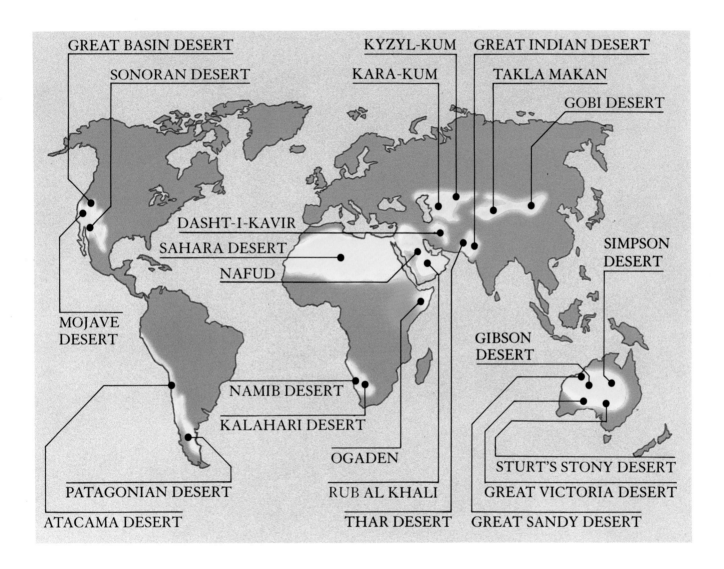

GREAT BASIN DESERT

SONORAN DESERT

KYZYL-KUM

KARA-KUM

GREAT INDIAN DESERT

TAKLA MAKAN

GOBI DESERT

DASHT-I-KAVIR

SAHARA DESERT

NAFUD

SIMPSON DESERT

MOJAVE DESERT

GIBSON DESERT

NAMIB DESERT

KALAHARI DESERT

OGADEN

STURT'S STONY DESERT

PATAGONIAN DESERT

GREAT VICTORIA DESERT

RUB AL KHALI

ATACAMA DESERT

THAR DESERT

GREAT SANDY DESERT

1
A GALLERY OF DESERTS

Desert regions, despite the harshness of their environment, can produce some of the most picturesque scenery in the world. Sometimes the landscape is rugged; often it is attractive in the aesthetic or artistic sense, in the textures created by patterns of light and shadow amongst the sand dunes. There can be a serene beauty in the light of dawn, which, though lost to stark realism in the midday sun, returns, changing by the minute, through a swiftly descending dusk to the unequalled clarity of a starlit desert night. No two deserts are the same, and within any desert lie an infinite number of scenarios. Some are on the grand scale, others much more of a cameo, but all reveal some element of the very special nature of deserts.

NORTH AMERICA – THE GREAT BASIN

Many of the world's deserts are given their visual characteristics by the soils and rocks from which they are formed. Often there is a typical topography – the flatness of the Australian desert regions, for instance; or the land may derive its appearance from a prevalent substrate and its colour – the bleached gold of the dunes in the sandy quarters of the Sahara and the Arabian deserts are good examples. However, this is not so in

Sun, wind and sand erode the toughest of rocks to create spectacular desert scenery, as shown here in the Ahaggar Mountains of central Sahara.

North America, where it is most of all the plant life that gives the desert areas their special character.

A tremendous variety of desert types are contained in that vast tract of inhospitable terrain running in an irregular belt right down the western side of the United States and into Mexico. Its western and eastern boundaries are formed respectively by the north–south ridges of the Sierra Nevada, close to the coast, and by the massif of the Rocky Mountains, sometimes almost 1000 km (some 600 miles) inland. This is the legendary 'Great American Desert', first graphically described to Western geographers by the engineer and explorer Stephen H. Long in the 1820s.

From British Columbia, just north of the Canadian border at about latitude 50°N, south through the Great Sandy Desert of Oregon, the Snake River Desert of Idaho, the Black Rock Desert of Nevada and the Great Salt Lake Desert in Utah, this is 'cold' desert. The typical plant that gives this enormous section of what is sometimes called the Great Basin its character – in both colour and aroma – is the scrubby sagebrush. Grey-green, bristly, low-growing but tangled sometimes to the point of impenetrability, this resin-rich plant dominates the scenery. Its aromatic foliage and distasteful sap are good protective or deterrent measures against insects, so there is little here for entomologists.

Further south still, the Great Basin truly merits classification as 'hot' desert. From the Grand Canyon of the Colorado Desert (where geology and soil colour provide a stunning sight), southwards through Death Valley (one of the hottest places on earth) to the Sonoran Desert of Arizona, the Mojave and Yuma Deserts, and ultimately to the Chihuahua Desert in Mexico, it is the cactus family that stands out. Particularly dominant are massive and spectacular species such as the organ pipe, the prickly pear and, above all, the majestic giant saguaro. Minor players from other plant families on this botanical stage include the yucca or Joshua tree; the tall, spiky sotol and agave, both with saw-edged leaves just as sharp as the real thing; the brittlebrush and creosote shrubs; and the paloverde, Arizona's state tree, at its best when smothered in yellow blossom.

Although plant life is the major distinguishing characteristic, the topography of the landscape also has a role to play in shaping the appearance of the North American deserts. The 'bedrock' of American deserts is comparatively young – far, far younger than that of Australia, for example. The flatter land is thought to be only just over 2 million years old, the mountain ridges along the margins probably resulting from upfolding of the earth's crust perhaps no more than 5 million years ago. Such relative youth means that the weathering of the rock by erosion and fragmentation is, in geological terms, fresh: so the topography is angular, with sharp edges – nowhere more clearly illustrated than in the Grand Canyon.

Beneath, or pushing through, the characteristic plants within Long's 'Great American Desert' can be found examples of most of the classic forms of desert (see Chapter 2). There are massive plateau areas, deeply eroded by gorges and ravines. There are bolson deserts, based on long-dried-out salt lakes and mudflats. There are rocky hamada-type deserts, with extensive exposed rock surfaces often clad with boulders or gravel, featuring flat mesas and the isolated, vertical-sided buttes beloved by the makers of Western movies. And in the Yuma Desert of Arizona and the monster dunes of El Gran Desierto, just over the Mexican border at the head of the Gulf of California, there are even sand deserts with extensive dune systems forever on the move – the ergs of the Sahara and Arabia.

Cactus plants, varied in size and form, dominate the vegetation of Arizona's Sonoran Desert.

SOUTH AMERICA – THE ATACAMA AND THE PATAGONIAN DESERTS

The two major desert areas of South America are very different from each other in appearance. Between them they illustrate many of the geographical and climatic principles associated with desert formation.

The more northerly, the Atacama Desert, lies mainly in Peru and Chile and occupies a long, narrow section of the west coast of the continent, stretching almost from the Equator south to about latitude 20° – a run of some 3000 km (1875 miles). Only rarely does this coastal strip of desert exceed 200 km (125 miles) in width, essentially the distance between its two natural boundaries, the Pacific Ocean to the west and the immense north–south cordillera of the Andes to the east. Both these physical features contribute to the climatic factors which create the desert zone.

The Andes, which rise to heights exceeding 6000 m (19,700 ft), effectively block the passage of any moist winds coming from the east and carrying the extremely humid tropical air of the Amazon Basin. Such easterly winds that do pass over the ridge shed their moisture content as rainfall when they are lifted by the Amazonian Andes foothills.

Running close inshore to the west is the famous Humboldt Current, which rises in the Antarctic and in most years flows strongly almost as far north as the Equator; here warm tropical ocean currents deflect it out into the Pacific, westward towards the Galapagos

Many desert regions contain mountains, contrasting in form to sandy or stony plains, but equally inhospitable to life.

Islands. This cold current and the cold air above it create what is called a thermal inversion. Westerly breezes coming in off the Pacific are unusual, but should they occur, the chill of the thermal inversion dries the air by extracting any remaining moisture and condensing it into insubstantial and often short-lived mists. Sometimes stratus clouds are built in the warmer, higher air layers – but these clouds produce no rain.

The Atacama is perhaps the driest desert in the world: much of it endures continuous drought for many years in succession. Nor is there much in the way of deep subterranean moisture reserves, and such boreholes as do exist are heavily contaminated with the element boron, which is damaging to plants and wildlife. Geologically this is a mineral-rich area, particularly in its deposits of sodium nitrate. These, together with the seabird guano gathered from the offshore breeding islands, made it the centre of the agricultural fertilizer industry; 3 million tons of nitrate were exported annually. But the steady development of synthetic fertilizers from the 1920s onwards caused the collapse of the industry and the abandonment of mining settlements deep in the desert.

Despite its subtropical location and its categorization as a 'hot' desert, the Atacama is far from being one of the warmest: mean hot-season temperatures rarely exceed 20°C (68°F). In appearance it is not the uniform, arid coastal plateau or shelf that might be expected. Over a considerable proportion of its length a range of low mountains rises, sometimes almost sheer from the sea. Behind cliffs 450 m (1475 ft) high, rocky crags tower to some 2000 m (over 6500 ft). Beyond this, in turn, stretches a valley corridor whose other boundary is the foothills of the Andes.

Much of this region consists of salt pan, with intrusions of alluvial fans (see p. 36) from the mountains. Most of these fans, and substantial areas of the desert itself, are pebble or gravel, but there are some sand desert areas where dune systems have developed. Further south, this coastal belt becomes a raised plateau at about 1000 m (nearly 3300 ft); in some parts occasional volcanic cones give it a 'moonscape' appearance. At its south-eastern extreme is a high-altitude arid plateau, called the Puna de Atacama, set in the valley between the eastern and western ridges of the Andean cordillera at about 4000 m (13,100 ft).

Vegetation is extremely sparse over the Atacama, restricted mainly to deep-rooting desert grasses and scrub. Some members of the cactus family have established footholds, but rarely do they become the visual

The cactus wren, one of an astonishing array of desert specialists.

feature that they are in North America. The scrub is usually mesquite, interrupted occasionally by the pallid branches of a stunted paloverde tree.

Animal life, too, is very scarce. Often the only movement is the infrequent passage high overhead of an Andean condor, soaring on broad wings and looking – as a carrion feeder – not for signs of life but for those of death. In the cactus areas, cactus wrens breed, while in more open but not totally desiccated areas one of the South American endemic families, the oven birds, are characteristic. They build domed mud nests, often on a stump or post, that are proof to a degree against predatory reptiles seeking eggs or nestlings and that offer some thermal insulation – their own adobe haciendas!

As in several other desert regions, probably the dominant animal group (though even they are far from numerous) consists of lizards. South America is home to almost all the species of *Iguana*: several colourful, pot-bellied, smaller species occur in the Atacama, along with the giant species called colloquially *the* iguana. At almost 2 m (6½ ft) long it is quite dragon-like in appearance, though in reality it is a comparatively timid scavenger rather than a ferocious predator. Offshore on the Galapagos Islands, 960 km (600 miles) west of Ecuador, lives another large member of this family of lizards – the marine iguana. This unique creature is the only lizard that lives routinely in the sea, diving through the surf for its seaweed food.

Further to the south, and this time on the east coast of South America, is the Patagonian Desert. It is classified as a 'cold' desert: even during its warmest months the central region only has an average maximum temperature of just over 12°C (54°F), while in the colder months sub-zero temperatures coupled with icy winds and snowfalls are regular features.

The Patagonian Desert lies between latitudes 40° and 50°S – the 'Roaring Forties' and 'Furious Fifties' beloved of old sailing ship captains anxious to make a swift return to Europe with their cargoes. Only a few degrees of latitude nearer the Equator the prevailing winds come from the east, blowing out of the Atlantic on to the eastern shores of Brazil and Argentina. South of about latitude 40° the winds are stronger, often gale force, and blow on to the narrow 'horn' of South America from the west, out of the Pacific.

In consequence, the Patagonian Desert lies in the rain shadow of the Andes as they taper towards Tierra Del Fuego and Cape Horn. These westerlies have blown across the cold Humboldt Current and have already lost as offshore mists much of the water content they gathered during the long sweep across the milder expanses of the Pacific. What little moisture remains condenses as the air rises over the slopes of the Andes, falling as light rain or swirling mists on the forested mountainsides. And so the air sweeping down on to the Patagonian plateau from the west is very dry.

The Patagonian Desert landscape is dominated by a series of extensive plateaux, rising from about 100 m (330 ft) above sea level close to the Atlantic coast in a series of giant steps to the base of the Andes, where the tableland lies at 1500 m (around 5000 ft). In some places the plateau is covered in extensive salt pans, in others by sheets of basaltic lava. In yet others, intrusions of basalt penetrating through the flat sedimentary rocks form isolated, rugged clusters of mountains – inselbergs – that dominate the surrounding landscape.

The plateau land is cut by many broad valleys with steep, rugged, cliff-like walls. Only a few still carry a trace of water in the form of streams of melting snow run-off from the high Andes, although in the distant past all of them would have been cut by torrential rivers of the same origin. Where there is still a little water, stunted shrubs and trees grow along the margins. Elsewhere, the vegetation is scanty and steppe-like, lacking trees but with widely spaced patches of dense, waist-deep thicket. Further south, rough grassland and saltbush scrub give way eventually to even sparser desert grassland.

Long a target for hunters, an alert guanaco prepares to flee in the Atacama Desert.

Reptiles are numerous here, but the most characteristic animal life consists of mammals. The mara or Patagonian hare would perhaps be expected, as almost all desert habitats outside Australia have a representative hare. More fascinating in anatomy and habits, and endemic to South America, are the armadillos. With their plates of horny armour, including a shield on the pig-like snout, their speed across the plain as they race away, and the speed with which their powerful forelegs dig them into the safety of a sheltering burrow when cornered, armadillos typify Patagonia. So too does the guanaco, llama-like and clad in long, fine hair that produces excellent insulating warmth for the guanaco itself in winter, or, when plucked and woven into a blanket, weatherproofing day and night for humans. Once hunted to the brink of extinction, guanacos are making a slow come-back based on herds grazing undisturbed in the most remote quarters of the Patagonian Desert.

NORTH AFRICA – THE SAHARA

Greatest of the world's deserts without question, the Sahara occupies almost the northernmost third of Africa in a belt stretching from the Atlantic Ocean in the west to the Red Sea in the east, and 2000 km (1250 miles) or more from north to south. Not only is it the largest, but also overall the hottest desert on earth, and one of the driest. Regular rains are unknown, torrential storms rare, and in some areas the amount of moisture provided by dew exceeds that received annually as rainfall.

Everything is on a grand scale. What seem to be almost limitless flat or gently undulating plateau areas are interrupted, almost rudely it seems, by occasional impressively jagged mountain ranges. Water is, of course, scarce, limited to a few pools conserved in the shade and slightly lower temperatures of mountain gorges, and to oases, bright green havens of plant and animal refuge against the yellows, buffs and browns of the desert, deriving their moisture from subterranean reserves which mostly reflect moister conditions in times long past.

Physically, although their occurrence is strikingly piecemeal rather than orderly, there are three major desert types to be found in the Sahara. These are hamada (or hammada) – rocky highlands, ranges and plateaux, some exceeding heights of 3300 m (11,000 ft), often deeply dissected and usually spectacularly weathered; reg – vast, seemingly endless areas of silty gravel and stones, deposited aeons ago by flood waters, but today providing by far the best surface for travel by all-terrain vehicle; and erg – the sand dune areas which, though extensive, cover the smallest area of the three desert types and are far from being typical of the Sahara, as is popularly imagined.

Limitless, vast and wide open though the Sahara may be, it is not monotonous, although the enormous distances impose additional hardships and hazards on those humans who venture into its interior. The bedrock here is of extreme antiquity, consisting of gneiss, schists and granite. These crystalline metamorphic rocks were created under the massive pressures and extreme temperatures of the earth's formative period, some thousands of millions of years ago. Most lie deeply buried, but subsequent turbulence and flexing of the earth's crust forced folds of rock upwards to create the apparently random ruggedness of the Ahaggar and Tibesti Mountains. In places there are also extensive exposed hard, smooth surfaces, with only the occasional cracks or fissures formed as the rock cooled down, or at a later date was eroded by wind, sun and probably water.

Overlying this is a mantle of sedimentary rocks, usually limestone and sandstone, mostly laid down in the geological eras of the Tertiary epoch that began some 65 million years ago; at this time successive shallow seas, lakes and sandy beaches covered the area. The limestone is composed of the fossilized remains of countless millions of planktonic creatures that swam in the warm seas of that period. Mudstones and sandstones were laid down second-hand, as it were, created from silt or granite fragments resulting from the weathering of the bedrock, redistributed as sediments by the waters of the day, and recemented into rock by geological processes equivalent to the fossilization of plant and animal remains.

The sandstone landscape differs markedly from the older granite. The rock is much softer, and has been shaped by erosion into an infinite variety of forms including mushrooms. Elsewhere, it has been cut into fairytale castle turrets and battlements, separated by deep, narrow canyons carved out by water rich in gravel fragments. Often the sandstone surface shows the striking dark burnish of what is called desert varnish.

Again in the long-distant past, volcanic activity of major proportions played its part in shaping the scenery of the modern Sahara. The Ahaggar, Tibesti and Air massifs all show the outcome of eruptions in Pliocene times some two million years ago. Plentiful streams of rock lava flowed over the surface rocks, and in places deeply fissured polygon-shaped columns of basalt foot the much bulkier blocks of pure granite above. Elsewhere in these regions, volcanic 'plugs' protrude through the surface bedrock. These are the cores of extinct volcanic cones, left standing as pillars or chimneys of solidified lava when the softer rock and ash of the cones themselves eroded away. These mountain ranges, with various extensions or promontories running north or south, form what amounts to a central east–west mountainous spine to the Sahara.

Stretching away in all directions from the mountains and the high plateaux are extensive stone and gravel plains – the regs. Close to the foothills of the mountain massifs these plains are covered in large stones, rocks and even boulders, in a very rough 'pavement' that may constitute quite hard going for vehicle or camel. Further away from the mountains the reg is smoother, the much finer pebbles and gravel of which it is composed smoothed and rounded by the passage of

Overleaf *The windswept ripples give a Saharan dune a special textural beauty.*

water: this is the ideal landscape for desert travellers.

In places the rock plateaux, the hamada, remain clear of gravel, but are cut up to a greater extent by narrow ravines – tassilis, as the Tuareg people call them – and the surroundings of the Ahaggar. At its extreme, this produces a network of canyons of various widths and depths, known as chebkas. At the edge of the plateau are some free-standing rock pillars or table-plateaux, rising sheer from the plain. In America these would be called buttes – here they are gours.

The sand seas or ergs occupy around one quarter of the Saharan surface. The desert winds are continously creative amongst the dunes, sculpting lines and curves of sand, basically stable in the long term, but changing by the day in their finer detail. In places, the dunes may reach 300 m (1000 ft) in height, and the total quantity of sand involved is unimaginable. Although they are not typical of this desert as a whole, the ergs – and the verdant palm-fringed oases they contain – are amongst the most picturesque of all Saharan landscapes.

SOUTHERN AFRICA – THE NAMIB AND THE KALAHARI

Despite the fact that they are close together in the south-western corner of Africa, there are enormous differences between the Namib and the Kalahari. The Namib is far more the true desert of the two. Until comparatively recently much of what was known about it was derived from travellers' tales, the stories of fabulous wealth gathered by those lucky enough to find diamonds on the beach *and* to escape from the dangers of this remote and hostile coast. However, the past few decades have seen far more detailed exploration of the Namib, not just by geologists in search of its mineral wealth but by biologists seeking to unravel its unique ecology.

Bounded by the Cunene River in the north and the Orange River in the south, the narrow coastal strip of the Namib Desert extends from latitude 17°S to 28°S. Even at its widest this arid belt hardly exceeds 120 km (75 miles), and for much of its length it is only 40 km (25 miles) wide or less, backed by the foothills of the rather better-watered 'subdesert' plateau between the Namib and the Kalahari. Much of the northern half of the Namib is composed of rock overlain with gravel, while the southern half is predominantly sandy desert with some areas of spectacular dune systems, some of them 300 m (1000 ft) or more high. The rock-strewn northern coast is frequently shrouded in fog and subject to onshore winds; this makes it an especially treacherous strip of coast, particularly for sailing vessels.

This northern mixture of heavily wind-eroded rock and extensive stone or gravel pans and plains is called the Kaokoveld. It is the richest area for gems, particularly diamonds, which in the extensive gravel banks are from time to time exposed and dispersed by torrential rains. Such wildlife as there is gathers near permanent waters; it is particularly rich at Etosha. The dune system further south may appear barren in the extreme, but it is here that many plants and creatures unique to the Namib are found, having evolved lifestyles that allow them to cope with their harsh surroundings.

Rains are rare, however, and between the Cunene and Orange Rivers run a handful of normally dry, sandy river beds. Should it rain, flash floods occur, causing considerable further erosion – but the water vanishes as quickly as it came. The Namib is sheltered from any easterly winds by its mountainous hinterland, and before that by the dry plains of the Kalahari: these two features effectively dry out any moisture in winds originating over the Indian Ocean. But all along its length the Namib is exposed to those onshore winds so dreaded by sailors. They blow on to the Namib from the Atlantic, but the plentiful moisture they carry is not deposited in rainfall as they reach the hills just behind the coast; instead dense clouds of rolling fog are produced, adding to the navigators' worries.

The reason is the presence close inshore of the extremely cold Benguela Current, generated in the Antarctic – a close parallel to the Humboldt Current off the west coast of South America. Crossing this band of cold water causes the water vapour in the air to condense into fog, creating air as humid as anywhere on earth. These fogs are an almost nightly event in the Namib, penetrating inland as much as 30 km (about 20 miles), and they have a profound effect on the survival of wildlife in an area otherwise devoid of moisture for months or years at a time.

The 'primary producers' of the Namib, those plants and animals on which other wildlife depends, have been selected by the natural processes of evolution for their ability to trap wind-borne fragments of decaying plant life blown down from the interior and to extract the moisture from the fog. Here live tenebrionid or darkling beetles that stand 'on their heads' at night on

From small 'dust devils' to full-blown tornadoes, winds play a major part in shaping deserts.

the dune crests, so that mist condensing on their bodies and limbs runs down into their mouths as water. It is also the home of the strange, dried up welwitschia, a plant unique to the Namib and one that may live, despite hardships, for two thousand years or more.

Not far to the east, separated from the Namib by the high plateaux of Nananib, Hanam and Tiras, mostly exceeding 1500 m (5000 ft) above sea level, lies the Kalahari Desert. Far larger than the Namib, the Kalahari dominates most of Botswana and a good deal of eastern Namibia and the northern fringes of South Africa.

For a desert, the Kalahari has a comparatively rich plant life: it supports a reasonable covering of grass species and scrub adapted to dry conditions. So well vegetated and stocked with game is the Kalahari, in fact, that some would argue that this is steppe or bushveld country, not desert. The term 'desert' is clearly open to interpretation; perhaps the best definition of all is that found on a number of old maps: 'land of thirst'.

The Kalahari is an almost featureless sandy plain, lying over 1200 m (4000 ft) above sea level. It undulates gently and has few topographic intrusions other than some rocky ridges round its margins; the extraordinary Okavango Swamp – an 'inland delta' phenomenally rich in wildlife, particularly in the dry season; and occasional fossil river valleys. So secure is the plant cover that the soil has been stabilized, except where over-grazing has denuded the vegetation; where this has happened erosion has taken place and small sand deserts, often with crescent-shaped dunes known as barchan dunes, have formed. Wind and rainfall erosion are minimal in most other areas. In some areas, usually amongst fossil river valleys, various types of salt pan have formed – some largely of clay and not demanding much in the way of salt-tolerance by the plants that colonize them, others appreciably more saline, with white-encrusted surfaces which few plants and even fewer animals can tolerate. But these are very much minor features – dents in a desert landscape that is, unusually, uniformly flat.

Salt-pan conditions following flash floods quickly reduce trees to skeletal form.

ARABIA

Set between the Sahara to the west and the Desert Corridor that stretches from the Iranian Desert as far east as the Gobi, the Arabian peninsula could hardly be anything but desert itself. Apart from comparatively lush and fertile corners to the south-east and south-west, almost the entire landmass – essentially large enough to qualify as a subcontinent – consists of desert. It is perhaps easiest to visualize Arabia as a wedge of cheese lying on its side. The rough, ragged 'rind' rises steeply from the full length of the Red Sea coast, while the bulk of Arabia slopes gently away eastwards as a plateau, eventually sliding into the shallow seas of the Persian Gulf.

Though its wildlife comes both from Africa and Asia on either side, and from Europe to the north, in geological terms Arabia is unequivocally part of Africa. Some 65 million years ago one of the great supercontinents of that time, Gondwanaland, began to break up. Africa, with Arabia firmly attached, drifted north as a section of the earth's crust floating on a semi-molten core; there collided with the northern supercontinent, Laurasia. Arabia took the force of this very gradual impact, the effect being that the eastern margin of the landmass tilted and slid slowly under Asia, beneath what is now Iran. The break with Africa is thought to have taken place about 35 million years ago. A comparatively simple split occurred along a line of weakness, forming a trench which rapidly filled to form the Red Sea. At a very gentle pace, of the order of centimetres per century, the Red Sea continues to widen as the earth's crust evolves.

On the Arabian side of the Red Sea, once the tension was released the Sarawat Mountains reared up, fronted by the Asir and Yemen ranges which run roughly north–south to form the rind of the cheese wedge. As not infrequently occurs during such major upheavals on the earth's crust, volcanic activity was generated. This is reflected in the volcanic craters and cones in the Sarawats, and in the enormous fields of basaltic lava, the Harrats, to be found from Harrar in the north at intervals southwards down to the hinterland of the Asir Mountains behind Mecca.

On the other side of Arabia the shallow Persian Gulf, occupying a much greater area than today and hardly anywhere deeper than 30 m (100 ft), became immensely rich in plankton. When they died, the plankton sank to form thick organic deposits. Trapped and capped by domes of crystalline salt as the shallow seas evaporated during climatic changes, then compressed and covered by sedimentary rocks, these hydrocarbon deposits became the world's richest oilfields, the basis of the prosperity of this superficially barren and hostile landscape. Interestingly, deep in the rocks there are also vast reserves of water, accumulated during long-distant wetter periods in the earth's climatic history.

But above, the landscape is of unrelenting desert from horizon to horizon. Antique maps label the narrow coastal belt abutting the Indian Ocean as 'Arabia Felix', or 'fortunate Arabia', reflecting the fact that it was well-watered and agriculturally productive – at least in parts. To the north on these old maps lay 'Arabia Deserta'. When the great plateau was tilted millions of years ago, it was flooded by the sea. Besides trapping the oil deposits, the resulting sedimentary sea floor became in time the limestone plateau which forms the substrate for much of the Arabian Desert.

Particularly round its southern margin, the plateau may be cut by deep ravines called wadis. Elsewhere, the desert centre may consist of bare, windswept rock, sometimes cut deeply by wadis or interrupted by rocky escarpments – always ruggedly weathered by intense heat, sand-blasting and occasional rain, and sometimes eroded into fantastic shapes. More commonly, rock, sand or gravel deserts extend as far as the eye can see. The sand and gravel overlying the rocky plateau are largely derived from the wind- and sun-induced weathering of the mountain ridges along the western side of the peninsula; this weathering process adds to the starkly jagged outlines of mountains that are, in geological terms, comparatively young. Sweeping into the interior of Arabia Deserta, carried by the wind – especially the seasonal shamal, which blows in December, and again in May and June – and by floods following torrential rains, these mobile deposits give the Arabian Desert its essential characteristics.

Much of the southern third of the peninsula – the sinisterly and suitably named 'Empty Quarter' – is occupied by an immense sandy desert, the Rub al Khali. So large and old-established is the Rub al Khali (estimates suggest that it has existed for two million years) that the linear dune system has giant sand valleys some 200 km (125 miles) long, running between dune ridges with crests 330 m (1100 ft) high. Sand desert also occurs further north, in the An Nafud – altogether on a smaller scale but with spectacular crescent-shaped dunes. Along the coasts of Arabia, the rises and falls of sea levels which have helped give rise to the oil deposits have also created salt or salt-flat deserts up to 30 km

(about 20 miles) wide. These are called sabkha – a name derived from the Arabic for 'salt pan'. They are treacherous, as their crystalline, salty crust overlies a soft, muddy quagmire – but not as treacherous as the murderous quicksands that occur in the Rub al Khali.

Crescentic dunes, or barchans, backs to the wind, typify the vast sandy deserts of Arabia's 'Empty Quarter'.

Overleaf   Many deserts like the Sahara have oases, scattered sources of permanent water invaluable to man and wildlife.

THE DESERT CORRIDOR

From the shores of the Caspian Sea in the west, a vast, sinuous tract of deserts and parched, wind-blown steppe sweeps across central Asia to Mongolia and western China. Often, and appropriately, called the Desert Corridor, it embraces desert areas from Iran and Turkestan, the Kara-Kum and the Kyzyl-Kum, the Takla Makan, the arid highlands of Tibet and, at its eastern extremities, a cluster of Chinese and Mongolian deserts – the Alashan, the Ordos and (perhaps the best-known) the Gobi. Fittingly enough, the name 'Gobi' is derived from the Mongolian for a 'waterless place'.

This is land-locked wilderness country, set in the dry heart of the largest landmass on earth, Eurasia, equidistant from the Arctic Ocean in the north and the Indian Ocean in the south, the Atlantic Ocean in the west and

the Pacific Ocean in the east. The only interruptions to this broad belt of desert, which in places is over 2000 km (1250 miles) across, are the Tien Shan range and the Pamirs. Prevailing winds tend to be northerly, devoid of moisture for much of the time because of the arid chill of the Arctic where they arise. Winds from other quarters have their moisture effectively removed both by the mountain ranges (such as the Himalayas) between the nearest ocean and the desert corridor, and during the tremendous journey overland before they blow into the desert interior.

Set between latitudes 35°N and 50°N, this corridor is classified as a 'cold desert'. In the Gobi, seasonal temperature extremes range from −40°C (−40°F) in January to 45°C (about 115°F) in July. There are distinct seasons. During the long winter temperatures are held low by winds sweeping down uninterrupted

23

from the frozen wastes of the Arctic Circle, and some areas are heavily snow-covered. This is followed by a brief spring, with rising temperatures; occasional brief and often insubstantial rains combine with snow melt-water to provide the moisture needed for a spectacular flush of growth and a brief rainbow of bloom from the desert plants, many of which are ephemerals. Summers are dry and warm, sometimes hot, with maximum temperatures over 35°C (95°F) in places, and staggering temperature differences between day and night – falls of as much as 40°C (about 100°F) in twelve hours are on record. Autumn is but a brief respite, sometimes with a little rain, before the extreme cold and snowfalls of winter set in once again.

The Desert Corridor varies considerably in its geology, but rather less in its structure. For much of the time, the vista is of an endless, gently undulating plateau, sometimes of sand, sometimes gravel, sometimes rock and clay. In some areas there are deeper dry river valleys, and occasional rocky mountain ridges penetrate the tableland. In a few parts of the Gobi, the clay plains are interrupted by table-topped mesas or buttes. Generally speaking, the northern half of this long corridor is of dry clays, sometimes rich in minerals such as gypsum; it is generally more stony towards the east, where the shallow undulations may be filled with stones or gravel. Between the Caspian and Aral Seas, at the western extremity of the corridor, the region is basically sandy, and the Kara-Kum, Kyzyl-Kum, Takla Makan, Alashan and Ordos are all sandy deserts where extensive dune systems have developed overlying clay pans.

On the broader plains there may be huge saucer-shaped depressions, the relics of major lakes in times past. Sometimes their edges are stepped, an indication that the lakes dried up irregularly. Elsewhere, in some of the clay-based valleys, salt marshes still persist, with their characteristic salt-tolerant plant life. Throughout the region vegetation is extremely sparse, the largest plants usually being tamarisk bushes. Two smaller shrubs, both saxouls, are typical of the plants here – both have special ways of preventing moisture loss. One, the white saxoul, characterizes the sandy deserts and has much-reduced leaves; it relies largely on chlorophyll within the stem cells for photosynthesis – the manufacture of food by converting carbon dioxide and water into carbohydrate. The other, the black saxoul, is completely leafless, ensuring that moisture is retained which would otherwise be lost during the normal process of transpiration – evaporation of water through the leaves, to encourage the sap to rise.

This flat landscape with its scanty vegetation is the home of the double-humped bactrian camel, of the onager or wild ass, and of some sixteen different species of jerboa; these rodents range in size from mouse almost to rabbit, all with long, kangaroo-like hind legs. Knowledge of this group of mammals has increased considerably in recent years, but as they are extremely fast-moving, shy and nocturnal in their habits, it may be that even more species remain to be discovered. Since European eyes and ears first heard of the Gobi and saw examples of its life in the accounts of Marco Polo, as long ago as the thirteenth century, there has been a long interval of silence. Now modern geographers and biologists are adding to our understanding of this region at an extraordinary pace.

AUSTRALIA

If just one word was to be chosen to describe the vast arid centre of Australia, that word would be 'flat'. To the traveller standing on the ground almost anywhere in the Australian desert, the distant shimmering horizon is usually as flat as the ground beneath his feet. Even in the much clearer air of dawn, only rarely is it possible to find a viewpoint where rocky hills disrupt the skyline. It is dispiriting country for explorers, and immensely difficult terrain for the nomadic native peoples, the Aborigines, when it comes to remembering navigational landmarks for their irregular migrations.

Flatness, though, should not be taken as synonymous with uniform, for the Australian desert is far from that. To fly across the country reveals the changes in colour, themselves often reflecting the nature of the ground surface. The narrow western coastal belt of green, or rather an already parched-looking grey-green, relieved only by the occasional dark green ribbon of mangroves along a coastal creek, soon gives way to the pallid sandy or sometimes reddish-green of land grazed by cattle and sheep as well as by the native kangaroos. This settled outback is criss-crossed by tracks and punctuated very occasionally by a homestead or ranch, newer corrugated iron buildings glinting in the sun, and almost inevitably with a red-earth landing strip close by.

Gradually this steppe habitat becomes sandier, sometimes reddish, sometimes yellowish, and soon the dune desert lies beneath the airborne traveller. At the margin the dunes are in a chaotic jumble, but soon the choppy waves become more stable and immensely long, linear dunes appear, sometimes totally devoid of any vegetation, but more often with plants like spinifex on their

Widely spaced plants give little indication that the volcanic soil is packed with roots seeking any available moisture.

flanks and more robust scrub like mulga in the valleys between. From then on, occasional dune deserts are interspersed with rocky deserts; the major dune area falls in the Simpson Desert, where the Northern Territory and the states of Queensland and South Australia abut. To the west the dune systems run east–west, but by the centre their alignment is more south-east–north-west, thanks to the prevailing wind.

The rock desert in central Australia does show some variation in topography; it is interrupted by craggy ranges like the Macdonnells, the Musgraves and the Everards, and by extraordinary rocks of deep spiritual significance to the Aborigines, like the Olgas, and Ayres Rock or Uluru, which are quite staggeringly beautiful at dawn and sunset. In places, dressed in scant, scrubby vegetation, the rock desert seems like fossilized dune country, so linear are its weather-worn, sand-blasted, hump-backed ridges. Further east, Sturt's Stony Desert recalls in its name the explorer to whom its sharp-edged flints gave so much trouble. This region signals a return to the flat lands, the gibber country, made of stones polished and faceted like giant gems.

Between the Everards and Sturt's Stony Desert lies Lake Eyre, surrounded by rock and sand bearing the imprint of the antique watercourses that come to life perhaps only once or twice in a decade to fill the lake with strongly brackish, saline water. For much of the time Lake Eyre is an irregular crust of salt and sand about 80 km (50 miles) long, lying perhaps 15 m (50 ft) below sea level and blinding white when seen from a distance. When it is flooded, this huge lake, together with numerous adjacent lakes, pools and billabongs, forms a fabulous area for wildlife. To the east of Lake Eyre lie the North Flinders ranges, then the Murray-Darling Basin and the outback of Victoria and New South Wales, separated by the Great Dividing Range from the surburban civilization of the green eastern coastal belt with its lush vegetation. But the relentless reds, fawns and buffs of the centre – often called the 'red centre' – are themselves from time to time relieved. Those irregular rains that fill Lake Eyre with birds, shrimps, frogs and fish have an immediate impact on the landscape, clearly visible from the air, as the desert vegetation, parched or dormant for so long, springs into life in a riot of colour.

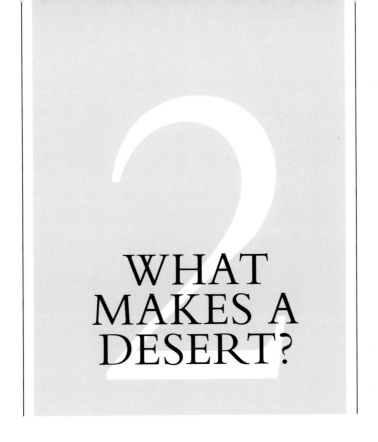

WHAT MAKES A DESERT?

The word 'desert' immediately conjures up the mental image of a hot and arid landscape. This image is usually formed in some detail – the picture is in full colour, with vast expanses of pale sandy to reddish soils. These mental images may well include sweeping, crescent-shaped dunes, reminiscent of an ocean but with its massive, rolling waves frozen in sand. Perhaps the background will be of sunbaked rocks or crags, or of mountain ranges, heavily sculpted and eroded by the weather, but devoid of plant life. The sky will be a hard, brilliant blue, and the intense heat of a burnished bronze sun can almost be felt. There will be few plants, but what there are will be clearly recognizable as either tall, spiny cacti or palms. In most minds, this image will contain no animals: if it does, the chances are high that they will be camels, possibly accompanied by a heavily robed driver.

How does this vision compare with reality? Despite the fact that few of us have seen true desert conditions, the popular image contains much that is authentic. Depending on how a desert is defined, deserts occupy between one-fifth and one-third of the earth's land surface – which astonishes most people. Perhaps

because they are so widespread, but more probably because their climatic conditions are so extreme, most of the major desert areas are well known to us all. But how well known and documented are they in detail – and indeed just what *is* a desert?

THE GEOGRAPHICAL CRITERIA

Surprisingly, this is far from easy to answer. Geographers and climatologists differ in their views, and biologists of varying disciplines also wish to have a say. But most would agree that 'desert areas' are those with less than 250 mm (10 in.) of rainfall on average during the year.

Sometimes this rain may follow a seasonal pattern, but more often it falls in the form of sudden, torrential storms. In some years there may be several storms, in others none – so the 'average' must be a long-term one; parts of the Atacama Desert in Chile, for instance, had no recorded rain between 1570 and 1971. The Namib Desert easily fulfils the minimum rainfall criterion, but receives some additional moisture in the form of overnight mists sweeping in off the Atlantic. A number of plants and small animals in the region have evolved special strategies which allow them to capitalize on this additional water source (see p. 121).

Surprisingly, too, vast tracts of the polar regions fall within this definition. It is not so appropriate to the North Pole, which is essentially a sheet of ice floating on

The Atacama Desert of South America – created by oceanic currents and winds.

the Arctic Ocean; but it is certainly so in Antarctica. Where, despite the vast mass of water locked up in the icecap covering the rocky continent beneath, the average annual rainfall is well within the 250 mm (10 in.) limit.

Climatologists would add a further criterion based on the rate of evaporation, or on a 'Moisture Index' derived from it. In deserts evaporation rates are extremely high, and normally associated with very low humidities and very little cloud cover.

Temperature, though obviously a vital part of the definition of a desert, is more difficult to categorize. On the one hand, daytime air temperatures touching 58°C (136°F) in the Libyan Sahara and 57°C (135°F) in the aptly named Death Valley in North America are on record, and the soil surface temperature may reach as high as 80°C (176°F). At the other extreme, for half the year the average temperature of the Mongolian Desert is below freezing point at 0°C (32°F). And in Antarctica winter mean temperatures may fall as low as −30°C (−22°F) and below, while in summer only for a few weeks will day temperatures exceed 5°C (41°F).

So since climatic characteristics common to all deserts are difficult to determine, a subjective definition may be as good as any other. A desert can be described as an empty, arid region, capable of supporting comparatively few – and highly specialized – forms of plant and animal life. The soils are thin and wind-blown, lacking humus and general fertility. Normally much more moisture is lost through evaporation than falls as rain. Rainfall itself is usually irregular, with periods of drought often exceeding a year. If Antarctica is excluded on the basis that it is a special and atypical place, a further note can be added to this description of what constitutes a desert. The aridity and heat are so excessive that in most years it is impossible to grow any crops, although seasonal or nomadic pastoralism may be possible if, following the rains, enough vegetation grows to provide grazing for flocks and herds.

DIFFERENT TYPES OF DESERT
With the exception of Antarctica (a special case best put on one side for consideration elsewhere), there are about a dozen major desert regions around the globe (see p. 7), and they can helpfully be divided into two types. Hot deserts are characterized by high daytime temperatures year-round, though at night

Cacti typify the desert regions of North and South America.

temperatures may fall to below 10°C (50°F) or even below freezing from daytime maxima often exceeding 40°C (104°F). The major areas in this category are the Sahara, Namib/Kalahari, Arabian and Iranian Deserts, the complexes of deserts in south-western North America (Sonoran, Mojave, Colorado and so on), and the Atacama and Australian Deserts. Cold deserts are characterized by having hot summers counterbalanced by relatively, and sometimes extremely, cold winters. They include the desert complex in western North America (often known as the Great Basin), and the Patagonian, Turkestan and Gobi Deserts.

In terms of size, the Sahara is by far the largest desert at about 8·5 million sq km (3·3 million sq miles) and currently still increasing; it occupies roughly one-third of Africa – an area about as large as the entire USA. Next come the Arabian and Australian Deserts at about 1·5 million km (600,000 sq miles) each, the Gobi at 1 million sq km (390,000 sq miles), Patagonian, Kalahari and Turkestan at around 0·5 million sq km (19,300 sq miles) each, and finally the Sonoran, Namib and others at 0·3 million sq km (13,300 sq miles) or less.

In contrast to popular belief, sand is not commonplace in deserts. Most often small rocks, pebbles or loose gravel form the surface layer, or occasionally more or less bare rock, though often fissured: only 15 per cent of the world's desert surface consists of pure sand,

Winter snowfall in the butte country of the Great Basin 'cold' desert of Monument Valley, Utah.

and the bulk of it is found in the Sahara and Arabia.

Desert landscapes have traditionally been divided into five types – sand, stony, rock, plateau and mountain – despite the great variety of their more detailed aspects. True sand deserts, composed of vast areas of linear dune systems, or simply an undulating 'sand sea', are called ergs in the Sahara, koums in Turkestan. Stony deserts are comparatively level gravel surfaces – called serir in Libya and Egypt, reg in Algeria. Rock deserts normally have bare rock surfaces, a huge pavement kept almost clear of sand or gravel by the wind, and sometimes interrupted by features such as yardangs and zeugen (see p. 37). Plateau deserts (sometimes called mountain-and-bolson deserts – or, aptly, 'badlands' in America) are rocky plateaux, often deeply dissected by wadis and sometimes containing buttes or inselbergs (see p. 36). Finally come the mountain deserts, bare and arid arrays of jagged rock peaks such as the Tibesti and Ahaggar ranges in the Sahara, the mountains of Sinai, Arabia and Baluchistan, and the Macdonnell ranges in central Australia.

WHAT CAUSES DESERT REGIONS?

Essentially, desert areas can only form where one of the most fundamental of all natural processes has been interrupted or suspended for some reason. This is the rainfall cycle, by which water circulates from the sea to the land via the atmosphere before returning to the sea. On this cycle all life on land depends. Evaporation under the influence of the sun's heat lifts water (pure water, for the salt remains in the oceans), against the pull of gravity, into the atmosphere. Onshore winds, blowing from the sea, carry moisture-rich air over the land. Here cooling takes place as the air rises under the influence of upcurrents created by the warmer land surface. This makes the contained water vapour condense, leading to its precipitation as rainfall. This rain provides vital sustenance to plants and animals before making its way back to the sea through the ground water, streams and rivers. The scheme of global air circulation is therefore of major importance so far as deserts are concerned, because an onshore wind can bring water from sea to land whereas an offshore wind cannot.

The global climatic factors that establish and maintain desert areas are complex. A glance at the world map shows that the desert areas occur in two broad belts, running parallel to the Equator and, at 20–30° north and south of it, along the lines of the Tropics of Cancer (to the north) and Capricorn (to the south).

These arid zones develop under the influence of more or less permanent areas of high pressure (or anticyclones) between the trade wind belt beloved of sailing ship captains in days gone by, and the belt of mid-latitude westerly winds. The anticyclones are created when air that is heated over the Equator, where solar radiation is at its highest, rises and spreads north and south before cooling. It then condenses and releases its moisture over the tropical zone. Subsequently this denser air sinks towards the ground, establishing these two subtropical belts of high pressure. The atmospheric physics of this process dictate that these belts occur around 25° of latitude north and south of the Equator. As the air sinks groundwards it creates winds, the 'easterly trades' that blow, hot and devoid of moisture, across the Sahara, the Middle East and North America. Where these trade winds blow onshore – and, having crossed the sea, they have a higher moisture content – no deserts develop. This is particularly clearly demonstrated in Australia, southern Africa and South America.

At first sight, this appears to be a neat and simple explanation of the occurrence of the world's hot deserts with the world air-circulation pattern as the primary factor. An onshore wind can bring moisture from sea to land, while an offshore wind is unable to do so; and where major landmasses are concerned, any arid areas will tend to occur on the 'lee side' with respect to the prevailing winds.

But there are several other climatic and physical factors to be taken into account, and these create complexities. Sea temperatures influence both the ease with which water can be extracted to the atmosphere, and the global pattern of currents. These are established far from the desert belts – in the case of the Southern Hemisphere, close to the Antarctic Circle itself. Here, powerful currents flowing north from the polar region tend to bring cold water to the western sides of the comparatively few Southern Hemisphere continents, while their eastern coasts are bathed by warmer sea currents that are largely tropical in origin. In addition, steady offshore winds tend to draw cold, deep water up to the surface, while onshore winds tend to do the opposite, pushing warmer surface water close to the land. These warm seas readily release water vapour to the atmosphere by evaporation, boosting the moisture content of the atmosphere on eastern coasts. Cold seas off western coasts tend in contrast to extract water vapour from the atmosphere, condensing it into mists and sea fogs.

The other group of arid lands, the 'cold deserts', are

more a feature of the Northern Hemisphere, which has a much greater landmass compared with ocean than does the Southern Hemisphere. Here physical geography or topography plays its part. In the heartland of these massive northern continents, around latitude 40°N, the cold deserts form, including those in the United States and, most dramatic of all, the Desert Corridor of central Asia. This stretches from about longitude 40°E to longitude 120°E, approaching one-quarter of the earth's circumference. These deserts often become established in massive shallow basins, in the rain shadow of mountains. Moisture-rich air, carried on prevailing winds, rises over these ranges, releasing its water in the form of condensation and then rain. Once the summits have been passed, it is arid air that sweeps onwards, creating desert conditions.

ICE AGES AND GLOBAL WARMING

Considerable debate surrounds the longer-term history of desert regions and their influence on the plant and animal life of this planet. One argument suggests that, through much of the earth's history, its climate has remained generally warm and mild. Only during the various ice ages has this benign climate been interrupted. These interruptions produced not only the much lower temperatures expected but also severe aridity because so much of the global water, particularly the atmospheric moisture, was 'locked up' in the gigantic icecaps at the poles and elsewhere. It is thought that these icecaps had a profound effect on both oceanic currents and atmospheric air circulation, producing huge and arid high-pressure regions in temperate and subtropical zones.

The last major period of glaciation occurred only some twenty thousand years ago, and some climatologists suggest that the earth is at present only two-thirds of the way from a period of maximum coldness to a period of maximum inter-glacial warmth. As the climate improves further, global warming will produce not the expected extension of desert areas, but rather a reduction in their extent as the icecaps shrink and milder, moister, climates prevail.

Though the relationship between periods of arid climate and the various ice ages is generally accepted, another school of thought suggests that this association cannot be the dominant factor in the establishment of what in geological terms is a temporary desert belt. The argument for a permanent arid belt, though varied in extent and location, was set out by J. L. Cloudesley-Thompson and M. J. Chadwick in *Life in Deserts*:

The main meteorological factors determining the pattern and extent of the Earth's climate are themselves determined by the size, shape and movement of the earth and the physical characteristics of its atmosphere. These can have changed very little and thus the position of the arid regions, lying between the trade-wind belt and the belt of the westerlies, created largely by the extratropical region, can only really have shifted north or south within very narrow limits during post-Pliocene times.

In other words, it seems unlikely that, during any past epoch, the earth would have lacked a subtropical arid belt. As climates changed, the desert areas may have expanded or contracted; and the belt may have shifted a few degrees of latitude closer to the Equator during recent glaciation. But it is difficult to substantiate its total disappearance.

This is an area where the arguments are based on scanty or incomplete geological evidence. Much more hard information is needed before the picture can become clearer. It is important, too, that events should be set against a long timescale. Though the earth is currently enjoying an improving climate in an inter-glacial period, this has not been a steady process. For example, there was an unusually warm period between AD 1000 and 1300, when the Greenland discovered by Eric the Red was indeed green; capable of growing temperate crops, it was far from the largely ice-covered country of today. Similarly, unusually cold periods have also occurred: the 'Little Ice Age' of AD 1650–1850 is an example, amply illustrated by the snow and ice in winter scenes painted by numerous artists in what is now regarded as temperate European countryside.

There are parallel uncertainties in the biology of deserts, illustrated nowhere better than by the Sahara. A few decades ago, both popular and scientific belief held that much of Africa, including the Sahara, had been blanketed in forest until the geological Miocene epoch some 20 million years ago. Since that time, the theory went, the region had increasingly dried up to the extent that desert habitats had appeared, which plants and animals from the Asiatic steppes had invaded.

But current thinking re-evaluates the evidence and suggests that Africa has always contained a rich co-existing mixture of habitats including evergreen forest, savanna and desert – much the same as it is today. The arid belt will have shifted slightly north and south, possibly every few thousand years, but Africa will

A sheltered gap in the Macdonnell Range in central Australia. Gouged out by water erosion, this now remains as a valuable permanent water source.

always have had the right habitats to fit its position as a centre of evolution for plants and animals adapted to all these types of environment.

Taking the longer-term view, current concern at the rapid (sometimes tens of kilometres annually) southward extension of the true Sahara Desert into the Saheel – the arid but scantily vegetated sub-desert band stretching across the 'bulge' of Africa – should be tempered by the knowledge that in the past the mobile sand zone has penetrated even further south than at present. And Mediterranean-type woodlands once covered the area well to the south of the Ahaggar Mountains. Similarly, in Australia fossil remains found near the Macdonnell ranges in the currently arid interior indicate that in the (geologically) not too distant past, both more northerly and more southerly plant and animal life have ranged through this region.

THE EFFECTS OF TODAY'S CLIMATE

In a much more immediate way, climatic forces play probably the major role in shaping the visible features of desert areas, giving them both their general physical appearance as well as creating the character of individual deserts or desert zones. These forces are much the same as those that shape the landscape anywhere: wind, sunshine, rainfall and, in the cold deserts, even frost and ice. As lack of rain is one of the major determinants of a desert, it may seem strange to list rainfall as a major shaping feature; but it must be remembered that in most deserts the pattern of rainfall is not steady. Though rain may not occur for years, and sometimes not for decades or longer, when it does come it is often in the form of thunderstorms.

On a bone-dry landscape, the erosion and scouring effects of such torrential downpours can be very marked. In sandy deserts, the rain usually drains swiftly away and changes in the landscape are comparatively slight. In contrast, in rocky deserts the downpour drains rapidly into adjacent wadis; these steep-sided, usually dry valleys were initially created and then deepened by just such rainfall erosion. Depending on the size of the downpour it can speedily build up into a flash flood, carrying first sand and gravel and then large rocks and boulders before it; these add to the erosive power of the water as it rushes down the gorge. At the end of most wadis lies an enormous bank of sand and stone – an 'alluvial fan', composed of the sediment deposited by the flash flood as it emerges into a more open landscape and runs out of power. Into this bank the torrent subsides, dropping most of its contents to add to the fan. Any surplus runs on to form muddy lakes of variable size and duration.

These lakes are particularly typical of the Australian desert, lasting long enough to have a major ecological impact and to allow a 'breeding season' for creatures as diverse and unexpected as shrimps, frogs and wildfowl. The lakes may also be saline. Current thinking suggests that the salt content is derived from salt in the atmosphere originating as windborne oceanic spray, and not,

as was believed in the past, leached from the soil by the floodwaters. Most deserts' floods subsequently create a spectacular flush of plant growth and flowering.

Between wadis, most non-mountainous desert areas contain comparatively flat plateaux, varying in extent, called mesas. Should a small area of mesa become isolated by a steadily widening wadi, until it stands as an isolated, flat-topped, steep-sided island in the desert, it is called a butte. Not to be confused with the butte is an isolated hill, often craggy in outline and roughly conical (rather than distinctly flat-topped and vertical-sided), rising from the plain. These inselbergs are often derived from plugs or cores of a different type of rock, perhaps extruded aeons ago through the sedimentary rocks from the earth's molten core, and showing very different weathering characteristics from the buttes.

In sandy deserts the impact of heat and cold produces little or at best minimal evident effect, but in rocky

The grazing livestock of pastoral tribes contribute to erosion both by overgrazing and because their well-worn tracks to waterholes destroy the soil surface.

deserts the impact is much greater. In cold deserts winter frosts, and particularly occasional rainfall that is subsequently frozen by overnight cold, fragment rocks; naturally, the softer or more easily split the type of rock, the greater the impact. Water seeps into minute crevices and on freezing expands, steadily forcing the rocks apart just as effectively as a steel wedge.

In hot deserts the fragmenting force of temperature is slower and steadier. It is based on the extreme differences between midday heat, when some rock surfaces will reach 70°C (158°F) or 80°C (176°F) and maybe higher, and the cool of midnight – around freezing point. Although rock does not expand as much as metal under the influence of heat, day after day after day of even minor expansion under the burning sun, followed by contraction in the chill of the night, will gradually weaken the surface layers, causing flaking. Such weaknesses may be exploited or exacerbated by other erosion forces, particularly tropical downpours or abrasive desert winds.

Of all the climatic forces operating in deserts wind may be the most powerful – and not just in shaping the appearance of the landscape. In deserts of all types plants particularly, but also animals, are already under extreme stress because of the high temperature. Their desert adaptation is then even more stringently tested by hot, dry winds which seek to extract the last drop of moisture. But the major physiographic effect of desert winds is to move sand and dust particles – and incidentally, often to remove any vestiges of organic debris that might contribute to soil fertility. It is a vicious circle: the scarcity of desert plants contributes to the ease with which such wind erosion can occur.

At its extremes the wind can do great damage, as in the creation of the 'dust bowl' in the prairie States of North America. Here an arid but reasonably productive area was reduced in the 1930s to genuine desert by a combination of over-cropping, over-cultivating, and devastating tornado winds which whipped off the topsoil and blew it far away. The finest dust may be lifted thousands of metres up into the air and carried vast distances on high-level winds. Such a phenomenon is not unusual in northern Europe, as when cars and windows get covered in a reddish dust caused by rainfall pulling Saharan fine sand out of the upper atmosphere. Much of this fine dust comes to rest in either more temperate or better-watered regions, where it can form the basis of a fertile soil called loess.

Within deserts proper, sandstorms driven by fierce winds can blot out the sun, obliterate roads or tracks, swamp oases or wells with blown sand and generally make life extremely dangerous and unpleasant for both wildlife and humans. No matter how sophisticated their desert adaptations, nor how well organized the human survival strategies, these are hazardous situations. They are perhaps worst for the smaller forms of wildlife. Seeking adequate shelter from the stifling and abrasive blast is essential, but as the storms can persist for many hours, or even days, obtaining water when it is needed may present unsurmountable problems. To emerge is to risk suffocation or to lose track of the refuge. To remain concealed may increase the risk of death from dehydration. If the creatures survive the storm unscathed, they emerge from shelter to find a totally changed landscape.

Normally, though, sand grains are not carried quite so far, and rarely rise more than about 1 m (3 ft) above the ground. Most bounce along the surface before the wind as they travel, literally sand-blasting anything in their path. As the sand grains move along they become much more nearly spherical than sand grains from a river bed, and viewed under the microscope their surface has a ground or frosted glass appearance. Larger, firmly set pebbles which they encounter may be 'polished' by the sand-blasting – on only one side if there is a prevailing wind. If the winds blow from several quarters the pebble may acquire several polished faces, rather like a cut gemstone: in the Sahara, where such occurrences are not infrequent, such pebbles are called dreikanters or ventifacts.

The sand-blasting process also affects major rock faces. Some may become smoothly polished, and often at low levels faults or softer strata within the rock will be eroded to different degrees. Where the strata lie in a near-upright plane the sand-blasting may leave vertical ridges (called yardangs) and grooves of varying widths, similar in appearance to the crevasses in a glacier. If the rock strata are still roughly horizontal, the sand gouges out first the softer rock; in time it also wears away the lower levels even of tougher strata, leaving a slender pedestal supporting a so-called rock mushroom or zeugen. These rocks may be eroded into a variety of strange shapes.

It is in the sandy deserts that, not surprisingly, the effects of the wind are most dramatically evident, producing the landscape of popular imagination. Here wind action creates dunes, of which there are several types. At the margins of the deserts the sand layer is irregular and relatively shallow, and there are often intrusions of rock or scrubby, arid vegetation. Any such obstacle in the path of sand moving before the wind may lead to the formation of a head dune or attached dune. The head dune accumulates in front of the obstacle, sand filling the dead space as the air current rises up and over the crest. Behind the obstacle a more gently sloping tail dune accumulates, the whole structure making an ideal streamlined shape. During sandstorms, a couched camel may remain so motionless that a dune of this kind accumulates round it. More practically, planted vegetation some distance from the fertile moisture and wells of an oasis will collect a head dune. The effect is to help protect the oasis from further incursions of sand.

Almost at the desert margin, barchan or barkhan dunes may form if there is a persistent prevailing wind. Barchan dunes are shaped like the crescent moon and are comparatively small. The horns of the crescent point away from the wind. Sand grains blow up the gentle slopes of the windward side of the barchan before rolling more quickly down the inner slope of the cresent. This rolling exchange of sand grains causes the whole barchan to move horns-first downwind, at speeds varying from the barely detectable to as much as 15 m (50 ft) in a year – still nothing phenomenal compared with the speed with which sandstorms can destroy and recreate the landscape. Sometimes barchans will accumulate into a somewhat ragged line, their horns vanishing as they merge: this creates a transverse dune, and introduces a measure of orderliness into the barchan landscape, which otherwise tends to be rather chaotic.

Longitudinal or seif (or sif) dunes are individually much larger on the whole, and also occupy a far greater proportion of the sandy desert area. Seif dunes are essentially long ridges of sand, set along the line of (parallel to) the prevailing wind, normally with an expanse of bare rock between neighbouring dunes. Side eddies quickly pile back up any sand that slips down to the rocky corridor between the dune lines. Seif dunes may reach and even exceed 40 m (130 ft) in height and 600 m (2000 ft) in width. They can be of almost any length; some of the longest approach 400 km (250 miles) and are perhaps most typical of parts of the Sahara, the Thar Desert in Iran and the western part of the Australian desert. Where wind directions are less well defined, both barchan and seif dune systems may merge into areas of complete sand cover, where individual dunes lose their precise shape to become part of an irregular, wave-like surface.

Two other, related, weathering processes may help

to give desert areas their local characteristics; both are extremely long-term soil-chemical reactions. One, called desert varnish, is a patina akin to the dark reddish brown sheen of maturity achieved by antique furniture. In deserts this patina is accumulated over at least two thousand years, according to the experts. Desert varnish may coat sand, gravel, rocks and cliff faces and even man-made items (hence our ability to date the process), giving them a subdued dark polish. The effect is thought to arise from the very slow weathering and hardening of minute quantities of iron and manganese oxides extracted by overnight dews from the bedrock.

The other weathering process is the formation of what are called duricrusts, first found and described in the Australian desert but now known from many other locations. This would appear to be an even more time-consuming process than desert varnish formation. Again, dew plays an important role as the moisture source, creating hardened or rock-like soil layers which often occur as protective caps on ridges or djebels. Essentially this is a greatly slowed-down soil-producing process, frequently involving calcium carbonate or limestone, and alumina- or silica-rich compounds, often reddish in hue due to the presence of iron oxides.

Seif dunes have a serene beauty.

This, then, is an outline of the genesis of desert areas and of their subsequent shaping by natural climatic forces. What results is a climate and a habitat whose peculiarly harsh and inhospitable conditions have challenged nature to produce the amazing adaptations for survival that feature in the following chapters.

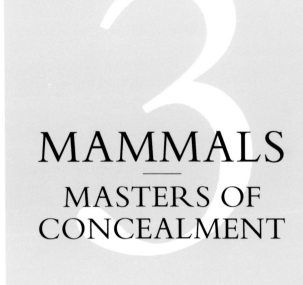

3

MAMMALS
MASTERS OF CONCEALMENT

There is a popular belief that the camel is about the only mammal in the desert. But the reality is very different, for a surprisingly broad spectrum of mammal groups has successfully tackled the problems of desert survival. Most are comparatively secretive: only a large animal, almost immune from attack, could afford to be seen against such a starkly revealing habitat. Many are assisted in their concealment (as are most desert birds) by a skin or coat that is cryptically coloured – patterned for camouflage against the desert backdrop. And many, too, are nocturnal, revealed only by the reflections from their eyes in the light of vehicle headlamps or in the beam of a powerful torch. A walk or drive through the desert at night reveals a startling number of pairs of watching eyes of all sizes, set in shadowy, swiftly retreating bodies. But during the day, careful inspection of freshly blown sand, or the moist ground around a waterhole, reveals a large number of varied tracks that amply confirm the level of night-time activity – though of course not all will be mammals, as much of the desert's insect and reptile life is also active after dark.

Almost all of the mammalian orders have their representatives in the world's deserts. Primates, however, are scarce: the apes and monkeys are absent or only occur on the desert margins, since many are tree dwellers. But several species of baboon succeed – notably the hamadryas baboon from Ethiopia, Somalia and elsewhere in the desert junction between Africa and Asia. The Rodentia (rats, mice and so on) and the related Lagomorpha (rabbits and hares) are represented by many species and occur in just about every desert area. Their adaptations to desert life are among the best, and of all mammal groups these two are probably the most successful in, and typical of, desert habitats. Even the European rabbit, accustomed to temperate grassland and woodland margin, has adapted to this alien habitat with extreme speed. When introduced into Australia it spread like wildfire through the bush and outback, penetrating deep into the real desert of the 'red centre'.

The hoofed herbivores are also represented: although they prefer semi-arid grasslands adjacent to real deserts, and temperate pastures, both odd-toed and even-toed ungulates can be found in truly arid country. The odd-toed (with a single hoof at the end of their leg, including the zebras, horses and their kind) are represented by various wild asses and indeed by the Grevy's or mountain zebra which flourishes in arid, lightly bushed uplands. The even-toed (or cloven-hoofed grazers – the deer, antelope and the like) are considerably more

A vicuna grazes the desert altiplano, 4300 m (14,100 ft) above sea level in the Chilean Andes.

41

numerous overall, and are represented in deserts by a number of gazelle and oryx species and by the addax, which has one of the most drought-resistant lifestyles of all the larger mammals. Into this category fit those well-known desert specialists the one-humped dromedary and the two-humped bactrian camels. Like the addax, they are supremely well adapted to desert life.

In contrast to the reptiles, of which a quite disproportionate and puzzling number of species lead predatory lives, true desert mammalian predators (rather than marauders from the desert fringes) are scarce. An abundance of smaller herbivorous mammals, as well as insects and reptiles, is preyed upon by a surprisingly small range of predatory carnivorous mammals. Larger vegetarians fall prey to various members of the dog family – the kit fox, dingo and coyote – while at the top of the food chain, and scarce, are hyenas and, close to the desert margins, the very occasional lion.

In Australia, things are very different. The landmass that was to become Australia broke away from the old supercontinent of Gondwanaland so far back in evolutionary time that only the most primitive of the mammals had appeared. On the island continent of Australia, isolated by a steadily widening gulf of ocean, animal life consisted of amphibians and reptiles, monotremes and marsupials. The monotremes – egg-laying mammals of the most primitive type – are today represented by the echidna and the platypus; marsupials are pouched animals such as the koala bear and kangaroo that give birth to tiny 'premature' young and have poorly developed mammary glands with which to deliver milk to their young.

On the residual landmass that is now America, Africa, Asia and Europe, the mammal orders that today exploit various habitats gradually evolved; their increasingly advanced structures and biology gave them a superiority over the marsupials that led to the latter's eventual extinction. In Australia there was no such competition from more advanced orders; as a result the marsupials developed, the slow process of evolution shaping them and their lifestyles to their environment, to occupy most of the available habitats, with the monotremes just managing to maintain a precarious toe-hold.

The marsupials have, however, by no means stood still – they have developed into various herbivorous and carnivorous groups, mostly still flourishing. Only where humans have introduced highly competitive advanced mammals from elsewhere (for example, dogs, cats, rabbits and sheep) have their marsupial equivalents been severely threatened or wiped out.

DEALING WITH DESERT CONDITIONS

When it comes to evolving structures and strategies to cope with the excessive heat (and sometimes cold) and aridity, there are three basic solutions which mammals adopt. They can evade the worst of the heat by hiding or sheltering from it, or by undertaking migrations or nomadic treks. They can passively tolerate it, relying on an advanced physiology to see them through. Or they can actively combat the heat, using the cooling effect produced by the evaporation of water.

By far the simplest way to avoid the heat of the middle of the day is to seek shelter underground, because not many centimetres below the surface the huge temperature fluctuations are ironed out and, most important of all, the extreme maxima are appreciably reduced. Sheltering beneath overhanging rocks or stunted trees may not offer adequate protection as the ambient air temperatures will still be excessive. Size is a limiting factor here. Retreating below ground level is a facility available only to the smaller mammals – an important facility, for they cannot sweat or pant. In consequence most are burrow-dwellers, emerging only in the cool of the night to forage for food.

So for larger mammals, like gazelles, oryx, asses and camels, remaining out on the desert surface, even in the shade of a rock or stunted tree, may cause their body temperature to rise to potentially lethal levels. To avoid death the animal concerned needs increased tolerance to high temperatures, or some mechanism of combating the heat by evaporation. But temperature tolerance, though present in some desert mammals, only increases their staying power by 2–3°C (3–6°F). Sweating is efficient, and effective at maintaining the body temperature at tolerable levels; but water has to be available, either from waterholes or from the natural moisture content of plant or animal food.

Here, it is the smaller mammal that is at a disadvantage. If a large rock and a small pebble, both at the same temperature, are placed together in the heat of the desert sun, the pebble will soon become intolerably hot; the rock, on the other hand, may take so long to heat up that night comes, allowing its temperature to fall. Similarly, the pebble will cool far more quickly than the rock. The reason is that heat gain or loss depends

Called, for obvious reasons, 'giraffe-necked antelopes', gerenuk stand on their hind legs to nibble scarce Acacia *shoots beyond the reach of other desert antelopes.*

heavily on the ratio of surface area to weight; the smaller the rock, the greater the surface area relative to its weight – so the more quickly it gains or loses heat. Much the same applies to desert creatures. Gain of heat *from* the environment (and its converse, loss of bodily warmth *to* the environment) is proportional to the surface area, not the weight, of the animal, following a curve calculated by a physiologist called Benedict and given an attractively non-mathematical name – the mouse-to-elephant curve! So the small desert rodents face much greater problems in keeping their body temperatures down to tolerable levels than do the antelopes or camels.

Large animals can sweat and pant, but this must be at the cost of replacing from their food or drink the water that they lose in the process. This creates a strong evolutionary pressure to reduce all non-useful forms of water loss. The desert animal most likely to survive successfully has a gut that allows maximum water extraction, enabling it to excrete almost dry faecal material, and possesses kidneys that extract the minimum water from the blood, secreting urine in a highly concentrated form. Another source of water loss that is unique to mammals is the milk produced by the mammary glands to feed the young.

Water losses have to be made good fairly swiftly. Apart from drinking and the natural water present in food, further water is released during the chemical reactions associated with food digestion and bodily metabolism. But although it does liberate a small amount of water, simply increasing the food intake and digestion to make water available is not an option. Digestion – essentially oxidization – demands oxygen, which must be obtained from the air by increased respiration. This extra use of the lungs results in a loss of water from the lung surfaces, and in most cases the result would be a net loss of water, not a gain. As a result, while increasing the metabolic rate is not a practical proposition, *decreasing* it can be very important in saving water at times of extreme stress. It forms part of the strategy employed by aestivating ('summer hibernating') mammals to avoid the worst climatic extremes.

THE SMALLEST DESERT MAMMALS

How, then, do the various groups of mammals cope with the severities of their habitat? Perhaps the simplest approach is to look at some case histories, starting with the smallest. Tiny desert carnivores, or near-carnivores, are not common. The grasshopper mouse from the south-western United States subsists, as its name suggests, largely on a diet of grasshoppers, locusts and any other desert arthropods (creatures with jointed limbs) that it can catch. From these it will easily satisfy its needs for both food and water. The mulgara, a marsupial from Australia, is much the same size and lives in much the same style. In laboratory conditions both animals have been shown to excrete nitrogen-rich urea in a very concentrated form. This is necessary for carnivores, which obtain their water requirements almost as a by-product of a diet rich in protein and, in consequence, nitrogen.

The planigale, at around 100–150 mm (4–6 in.) long, including a substantial tail, is perhaps the smallest of all the Australian marsupials. At this size, young planigales may get carried along by the grasshoppers that they attack. Attack – and ferociously – is the word, as their potential prey may be bigger than they are, heavier (planigales weigh about 5 g or five to an ounce), and quite well armoured and able to defend itself. It has been calculated that planigales need six or more 50 mm (2 in.) grasshoppers daily to supply their needs, so they lead active lives.

Larger, but just as determined in attack, are the desert hedgehogs. These are just as well protected from their own predators as are their European cousins, and can roll themselves into a fox-proof spiny ball. Their diet is catholic in the extreme, embracing most invertebrates; small reptiles and their eggs, nests of birds' eggs or young and nests of young desert rodents are also all acceptable. All these food items provide adequate fluid supplies, so drinking is not necessary. The desert hedgehogs are smaller, lighter and longer-legged than their temperate cousins – perhaps an adaptation, coupled with large feet, because they have to move swiftly over sandy soils. They also have noticeably larger ears than their relatives. These probably serve the dual function of increasing their nocturnal prowess as hunters and acting as heat exchangers or coolers – effectively dissipating, like radiators, excess body heat to the surroundings – since the spiny coat must produce an inflexible layer of thermal insulation.

Several species of reptiles – both lizards and snakes – have evolved predatory lifestyles in the uncertain, shifting habitat provided by sand dunes, pursuing prey ranging from insects to small mammals. In Australia, the marsupial that occupies this predatory niche is the marsupial mole. This quite extraordinary creature was first seen by western eyes just over a century ago: mole-like in size at 10–20 cm (4–8 in.) long, sandy in colour

Sheltered beneath an aloe, a Namaqua rock mouse forages for food.

with coarse hair rather than velvet fur, it possesses powerful fore-limbs with formidable shovel-shaped claws to propel it through the sand. Like its counterpart from temperate climates it has tiny, probably almost useless, eyes buried beneath the facial fur. The nose is long and sensitive and serves as the main prey-locating organ – although hearing may also assist. The bridge of the nose is protected by a tough, leathery patch of skin, and it seems that the head plays a major part as the marsupial mole ploughs through the sand.

It is a voracious feeder, preying largely on soil arthropods but also on young lizards, and is reputed to eat at least its own weight in food every day. Its feeding behaviour is astonishing. It will dash about frantically searching for food and gobbling up whatever it finds, suddenly stop dead in its tracks and doze off for a few minutes, then wake with a start and resume its feverish hunting. So far as is known, the female marsupial mole

produces only a single offspring each year, which would indicate a surprising survival rate and length of life for an insectivore in a habitat apparently so hostile to its survival.

In the Namib Desert of Africa another mole-like creature hunts through the sand dunes, spending much of its life underground. This is the golden mole, an infrequently seen and little studied mammal. Similar in size and superficially in appearance to the temperate zone mole, it is thought to be at best distantly related. Its fur is sandy or golden, and rather coarse; and it shares with the marsupial mole a leathery, wedge-shaped nose that, like a plough, greatly assists fast movement through the sand as the golden mole pursues its favourite prey, sand-dwelling lizards, particularly the legless skink. To further speed its progress through the sand, its ears are greatly reduced and so too are its limbs. The greater part of the bone structure is reduced and held within the body: only the hands and feet protrude to provide propulsion, which they do with great effect. Most moles can dig surprisingly quickly, vanishing underground within seconds; but in soft sand a golden mole surprised on the surface can tunnel out of sight and so deeply that it escapes even the most frantic digging of a fennec fox – or indeed a research zoologist!

True small rodents, specially adapted to desert environments, are found in all the major desert areas of the world. In North America, their representatives are the kangaroo rats and pocket mice; in the great belt of desert stretching across the heart of the Old World from Africa to Mongolia, the gerbils, jerboas and their allies (similar animals, either related zoologically or with much the same lifestyles); in the Kalahari of southern Africa, *Pedetes*; and even in Australia there is one – not a marsupial, but the kangaroo mouse.

Despite the vast distances separating them, all of these small creatures show similar structural adaptations to their desert habitat. They have elongated, kangaroo-like hind-legs with fewer toes than normal, with much-reduced fore-limbs. They spend most of their lives as bipedal animals, using only their hind legs to move about. Their main means of locomotion is a series of high-speed hops – again kangaroo-like. All have modifications to their skull structure, where cavities or bullae retain moist air around the ear and reduce the dehydration of the middle ear fluids. Most have cheek or throat pouches in which to carry food. All are nocturnal, remaining in the cooler, more humid conditions of their burrows through the heat of the day.

It seems that kangaroo rats can live almost indefinitely without access to 'free water' – in other words, water that is free-standing in pools or streams, rather than 'locked up' as a component of their food. In their American desert home rainfall is rare and unpredictable and even dew is unusual, so opportunities to drink may be few and far between. They seem even to avoid green plant food that springs up following rains, preferring to

A hairy-footed gerbil tidies up the last remains of its meal, a large millipede.

stick to their normal diet of dry seeds. From this they obtain adequate moisture, but only with the assistance of the most stringent water conservation strategies. They lack sweat glands and so cannot lose water through their skin; and while many mammals lose considerable moisture during breathing because air currents pass over the moist lung surfaces, kangaroo rats minimize this by keeping the temperature of expired air as low as possible. Spending the day deep in their burrows, at moderate and stable temperatures, they usually maintain a humidity four times moister than outside by sealing the burrow entrance behind them once they have entered. Their urine is highly concentrated, needing little water in its formation. Similarly, on its passage through the gut most of the nutritive value and water content is extracted from their food. So the faecal matter is small and very dry, giving a water loss only 20 per cent of that of a comparably sized temperate-zone rodent.

Many of these strategies are also employed by the gerbils, jirds and jerboas of the Old World. They too can live on dry seeds and plant matter, without the need for drinking water. They share typical rodent teeth, which need to be strong to cope with their tough food. The brunt of the work is carried out by the incisors of the upper and lower jaws, two in each. These teeth are 'rootless', which means that they are continuously growing and so never wear out. Additionally, they are fronted by brown, extremely tough enamel, backed by rather softer dentine. As the tooth wears in steady use the dentine wears away faster than the enamel, producing an effective chisel shape and a sharp, tough cutting edge.

Gerbils tend to move on all fours more frequently than jerboas, scampering as often as they hop. Most have bodies in the 8–18 cm (3–7 in.) range, with tails 8–25 cm (3–10 in.) long. They are remarkably prolific; the females often produce several litters of up to eight youngsters each every year, giving birth deep in 'humidity-sealed' underground nest chambers.

Jerboas are the most amazingly diverse group, with sixteen species in central Asia alone. All have kangaroo-like hind-legs, but their heads are startlingly diverse. Some are rounded and almost earless, some like rabbits, some like hares, some like mice and some like squirrels – all in miniature. All have long tails, usually slender and often tufted at the tip, which help the jerboas to balance as they leap at considerable speed across the desert sands. Although primarily nocturnal, they may be about in the cool of dawn or dusk; at this time of day they

become vulnerable to predatory desert falcons and hawks, as well as to the desert owls and foxes that are their main night-time enemies. The jerboas' escape strategy is bewilderingly swift – perhaps this is the basis of its frequent success. Using their long tails to alter balance they can change direction in mid-leap, leaving a swooping or pouncing predator striking at the air. Desert jerboas, only about 15 cm (6 in.) long but with a tail trailing 25 cm (10 in.) behind, can execute some prodigious leaps, often exceeding 3 m (10 ft).

The giant jerboa bears more than a passing facial resemblance to the chinchilla of the highlands of the Patagonian Desert of South America. But unlike the giant jerboa, in body chinchillas resemble small rabbits. Because they are upland creatures (ranging from 3000 to 6000 m, or 10,000–20,000 ft, above sea level in the Andes) they are extremely well insulated by a soft, dense coat of fur. As a result, chinchillas suffer tremendous pressure from trappers seeking their skins. So popular were they at one time that the price of a coat made of wild chinchilla skins went above US$ 100,000, making chinchilla one of the most expensive of all furs. Chinchilla skin exports from Chile have in the past exceeded two hundred thousand pelts annually. Today, with the spread of more humane attitudes and the belief that fur skins are better on animals than on humans, this persecution is fortunately reduced.

Although they feed on tough grasses and seeds, these rodents need not drink free water because they also eat fleshy or dew-covered leaves. For much of the time, chinchillas seek the shelter of rock crevices and hollows to avoid the chilling, desiccating wind. Less prolific than gerbils, they produce two or three litters each year, of four young at the most. While most young rodents remain naked and helpless for some time, young chinchillas are born with some insulating fur and are active amazingly quickly, moving about within an hour or two of their birth.

In stark contrast to the densely furred, well-insulated chinchilla is the appropriately named naked mole-rat from the eastern Sahara. Wrinkled, naked, to all intents and purposes blind and with just a few bristly whiskers, they seem almost embryonically helpless. But this is far from the case. The mole-rat must be one of the most bizarre of rodents: extremely specialized in a number of ways, with several unique anatomical and social features, it seems on the face of it to be totally unsuited to life in a desert habitat. Most desert animals show physiological adaptations which allow them to cope with extremes of heat and drought. But this is not so in the mole-rat, locally called the sand puppy, which has almost lost the ability to maintain its body temperature and is regarded by researchers as worse in this context than *any* other mammal. How, then, does it survive? The answer is simply that mole-rats spend their entire lives deep underground in an extensive tunnel system a metre (3 ft) or more beneath the surface. Here, in eastern Africa, the ambient temperature is naturally equable and even, removing the need for sophisticated physiological adaptations.

Burrowing is the naked mole-rats' speciality. They are social animals, living in clans or groups up to a hundred strong, and they do their excavating in teams. Beneath the sand they build a network of tunnels, some used for feeding, some as living quarters, some with chambers used as nurseries, some as storage larders, some as lavatories. The team leader uses its teeth to cut into the subsoil. The teeth themselves are of typical rodent pattern and strength, and protrude in an ugly way from between pursed lips to give the impression of a large, wrinkled sausage with buck teeth at one end and a stubby tail at the other! Cutting its way into the sand face, the lead mole-rat scoops the soil back between its legs with comparatively feeble-looking paws. The next mole-rat in line follows suit, pushing the soil further back down the tunnel to other team members in series until eventually it is ejected on to the desert surface, forming a conical heap reminiscent of a miniature volcano, out of which more sand shoots – like hot ashes from a crater. They can dig so fast that they face little danger from predators, most of which simply cannot dig fast enough or deal adequately with the facefuls of flying sand.

Pursed lips on the lead digger help prevent it taking in mouthfuls of sand as it digs. The same technique is used when feeding – a process also carried out completely underground. Their chosen foods are roots, bulbs and tubers, the last two providing richer feeding than leaves for a herbivore. Within the well-controlled and high humidity of their burrows these plant tissues provide sufficient moisture for the naked mole-rats' needs, and they apparently never drink. But clearly this lifestyle limits their distribution to areas where sparse grassland or desert shrubs have established a permanent roothold.

Socially, naked mole-rat organization is both complex and efficient; it is also extremely unusual in the animal kingdom, certainly amongst the vertebrates. It can perhaps best be likened to that of a colony of bees, with a single female – the queen or matriarch –

dominating the entire clan. Her hormonal secretions, plentifully evident in the communal lavatory area, are believed to suppress the hormones of other females in the clan and keep them from developing to a sexual maturity and activity that could provide competition to her dominance. Consequently she is the only breeding female, and the entire colony membership is her progeny apart from some mature breeding males who mate with her. The younger offspring form the tunneling and food-collecting teams, returning with stores just as bees do to the central chambers. Larger immatures see to tunnel maintenance and keep watch (better called 'sensory alert' in a blind animal) for intruders. These workers include pre-breeding suppressed females, whose own chances of reproduction depend either on a nocturnal emigration to found a new colony, or on the death of the matriarch.

But not all the small desert rodents can cope without drinking or access to a free water supply. An excellent example is the pack or wood rat of the North American deserts, which need a great deal of water. They obtain this not by drinking from free-standing supplies but by concentrating on fleshy, succulent vegetation. In Arizona and nearby states various cactus species feature in the pack rat's diet right through the year, along with seeds an other plant material. During the driest months, something like 90 per cent of its diet consists of succulent cactus. Like so many other small desert rodents pack rats are nocturnal, avoiding the problems of the main heat of the day by retreating underground.

Pack rats have no better ability to survive desiccation than the ubiquitous urban brown rat, but whilst the brown rat cannot survive on a diet of cactus the pack rat can. One specialization it possesses is the ability to neutralize various toxic chemicals in plant tissues. Many plants contain such chemicals as an inbuilt defence against attack by insects or grazing animals. The chemicals are often alkaloids or oxalic acid which, taken in small doses, do little harm; as the bulk of an animal's diet, however, they can be lethal. Cacti contain oxalic acid as well as large quantities of calcium, which is not toxic but in excess is likely to result in kidney stones. Laboratory experiments have shown that the pack rat, in contrast to the brown rat, can metabolize these chemicals successfully and so survive despite the large proportion of cactus in its diet, but the mechanism is not yet fully understood.

The various desert ground squirrels of the Americas, Africa and Asia similarly need to obtain a reasonable quantity of water from their food. Too small to make a periodic trek to a waterhole (even if there was one), they take advantage of fleshy plant material when it is available after the rains to supplement a basic diet of seeds, roots and other plant matter that all contain much less water. Although this vegetarian, low-moisture food forms the steady basis of their diet year-round, rarely does it constitute the major part of their daily intake. Once the flush of growth following the rains has passed, some at least, like the antelope ground squirrel, turn their attention to insects, other terrestrial invertebrates and the occasional small lizard. This diet, too, contains sufficient moisture for their needs. Another desert adaptation enables them to drink quite salt water and to eat various succulent 'salt-brush' leaves –

which indicates that they have highly efficient kidneys.

The ground squirrels are attractive small mammals, bushy-tailed and often with longitudinal pale stripes in their fur. They rarely weigh more than 200 g (just over 7 oz) and so fall into the 'small mammal' category of surface area-to-volume ratio, where heat loss through sweating or panting is too expensive on body fluids to be a solution to coping with the heat. Instead, though they feed in daylight they concentrate their efforts on the early morning and late evening, when temperatures

Cape ground squirrels use their bushy tails as sunshades.

are lower. During the day they may make short feeding excursions, but as the temperature rises these get briefer and much of their time is spent underground in the burrows they have excavated. Here the temperature is both more uniform and far more tolerable, and the humidity remains much higher than in the open desert air. The Namib ground squirrel, and very probably others too, uses its bushy tail as a parasol. Using small muscles beneath the skin it fluffs out its tail to its maximum breadth and holds it arched over its back and head to produce a patch of shade, in which it feeds with a little less discomfort.

Some ground squirrels from desert areas in the Americas and in central Asia adopt another tactic so see them through the period of maximum difficulty, when the heat is at its most intense and water in any form in shortest supply. Aestivation – literally translated as 'summer sleep' – is the equivalent of the better-known hibernation or 'winter sleep'. This stratagem has evolved also in a number of smaller rodents, such as the small kangaroo mouse *Microdipodops pallidus*.

Aestivation has been investigated thoroughly in the case of the ground squirrels of the North American desert. Here the Mojave ground squirrel regularly aestivates – and also hibernates to escape the worst of the cold winter weather. Over much the same geographical range, the antelope ground squirrel does neither. It may well be that this helps allow two apparently rather similar animals with similar nutritional requirements to co-exist in a single, harsh habitat. During aestivation, the body temperature drops to somewhere between 20 and 22°C (68°–72°F) compared with the normal 36–38°C (97–100°F); breathing and pulse are barely detectable, and the metabolic rate (which together with respiration is the prime user of body fluids) is reduced by 60 or 70 per cent – a major saving.

MEDIUM-SIZED DESERT MAMMALS

Compared with the small rodents and their allies, the several species of hare that dwell in the world's desert areas suffer one major disadvantage – they do not excavate burrows. Not for them is the option of escaping underground from the heat, nor of aestivating to provide a longer-term solution. And although hares are far more mobile than the various desert rodents and

Crouched on a ledge in the shade, a jack rabbit holds its ears erect to maximize heat loss from them for beneficial cooling.

squirrels, they are still too small to achieve the nomadic versatility that many desert antelopes exploit. So how do the hares cope?

The jack rabbit (which is actually a hare) from the desert of the south-western USA provides a good example. They are fairly common, and presumably therefore reasonably successful. Their habitat is genuine desert, with no free-standing drinking water, but with some vegetation, which itself produces flushes of much greener, moister growth after the sporadic rains. Hares and rabbits still fall into the 'small' category when it comes to taking in, or dissipating, heat. They have no sweat glands in their skin and therefore cannot cool themselves in this way; and cooling through panting is hazardous because of the potential water loss. Observations of jack rabbits in the wild show just how expert they have become at exploiting every small opportunity of shelter that their often varied 'badland' habitat offers. They feed almost entirely at dawn and dusk, when heat stress is minimal and, given that over the heat of the day they lose no appreciable body water, they can survive well on the moisture contained even in the driest of their plant foods.

During the hottest season, jack rabbits very often spend the greater part of the day in the shade, albeit scanty, of a mesquite bush or some other shrub. If they can, they will choose a shallow despression, preferably to the north of a bush and so in maximum shade. Even the shadow cast by the mesquite bush will lower the ground temperature appreciably, from a totally intolerable 70°C (158°F) at the surface to perhaps as little as 35–40°C (95–104°F) at the base of the depression. Direct heating from the sun is also limited, screened out by the mesquite, and any reflected radiant heat off the desert surface passes over the animal as it crouches in its hollow. But the jack rabbit has yet one more trick up its sleeve. The huge ears, which are extremely useful when it comes to detecting an approaching predator, also function like the radiators in car engines.

Size for size, the desert hares have ears appreciably larger than those of their temperate climate counterparts. These larger ears are correspondingly well supplied with substantial blood vessels, so that the creatures' blood heat may be effectively radiated to a cool north sky. Something like a third of the metabolic heat generated by a jack rabbit can be dissipated in this way – indeed in the absence of ample water, this may be the only way that a medium-sized mammal could survive.

In the Australian desert, the 'medium-sized' slot is occupied first by the hairy wombat, squat and stocky with quite small ears and short, strong limbs. These physical attributes accurately reflect its way of life, for the wombat uses the avoidance tactics of the small rodent to minimize heat exposure and water loss. It is a powerful digger: wombat colonies generate a labyrinth of tunnels and living chambers that may be a metre (3 ft) or more deep, and which over the years expand to cover many square metres of the surface, much like an ancestral badger sett. Within the tunnels the humidity is high and the temperature moderate, and it is here that the wombats retreat as the sun climbs into the sky creating baking temperatures. Feeding takes place almost entirely at dusk or during the night, which saves the wombats not only from the heat but also from predators. Young wombats, bulky though they are, are slow-moving and little match for a dingo or a swooping wedge-tailed eagle.

The other medium-sized desert marsupial from the Antipodes is the quokka from south-western Australia. At around 3–4 kg (7–9 lb) in weight, the quokka is reminiscent of a bulky rabbit. This species has a fascinating method of combating heat extremes: it produces copious quantities of saliva which it licks over its feet and tail, and sometimes over its belly. This stratagem may reduce the body temperature by a useful 2°C (4°F), but it is not known how the quokka copes with the water loss created by saliva production. There is also another potential disadvantage: cooling by licking can only be carried out by an animal at rest. A creature running from a predator must find another means of cooling by evaporation – and at what could be its time of greatest need.

On the cold desert of Patagonia live maras, sometimes called Patagonian hares but not closely related to the hare family. These unusual-looking rodents – resembling a cross between a small antelope and a large rabbit – are able to graze on the scanty grass all day, as temperatures rarely become intolerable. From grasses and other plant food they derive adequate moisture – enough for the female to produce milk to suckle up to three youngsters. This she does sitting upright, like a large dog, so that she can keep watch for danger – her rabbit-like ears are for ever on the move, listening for possible hazards. The mara's young are born with a proper coat – as protection from the cold – and develop swiftly, being able to walk, and even run, within a few days of birth. Depending on the urgency of the situation, maras are versatile in locomotion: strolling sedately, hopping like hares, bounding like antelopes or galloping as fast as a horse.

LARGER DESERT MAMMALS

On these same high, dry plateaux of the Patagonian desert live the various South American members of the camel family – the llama, alpaca, vicuna and guanaco. Like the bactrian camel and the dromedary, some of these have been taken into domestic use – the llama as a pack animal, the alpaca as provider of the most amazingly soft, thick wool.

These are the grazers of this cold desert, the equivalent of the antelopes of hot deserts, but facing almost the opposite problem. True, they need a digestive system and physiology that allows minimal water to escape during excretion or respiration (where it condenses in the long nose), and they must be able to derive much of their water needs from their food. But rather than excluding heat from outside, through effective insulation they must retain as much of their own body heat as possible; in this way they need make only minimal use of their metabolism to keep themselves warm. The necessary insulation is provided by their woollen coats.

All have excellent fleeces, but that of the vicuna, which lives at the highest and coldest altitudes, is exceptionally fine. Centuries ago, only South American

In prime condition after the seasonal rains, Grant's gazelles make the most of the last good grazing.

Indian royal families were allowed to wear clothing made from it – ordinary people had to make do with the alpaca and guanaco. Recently the wool became more widely available, which opened up a hunting trade which at one time threatened the vicuna with extinction, despite its inaccessible and inhospitable habitat. But under strict protection, the numbers are now increasing.

The antelopes of hot deserts have faced similar levels of persecution, though not for the same reasons. Arabia, including the desert regions, is believed to have been the cradle of development for a group of smaller antelopes, the gazelles. From here various species have radiated out into Africa and Asia, spreading not just geographically but into a variety of habitats, including forests. Lightly built, gazelles are slender, elegant and fleet of foot, and the human simile 'graceful as a gazelle' is totally appropriate. Both sexes grow horns – long, slender and often lyre-shaped when viewed head-on.

The horns are ringed, and those of the females are lighter-weight than the males'. Too large to burrow, the desert gazelles seek what shelter they can in the shadow of larger rocks or beneath the scanty desert vegetation, and during the heat of the day they minimize their activity.

They are large enough and mobile enough to roam extensively in search of feeding grounds where rain has most recently fallen, and many will be within reach of a permanent waterhole which they will visit daily. But not all: the Arabian and dorcas gazelles may rarely, if ever, drink free water, obtaining their needs from the vegetation on which they graze. Though they do have the ability to sweat, avoiding the main heat of the day is their major strategy; this is combined with exceptional heat tolerance, a very efficient pair of kidneys, and a gut adapted to extract as much water as possible from their excretory products.

In desert habitats, gazelles never gather in the vast herds that sometimes collect on the better-watered plains and bush of Africa: there is simply not enough food. Sadly, their rarity has made them a target for sportsmen eager for an unusual trophy, and even their extreme fleetness of foot cannot protect them from the rifle of a modern Arab hunter mounted not on a lumbering camel but on a high-powered all-terrain four-wheel-drive vehicle. Several of the desert species are now threatened with extinction.

Similarly scarce, and resident high in the jagged, arid mountains on either side of the Red Sea, is the Nubian ibex. Ibex are related to the goats, and like them the males joust for supremacy over harems of females, facing each other on a rocky ledge and lunging forwards in a clash of heads and horns that echoes round the crags. Ibex horns are huge, and much larger in the bearded males than in the females. Shaped like a curved scimitar with large knobs on its leading edge, the horns sometimes make almost a complete semi-circle perhaps 150 cm (60 in.) long and weigh almost 10 kg (22 lb).

Nubian ibex are amongst the surest-footed of all cloven-hoofed animals – they need to be, for the ledges and screes along which they move every day may overlook sheer drops of hundreds of metres – certain death should they lose their footing.

Obviously Nubian ibex have superb balance and reactions, but their horny hooves show special adaptations to this way of life. The edges project slightly from the side: they are knife-sharp and will secure a foothold on the slightest crack in the rock. Where the rock is smooth, the ridged, fleshy pad of the sole gives a grip almost as powerful as a vacuum suction pad.

Dense hair protects the species as much from the cold of its high altitudes as from the heat. The Nubian ibex seems able to extract its total moisture requirement from the plants that it eats, and drinks only rarely. Ibexes spend about half the day grazing and the remainder in sheltered spots, lying down and chewing the cud. The 'cud' is part-digested plant material eaten earlier and held in one compartment of the ibex's stomach, brought up and chewed thoroughly prior to further digestion.

The pronghorn antelope, fortunately, is far from rare. Classed as the fastest land mammal in North America, the pronghorn can sprint at speeds up to 80 kph (50 mph). The females lack the double-pronged, fish-hook-like horns of the bucks. In desert and other arid areas, in the past this open-land antelope would have been preyed upon by coyote, cougar, lynx and wolf: these predators are now scarce, but the pronghorn is a favourite target for hunters. Even so it flourishes, even in the true desert, where it seems able to survive for months without access to free water. In parts of the American desert, tall cactus and other plants provide reasonable shade and concealment during the heat of the day, and the pronghorn derives its water needs from its food. Specially adapted kidneys minimize water loss in urine, and additionally allow the pronghorn to graze not only on sagebrush but on saltbush, which has a high salt content.

Both sexes are for ever on the alert. Eyes placed laterally on the head give a 360° view of approaching danger; sensitive noses continually sniff the breeze; and their large ears are always cocked, swivelling independently to check and identify any sound. Easily scared (but doubtless surviving better because of this), they quickly take to flight. As they do so they erect the dense buff hair around their tiny tails to reveal a large white rump patch, signalling a very obvious alert to other members of the herd. As they sprint away, scent glands on their tails squirt out strong-smelling liquid that reinforces the alarm. Pronghorns also use this hair-erecting ability during the heat of the day; they erect the hair on different parts of their body as the need arises and position themselves so that the breeze channels the air down onto the skin for maximum cooling effect.

Another antelope in which only the males possess horns is the saiga, a numerous beast which gathers in large herds and is supremely well adapted to the dusty desert plains of the Desert Corridor of central Asia. Saiga are migrants, moving southwards to escape the extremes of snow and cold of the desert winter. They are certainly the strangest of all antelopes in appearance – angular and pot-bellied, with spindly, knock-kneed legs, bulbous eyes and a balloon-like nose reminiscent of a half-finished elephant's trunk. Normally, their walk across the plains could best be described as shambling; and although they can produce a fair turn of speed if pressed (about 60 kph or 40 mph), their joints severely restrict their ability to turn, spring, twist and change direction in mid-air, as most antelopes do when escaping from predators.

The bulbous eyes are surrounded by bulky tear glands – the copious tears produced are necessary to flush away sand particles. The bulbous nose, almost a proboscis, contains nostrils that, like a seal's, can be closed by a circular muscle to exclude dust. Inside, each nostril is protected by large numbers of hairs and leads to a chamber lined with a substantial area of folded mucous membranes. This may serve some temperature-regulatory purpose, but is more likely to be simply a sophisticated filtering mechanism to extract dust from the air that the saiga breathes.

The various wild horses and asses are the desert representatives of the single-toed grazing herbivores. There are species in the deserts of Africa and Asia, and feral animals descended from escaped domestic stock, called in Australia brumbies and in America burros and mustangs. They have solved the problems of desert existence by adopting a nomadic way of life, and wander in herds. The desert areas that they inhabit are studded with waterholes – not frequent, but their locations are well known to the herd leaders. Their wandering path is dominated by the rains; in some way the nomads sense this and move from one area of fresh, post-rains grasses and short-lived plants to the next. There are always some perennial shrubs, bushes and trees available to supplement their diet.

Grevy's zebra, one of the best adapted of the horse family to arid conditions.

Long ears give asses early warning of approaching danger and may also dissipate excess body heat like the long ears of the jack rabbit. Far-carrying braying calls – derivatives of the familiar hee-haw of the donkey – keep members of the herd in contact. Most – such as the khur of India, the Somali ass of East Africa, and the Nubian ass from beside the Red Sea – are sandy-coloured, presumably for camouflage. The related mountain or Grevy's zebra, a desert margin member of the horse family that copes well with hot and arid

Desert specialists par excellence, Beisa oryx may go for months or even years without drinking.

conditions, relies on the fine stripes of its coat to break up its outline. If predators are close, it is thought that the resulting jumble of stripes as the group panic and rush in all directions confuses the predator and distracts it from the individual animal it has selected as its target.

Much the same as the asses in colour, and sharing the same natural distribution in Africa and Asia, are the various oryx species. These are donkey-sized antelopes, most conspicuous for their immensely long horns. From the gemsbok of the Kalahari to the scimitar-horned and Arabian oryx to the north, all are adept at survival in extremely hot and arid conditions. They are amongst the most heat-tolerant of all desert mammals, coping with overheating that at 42–45°C (108–113°F) would prove lethal to most other animals. Their kidneys are very efficient, minimizing water loss in urine, and through digestive adaptations they can satisfy their water needs from the dry grass and leaves that they eat. During the heat of the day, they seek out whatever shade is available from the scanty bushes. At night, they may glean water by licking condensed dew (or fog in the Namib) off each other's coats, and only when in calf and after the birth does the female need to have trekked to be near a permanent waterhole. When she does drink, she takes in up to about 20 per cent of her body weight!

Oryx are known to travel over vast group territories, of the order of 3000 sq km (over 1150 sq miles) and the group will know almost every inch of the way. Unfavourable parts within this area will never be visited, but the feeding grounds will be exploited in turn. Oryx travel at night to minimize heat stress and to conserve water, and their navigation is marvellously accurate.

Their spectacular horns, a metre (3 ft) or more long, are used in battles during the mating season between rival bucks. Many of these are trials of strength, with the clash of horns being accompanied by twists of the powerful shoulders to throw the adversary to the ground. Sometimes, but probably quite rarely, these weapons are used in a fight to the death. One possible origin of the mythical unicorn is the narwhal, that strange, small Arctic whale with a single, long, spirally fluted tusk, whose skulls must occasionally have reached Europe in the Middle Ages. Another strong possibility is one of the oryx family, because not infrequently one horn gets broken off in a fight. The rest of the oryx skull and skeleton would look far more horse-like than that of a narwhal.

More recently, the Arabian oryx itself has come very close to joining the ranks of mythical beasts. So magnificent are its horns, and so prized as trophies by 'sportsmen' with lights, four-wheel-drive vehicles and high-powered rifles with telescopic sights, that hunting reduced the wild population to an estimated dozen

animals. Of course, as the population became smaller so these few survivors became even more valued as a hunter's prize, and even more threatened – despite the difficulties of finding them in the heart of the Arabian desert.

In 1961 the Fauna Preservation Society wisely decided to intervene, and using Land Rovers, helicopters, skilled trackers and tranquilizing darts captured two males and a female. These, with others gathered from zoos and private collections round the world, were mustered into a series of herds. During the captive-breeding programme the structure of each herd was strictly controlled: animals were mated with others from outside their group to ensure healthy progeny. By 1980 – almost ten years since the last sighting of a wild beast – there were several hundred Arabian oryx in captivity. In 1982 the first reintroductions were made, rapidly followed by several others over a wide desert area. All the groups were released in Arabian countries under strict protection – and all continue to flourish. 'Operation Oryx' has been an epic conservation success story.

Sadly, another of the desert antelopes, the addax, is also the victim of hunting to near-extinction. Closely related to the oryx and very similar in appearance, except that it has spirally twisted horns, the addax is even more a true-desert antelope, with a range that once spanned the Sahara. But now its distribution is fragmented, and the making of an accurate census is impossible because of the low numbers and difficult, broken terrain in which they lead their extremely shy lives. Nomadic tribesmen place great faith in the healing powers of its liquid stomach contents, and the calcareous lumps (called 'gazelles' eggs') that are sometimes found in the stomach. As a source of fluid *in extremis*, a nomad could kill an addax and open up its stomach to drain the contents into a container: it takes little time for an appreciable, if revolting, quantity of liquid to gather.

Talismans or charms of addax skin, or the 'gazelles' eggs' themselves, are still carried in remote areas to ward off dangers as diverse as snake and scorpion bites, witchcraft and magic. In addition to this centuries-old depletion of their numbers there are newer, more species-threatening sources of persecution. The advent of advanced weapons, and their widespread use in desert Africa in local and more major skirmishes between families, tribes, political factions or nations, has tragically put the addax, a slow-moving target, in its present precarious position.

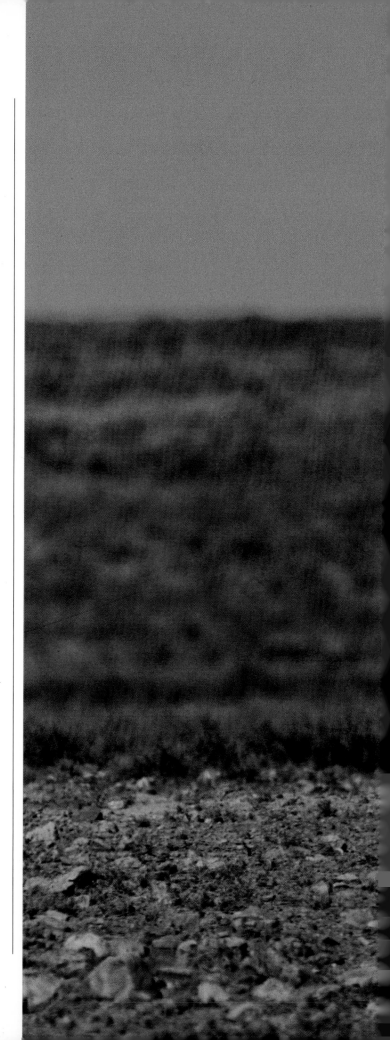

Several thousand miles away across the globe, the desert grasslands and bush of Australia are grazed by the largest of the world's marsupials, the red kangaroo. Just as they are commonly thought to be primitive, and therefore inefficient in their reproductive mechanism compared with the placental mammals, the marsupials are (equally incorrectly) supposed to have unsophisticated and ineffective methods of heat regulation. In fact some desert marsupials are poor heat regulators and some good – just like the placental mammals. And they use many of the same physiological or behavioural strategies: sweating, panting, and wetting the fur with copious saliva.

The red kangaroo is widely distributed through the arid interior of Australia. Though research has been scanty, it appears that its kidneys are extremely effective at producing very concentrated urine – as concentrated as that of placental desert 'experts' like the kangaroo rat and ground squirrels. So the red kangaroo should be able to go for long periods without free water if necessary. Only in periods of extreme heat should it need to drink to maintain its fluid balance.

Weighing as much as 100 kg (220 lb), the red kangaroo is a largely grazing animal. It can move swiftly and apparently effortlessly, covering long distances in its wanderings in search of fresh grazing and, if need be, to reach fresh standing water. It would be fascinating to know just how it derives the information required to set the targets and navigate on these journeys: it is a puzzle that rates, with bird migration, among the greatest unsolved biological mysteries. But the way the kangaroo moves its body is far from mysterious. Its back legs are much larger and stronger than its fore-legs. What looks as if it ought to be the knee, only bending the 'wrong way' in the middle of the leg, is actually the ankle – below that are the bones of the foot and toes. The knee itself is right up near the bulk of the body, hardly visible, and connected to the pelvis by a stout femur or thigh bone, far shorter than in man but similar to that of the horse.

Most jumping-specialist animals (such as frogs) take one leap at a time, collecting and repositioning their limbs prior to the next take-off. Not so the kangaroos. Using their substantial and weighty tails to keep themselves perfectly balanced, they bound across the

Australia's equivalent to the large desert antelopes, a red kangaroo bounds effortlessly across the arid plains of the Sturt Desert.

desert. Strong elastic tendons in the bent hind legs act like powerful springs each time the toes touch the ground. So, once the motion is started, the kangaroo can keep going at speeds approaching 30 kph (nearly 20 mph) for long periods, each leap covering up to 8 m (over 25 ft). This elastic-powered propulsion makes little demand on muscle power, and is one of the most efficient and energy-saving ways of getting around in the whole of the animal kingdom. In the context of the desert, energy-saving means more than anything water-saving; so the kangaroo's method of propulsion is of major importance in terms of its potential for survival.

Female red kangaroos will travel slightly more slowly than the males, depending on the presence and size of any youngster, or joey, in their pouch. Pouches are always a feature of marsupials, though the pouch itself may be vestigial (as in the possum) or vast (as in the red kangaroo), and face backward (as in the wombat) or forward (as in the kangaroo). The young kangaroo is born after only one month of gestation: at birth it weighs about 25 g (1 oz) and is about the size of a jelly baby. Given the size of a mature animal this represents considerable prematurity, but despite this the joey climbs and wriggles through its mother's fur into the pouch on her belly. Here it finds a teat from which it can suckle – its mouth is one of its better-developed organs at this stage, and so it is able to fasten on firmly.

For several months the joey lives in the pouch, growing rapidly, until it is large enough to venture out and graze on its own. Even then, if danger threatens it will clamber back into the pouch, long legs dangling outside as there is insufficient room for them inside. If the danger is really serious, the female will jettison the joey to make good her own escape: though to human eyes this may seem cruelly thoughtless and far from maternal, biologically this improves her chances of survival and of breeding again. When comparing the supposedly sophisticated placental mammals with the supposedly primitive marsupials, it should be remembered that a heavily pregnant female antelope easily falls victim to hunting lions or hyenas. In these circumstances, marsupials have the advantage.

DESERT CARNIVORES
Carnivores in the desert should be able to obtain most of their moisture requirements from the flesh or body contents of their prey. Members of the cat family (cougar, lynx, leopard, lion and several smaller species) and the dog family (various desert foxes, the wolf, dingo and hunting dog) seem to have powerful kidneys that produce concentrated urine. They lack sweat glands but pant freely, often with long tongues lolling from their gaping mouths. The cooling that this produces is only achieved by losing considerable quantities of water in evaporation so these families' potential for success in the desert is limited. Most are found at the desert margins, probably near a permanent supply of drinking water.

Some, however, can and do succeed. The smallest, like the grasshopper mouse and primarily insectivorous, have already been mentioned. Rather larger are the desert members of the mongoose family. With the sinuous agility, short legs and fast reflexes associated in temperate climates with the stoats and martens, they are catholic in their choice of prey. They will eat small invertebrates, young birds in ground nests (and eggs if they find them), reptiles, including venomous snakes, as well as small or medium-sized rodents which may be heavier than themselves. Typical of these is the suricate or meerkat of the Kalahari. Suricates avoid the impossible heat of the midday sun in the same way as many of their prey, by retreating to underground burrows dug by themselves. They live in family clans, and their lives are closely geared to the social necessities which such a system demands.

Recognition of other members of the group depends heavily on scent, and the group territory in both suricates and mongooses is marked with scent by the males. Hunting is a group activity: the team move quickly through their area, using their noses to scent potential food, digging here for a large grub, pouncing there on to a small mouse or even a scorpion. All the time a continuous purring chatter keeps group members in contact with each other should they dive down a rodent burrow or vanish into some thicker scrub.

In the group tunnels, sub-adult animals help the females with small young, watching over them at play; play is important in developing their appreciation of social positions within the clan, and in sharpening their hunting reflexes. The 'nurses' will carry the young to fresh quarters if danger threatens in the form of a large snake. Danger in never far away, with snakes at ground level and birds of prey overhead. The group will always post one or two watchmen as they forage. These animals stand upright on their hind legs without difficulty, which gives such a low-slung creature a much better view over the scanty vegetation and rocks, and quickly sound the alarm when necessary. Ever on the alert, females suckle larger young in the open, but standing upright.

Hyenas are also clan animals, and surprisingly for their size (at a weight of up to 80 kg – 180 lb – on a par with some of the largest breeds of dog) also live in underground dens dug by themselves. Dog-like in appearance, with the strongest jaws of any animal, but much higher at the shoulder than the rump, hyenas share the catholic diet of most dogs, taking carrion and occasionally some plant matter along with animal prey

Ears alert to detect danger or a possible meal, bat-eared foxes relax by their den in the Kalahari.

caught by themselves or stolen from another predator.

The hyena is found over much of Africa and in Arabia. Hunting is a group activity, much as in hunting dogs and wolves – it is perhaps because of the sparse density of large prey that pack hunting animals are relatively unable to penetrate the desert habitat. The hunting group of males and non-breeding females will find prey, either by running down an antelope, or by snatching or taking over by sheer weight of numbers the prey of another carnivore. If they are to hunt by running, the hyenas take turns in loping along in the lead. What they lack in speed they make up for in persistence, pursuing relentlessly until they bring their tiring victim to bay. The end is swift, the antelope being submerged in a snarling mass of hyenas. Both at the kill and when dealing with carrion, the powerful jaws and the teeth of the hyena – amongst the strongest in the animal kingdom – stand it in good stead. Once the kill is accomplished, the first priority is to take food to any brood female with young back in the subterranean den.

The smaller members of the dog family that do survive well in the desert are usually solitary hunters. Light and lithe in build, they behave more like cats in their agility as they capture prey. The kit fox of the North American desert is smaller than most temperate-climate foxes, and has rather larger ears. It excavates earths below ground and, like its prey, shelters below ground from the heat of the sun. Hunting is most active towards dawn and dusk, when most prey – usually small rodents such as kangaroo rats – is about. Good eyes help the kit fox, but it usually locates its prey by using its phenomenally good sense of smell and acute hearing. A stealthy stalk is completed by a cat-like pounce, as it pins the victim to the ground beneath its front paws. Sharp teeth in the long snout quickly terminate the hunt.

In Africa and Arabia, the kit fox's role is undertaken by the fennec fox. This species too lives sometimes a solitary life, sometimes as a member of a small group of animals, in an earth excavated in the sand. It shares with the kit fox an agility that allows it to leap about 70 cm (about 30 in.) vertically and 120 cm (48 in.) horizontally from a standing start. The fennec fox is known to be able to survive for long periods without access to free-standing drinking water, and has been seen wandering many kilometres away from the nearest oasis or waterhole. Its dense fur helps keep it warm as it hunts in the cool of the night, and over-large feet allow it to make good speed over loose sand without sinking in.

They also increase the 'catching area', as it pounces feet first on to its prey.

Like all foxes, it has a catholic taste in small animal – vertebrate or invertebrate – meals, but will not pass by any opportunity to eat ripe fruit. Its eyes are comparatively large, facing forwards to give range-finding ability and 'binocular vision' – very different from the eyes of its prey. These, on the sides of the head, cover the widest possible field of view to protect their owner from attack. The fennec fox's sense of smell is superb, and it has well-developed whiskers which are of particular use after dark and in the confines of crevices and burrows. But the most conspicuous of its features are the huge ears, relative to its body size the largest possessed by any carnivore, and reputed to be able to pinpoint moving animals an astonishing 1·5 km (1 mile) away. Long fringes of hair protect the ears from sand, just as long eyelashes protect its eyes. Though small, the fennec is perhaps the best adapted of all carnivores to harsh desert conditions.

THE CAMEL

It seems certain that no truly wild individuals remain of that most obvious symbol of the desert – the camel. This, the 'typical' one-humped Arabian camel, ridden by the Tuareg tribesmen across the Sahara, is more properly called the dromedary. The true camel, or bactrian camel, has two humps, and it is quite possible that a few wild groups exist still in the remote fastnesses of the vast Desert Corridor of central Asia.

The camel fully merits its position as the most famous of all desert animals: it is supremely well adapted to the conditions, and certainly it is indispensable to humans living in or exploring desert areas. It has the reputation of being able to cross vast distances of sand desert, to drink from waterholes far too bitter or saline for most other animals, to eat almost anything, no matter how tough or how thorny; and, in extremis, the camel rider can kill his beast and survive on what he finds in its stomach. Additionally it provides milk, fuel (its dung is almost immediately burnable, so dry is it on excretion) and a form of currency for the desert tribespeople. Although to strangers riding camels is an acquired skill, their usefulness as both riding and pack animals in this savage terrain must be accepted without question.

Naturally the camel's physiology includes many desert adaptations. Its leathery mouth and tongue, and tough tooth enamel, allow it to eat the thorniest of desert plants, notwithstanding the sand or salt encrustations commonly covering them. It used to be thought that the camel 'drank for the future', and that its prodigious intake at a waterhole (measured as in excess of 100 litres – over 20 gallons – inside ten minutes!) was held in some form of reservoir for its journey over the next few days. Certainly camels can trek for three or four days until the next oasis is reached, maybe 150 km (nearly 100 miles) away; but detailed investigation has shown that water is not stored in the animals' large and complex stomach.

Nor, as is often imagined, does the hump or humps contain a water reservoir. The origin of this belief probably lies in the fact that, as the camel travels further and further without water, the hump shrinks noticeably and slumps over to one side. The explanation is that the hump, far from being a water tank, is a fat store containing up to 40 kg (90 lb): but this does not dissociate it from the animal's water metabolism and balance. As the camel marches, with limited ability to feed effectively, the fat in the hump can be metabolized to provide the necessary energy. Were it to be used up completely (an unusual occurrence), each gramme of fat could yield about a gramme of water – so the potential body-water supply stored in the fat hump amounts to some 40 litres (9 gallons). But were this to be used simply as a water reserve, the physiological equations would not balance. To metabolize the fat reserves demands oxygen, which is taken into the blood through respiration, which in turn causes moisture evaporation within the lungs. This evaporation would lose the camel one and a half times the water that fat metabolism liberated.

Camels have thick fur, thicker on the back than on the belly. It provides maximum protection but, if the camel is standing during the day, allows excess body heat to radiate out to its surroundings. In the warmest seasons this coat moults and is replaced by thinner fur. Even the thin coat, though, offers them protection both from the cold nights and from radiant heat during the day. It is important to realize that the insulation taken for granted as preventing heat loss in a cold environment can be just as important at preventing, or minimizing, heat gain. For many years, animal physiologists regarded camels' variable body temperatures as indicative of a relatively crude and insensitive technique for temperature control. This is far from the case. In the desert, striving to achieve a steady temperature, often below that of the surrounding air, can be a costly process. How much better to do as the camel does, allowing its large body to 'soak up' heat, with an accompanying temperature rise that is not enough to damage the specially heat-resistant tissues, during the day, in order to dissipate it to a cold environment after dark.

Camels have another apparently anomalous means of dealing with heat, at first sight quite contrary to the behaviour that would be expected in hot surroundings. In the extreme cold of the Antarctic pack ice, young penguin chicks crowd together in their rookery to keep warm. So it comes as a striking surprise to discover that camels, sitting out the midday heat of the Sahara in summer, couched by their drivers, huddle together in groups to keep cool! The principle that both groups of animals are employing is the same: the larger the organism (or the 'collective' organism formed by the closely huddled group members) the smaller, relatively speaking, is its surface area. The smaller the surface area relative to bulk, the less the heat lost *or gained* through that surface.

Although camels do not pant, they can sweat to reduce their temperatures. Unlike racehorses, for example, which work themselves into a frothy lather, sweat on a camel is almost never visible. It remains moistening the skin surface, beneath the hairs, where evaporative cooling is most effective and least damaging to the animal's water reserves. Camels' kidneys are powerfully effective, producing strong urine with minimal water loss, and their droppings too are almost dry on voiding. Not only this, but over the long days of exposure to heat and thirst camels can tolerate a weight loss of about 25 per cent. This is almost double the dehydration level that in other mammals would precipitate an explosive heat rise – the blood would thicken, almost always leading to death. But in the camel, the blood plasma is the last part of the body to lose water.

When it comes to the birth of its young, the camel – and its master – seem able to judge the timing to a nicety. Close to a waterhole to provide both the water and the lusher vegetation needed for the female to provide milk for her new-born foal, the birth is swift. Within minutes the young camel is on its feet, within hours walking and feeding, and within just a very few days it too can undertake long desert treks at its mother's side. Desert antelopes and goats manage in exactly the same way but without the guiding hand of man, behaving as nature intends that they should.

Anatomically, the camel may seem to have evolved to a strangely awkward shape – the well-known 'horse designed by a committee'. It does, however, possess features with clear relevance to its desert lifestyle. A camel's eyes are protected from blowing sand by both substantial tear glands and double rows of long, curled eyelashes, which exclude sand and do not deplete its water resources. The nostrils are protected by guard hairs but, more important, have circular muscles which enable them to be closed during a sandstorm and only opened when a breath is necessary. Above all, camels move at a leisurely, even-paced gait, economical on energy; and they have feet with two broad, padded toes which are well insulated from the sand's heat and, as they are connected by a strong, flexible web, prevent the camel sinking into soft sand. So although some aspects of camel anatomy, physiology and behaviour may relate to the realms of fiction, at least as remarkable are the facts that make the camel the ultimate beast of the desert.

Camels rest at a palm-fringed oasis. The camel is perhaps the masterpiece of evolution to desert life.

4 BIRDS
BOTH LARGE AND SMALL

Desert birds face the same hazards in this hostile environment as are faced by humans and by other animals of all sizes. These are the extremes of dryness and heat (and sometimes also of night-time cold); the need to find shelter from these extremes, particularly for the nest with eggs or helpless young; the need to find adequate water; and the paramount need to find adequate food. Despite this daunting catalogue all the desert areas of the world have bird populations, usually from a wide range of families; they include some, like the waders or 'shorebirds', that would seem automatically excluded from such surroundings.

MIGRATORY VISITORS

Many of these are true desert specialists, and it is on these that this chapter will concentrate. There are also others – and in terms of sheer numbers either of species or of individuals they are the majority – that may from time to time be seen in desert or semi-desert habitats. Particularly in Africa and Asia, the desert belt stretches east–west for vast distances, with relatively few north–south corridors with more favourable climates running through it. This tropical and subtropical desert belt lies across the migration routes of enormous numbers of

On aerial patrol, alert that others' misfortune may provide a meal, a white-backed vulture soars effortlessly on broad wings.

birds that breed in the temperate and subarctic zones of the Northern Hemisphere. Twice each year hundreds of species of migrants, ranging in size from the smallest of warblers to giant storks and cranes, must cross the formidable desert barrier. All have evolved strategies – sometimes involving nocturnal flights, sometimes involving stop-overs at food- and water-rich oases or wadis – which allow them to do so successfully. Fascinating though these migratory strategies are, they are not relevant to a discussion of the means by which desert birds survive for long periods with no relief from the intensely arid conditions of their permanent habitat. But it should be noted that on occasion (and particularly near oases and other water sources) many non-desert birds may be encountered within the desert bounds.

COPING WITH HEAT

Birds seem able to cope with the stresses of desert life without obvious anatomical change. This apparent readiness to cope with the hazards of a situation is called 'pre-adaptation' by biologists. A prime example is the cladding of feathers that all birds possess – the one unique feature that birds but no other animals have. Feathers provide admirable insulation, not only for retaining body heat and keeping out the external cold in polar birds, but also for protecting the body within from the heat of the external environment in desert

67

birds. An obvious analogy is the Bedouin Arabs' all-enveloping, thick clothing. Feathers are formed from the protein keratin, and their complex interlocking network of barbs and barbules effectively traps a layer of insulating air next to the birds' skin.

Although many feathers are water-resistant, and some are more or less waterproof (as in ducks), this happens from the outside inwards. The fine, downy interior structure would quickly be destroyed, and with it much of the insulation, were the plumage to become wet from within. This precludes sweating, the standard mammalian technique, to assist heat loss in birds: the mental image of a bird with bedraggled, sweat-soaked and ineffective plumage is readily conjured up!

However, most of a bird's feathers are under muscular control beneath the skin, and this provides an alternative cooling stratagem. With body feathers held erect, rather than in the normal flattish streamlined posture, birds can turn tail into any breeze that is blowing, the upright feathers serving the role of ventilator slots or louvres and directing the air movement down to cool the skin.

But being unable to lose heat by sweating may not be such a disadvantage, because sweating results in appreciable losses of salt (which might be difficult to replace in desert surroundings) and, more important, in a dangerous loss of body water. Panting, too, exposes the moist surfaces of the mouth and throat: though the evaporation that takes place may lower the body temperature briefly, it does so only at the expense of body moisture loss. In birds, panting – or the equivalent, called gular fluttering – is rarely employed by true desert species.

The simplest strategy is the one adopted by most animal groups in desert habitats – seeking some form of shelter. Most desert birds will reduce all activity over the hottest hours, roosting in the shade of rocks or bushes, or sometimes entering underground burrows. This enforced siesta means that the search for food and water must be concentrated into a few hours at the beginning and end of the day. In predatory and insectivorous birds the feeding time lost is probably more than compensated for by the fact that their prey is much more active, and thus more readily available, during dawn and dusk.

In deserts where heat or drought reach seasonal or occasional extremes that are impossible to live with, then birds, with their powers of flight, are better able than most desert creatures to move on to more tolerable areas often a great distance away. Debenham, writing in 1954, suggested that 'the whole secret of life in arid regions is movement, a readiness and freedom to migrate'. This statement is particularly applicable to bird populations, with no better example than Australia; Alan Keast estimated that almost one-third of the total number of Australian species could be classified as nomads – an amazingly high proportion.

On a more local level, the broad-winged vultures, eagles, kites and buzzards may take advantage of their powers of soaring flight to escape the heat. By exploiting rising currents of hot air they require little energy output to spiral to a height of 1000 m (3300 ft) or more, where the temperatures are appreciably lower and high-altitude breezes assist in cooling them.

Pre-adaptation has a part to play in heat tolerance, too, giving birds appreciable advantages over mammals. When it comes to keeping relatively cool in conditions of 'dry' heat, the fact that, of all groups of animals, birds have the highest normal body temperatures is a considerable asset. The 'normal' temperature of a bird is around 40°C (104°F). Until the ambient temperature exceeds their own, birds need to resist or limit heat losses from their bodies to their environment.

An analysis of hot summer days in the deserts of the United States showed that on many days birds did not need to invoke any heat-loss mechanisms at all; if they did need to employ cooling strategies, it was only briefly at midday. In contrast, mammals needed to lose heat for several hours of almost every day over a three-month summer period. Linked to this is another pre-adaptive feature – hyperthermia, or heat tolerance. Birds seem better able than mammals of broadly similar size and shape to tolerate, on a regular basis, their body temperatures rising as much as 3°C (about 5°F) above normal. However, there does seem to be an upper limit of about 45°C (113°F) at which no bird can survive. Be it a desert specialist or not, at this stage some form of temperature reduction strategy is vital if death is to be avoided.

DESERT CAMOUFLAGE

As well as providing two-way insulation, feathers also offer desert birds valuable assistance with camouflage. The cryptic coloration of some of the desert species of lark is an excellent example: here geographical races may differ quite strikingly in colour, ranging from ashy grey to reddish grey depending on the place of origin – but the plumage colour always matches that of the sand, soil or rocks of the locality. Such camouflage has obvious benefits, in open habitats like deserts, in concealing small birds from potential predators.

Interestingly, the generally pale sandy coloration of desert animals also conforms to a 'biological rule' called Gloger's Law, which states that races of animals living in warm, dry areas are lighter in colour than those from more humid regions. This is because of a reduction in the amount of the dark pigment melanin. Though the physiological implications of Gloger's Law are poorly understood, it does seem valid as even the soles of the feet of the creatures concerned are paler – and this of course will not be a camouflage effect.

There are some striking exceptions to the generalization that desert birds (and a few other animals) resemble in their coloration the substrates on which they live – in many deserts a number of the native or indigenous birds are black. Considering the excellent ability of black objects to *absorb* heat, this seems to be a most remarkable, almost suicidal, situation. Examples come from a wide range of birds, including ravens, wheatears, chats, finch-larks and bustards. Two reasons are suggested for this curious state of affairs. Blackish birds take up some heat from the sun, and in so doing reduce the 'metabolic cost' of staying warm: in other words, they need to eat less food to maintain their bodily functions than would a pale or white bird. Given that they were able (as most do) to shelter from the heat of the day, this could be a positive advantage to birds from those deserts characterized by extreme daytime heat and nocturnal cold. These birds will hunt for food in the cool or even chill of early morning and evening – and because of their dark colour and the solar energy they soak up, they are saving some feeding time.

The second suggestion relates particularly to species like the wheatears and the black-bellied bustard, which are only partly black. Here, field observations suggest that another form of camouflage – disruptive – may be created. In bright sunlight any shadow cast is intensely black, especially against the normally pale sands, soils and rocks of desert habitats. Bold black or partly black mammals and birds improve their concealment if they stand close to patches of shadow, because their natural outline is disrupted and becomes unrecognizable where black plumage and shadow merge into each other. Such patterns have been widely used by human beings in desert warfare.

DEALING WITH WATER REQUIREMENTS

When it comes to obtaining the water necessary for life, birds use a variety of strategies. Naturally enough, around the few and far between permanent waterholes that are a feature of most deserts bird populations tend to increase in both numbers and diversity. Should the waterhole support enough vegetation to make it a wadi or oasis, then the 'ecological island' of tropical or subtropical vegetation may support some birds quite uncharacteristic of the desert, no matter how arid the distant surroundings may be, as well as some genuinely desert species living a life of some luxury compared with their counterparts actually out in the desert.

Where water is not regularly available, the ability of birds to move appreciable distances comparatively quickly is of paramount importance. Their powers of flight and highly accurate navigational skills endow them with a mobility unequalled in other animal groups. In some cases (for example the sandgrouse) flight enables the birds to visit permanent waterholes to drink on a daily basis, even though the water may be tens of kilometres from their usual habitat. In others a striking nomadic ability has developed, allowing dry-country birds to follow rainfall, even though it may be erratic in both timing and location. They can then exploit either the residual water in creek-bed lakes or pools, or the flush of vegetation and insect life that follows the rains. The best examples of these strategies come from the desert heartland of Australia, where the grey teal swiftly establishes breeding colonies following substantial rains, moving on as the terrain dries out. The other classic example is the budgerigar, that small grass parakeet now so popular as a cage and aviary bird. No matter how long ago or how far away the last rains were – even hundreds of kilometres – huge flocks collect, as if by magic, to feed on the seeds of the desert plants that spring rapidly but briefly into life following new rainfall. Several other species behave in the same way, including bronze-winged and flock pigeons and the small passerine warbler, the whiteface.

Some of these nomads also exploit their vegetarian diet. Budgerigars and several other seed-eaters can derive their daily moisture needs from apparently dry, ripe seeds, while other finches, pigeons and larks consume leaves, which have a much higher water content. Although this habit is sometimes regarded as an effective strategy for desert survival, experiments do not support the theory that the moisture released during the chemical reactions of digestion plays any worthwhile part in supplying desert birds with their moisture needs.

Even the zebra finch, an Australian bird better adapted to using this kind of water than most, loses more water through evaporation during the digestive process than is gained from the totally dry food.

But of course many desert foodstuffs, besides fleshy leaves, provide usable sources of 'pre-formed moisture' for those birds adapted to exploit them. Most insects and other invertebrate animals have as an exoskeleton, an impervious cuticle that very effectively protects their often highly fluid body contents from evaporation. Many desert birds feed largely on insects and the like, and they appear to provide for all the birds' moisture needs. Much the same is true of the birds of prey, including vultures, which derive their water from the flesh or carrion that they consume.

On occasion, desert seed-eaters (the African estrildid finches, for example) may prolong their ability to survive for months on end in desert areas lacking free water by supplementing their diet with insects. Specialist insect-feeders like the shrikes and some of the wheatears and chats may rarely, if ever, drink. This kind of behaviour is, however, not universal, even between closely related species. The two desert species of Australian robin rarely if ever drink from open water, while their close coastal relative from south-western and south-eastern Australia, the scarlet robin, drinks frequently and is even a common visitor to garden birdbaths and drinking troughs.

Hand-in-hand with the need to locate sources of water runs the need for a body highly geared towards water conservation, particularly during the excretion of waste products. Here again the pre-adaptations of birds as a group come into play, giving desert birds from the outset distinct advantages over mammals of similar size. Birds' kidneys extract water with great efficiency, and the renal excretory product from metabolizing protein comes in the form of semi-solid or jelly-like uric acid, instead of the fluid urine, containing urea, of the mammals. To dispose of similar amounts of nitrogenous waste products in this way, birds need usually less than 10 per cent of the amount of water required by mammals – a major saving.

One of the smallest of the pigeon family, a Namaqua dove visits a waterhole for its daily drink.

THE CHALLENGES OF DESERT BREEDING

At no stage in the yearly biological cycle of desert birds are the challenges greater than during the breeding season. Here is one situation where they may be at a disadvantage compared with mammals. A pregnant female mammal, though bulky and probably slower than normal in her movements, retains her mobility until the time of birth. This does allow her some choice, depending on the current climatic conditions, over where she produces her young. In birds similar in size to small mammals, once a breeding territory has been established and a nest site chosen (often some time before actual egg laying begins) this flexibility is lost. Once the process is under way, the location of at least the female (but normally both birds of the pair, or all birds of the clan) is fixed for the two to four weeks of incubation plus the rather longer period during which the young birds, either as nestlings or as juveniles, have

Excellent camouflage protects the two-banded courser and its chick from predators.

to be cared for. The young of comparable mammals would normally reach independence far more quickly.

But this is not to say that desert birds lack flexibility in their approach to the problems of breeding. The tactics that have been evolved are varied and fascinating. Most of the world's birds breed at regular intervals, the majority being 'timed' by the differences in light levels and day lengths occurring with the changing seasons; occasionally other factors are involved as well. There was once a generally held view that desert birds had adapted their breeding habits to take advantage of unpredictable rainfall, breeding when conditions were 'right'; rainfall, it was thought, took the place of day length as the dominant factor. This irregular breeding cycle now seems to apply only to Australia, where nomadism is prevalent and where even sedentary species may go for years between breeding cycles, depending on sporadic rains.

Elsewhere, in Africa, Asia and North America, breeding seasons seem to be more regular than in Australia, despite the fact that in some of the deserts

concerned the rainfall is at least as erratic as that in Australia. Interestingly, in these deserts sudden rains will not disrupt the regular pattern by triggering frenzied breeding activity, as would almost certainly be the case in Australia. The speed of reaction of Australian birds is phenomenal: in one reported case a bush chat was nest-building three days, and laid its first egg six days, after the rains broke a drought which had lasted for more than a year.

Otherwise, when choosing nest sites desert birds will frequently seek the benefit of any shade from rocks or stunted vegetation. Many nest in crevices, and some in disused rodent burrows, occasionally penetrating to the comparative cool found almost 1 m (3 ft) below the surface. Many, if not most, desert birds are best classified as 'ground nesters', for there is little suitable vegetation for them to nest in. Several unrelated species which nest in the open build small pebble mounds or barricades round the nest. These walls may act as windbreaks, or sometimes as dams to minimize damage caused by surface flood waters following the sudden torrential downpours typical of desert rains. They may also provide effective insulation. When the nest cup excavation is deep and its walls are pebble-lined, the air

Panting, and with back feathers erected to maximize cooling, a three-banded plover crouches over its eggs, sheltering them from direct sunshine.

pockets trapped between the pebbles can give substantial protection from the surrounding soil heat.

Many desert birds may crouch over their eggs in a 'sunshade' posture in extreme heat, but for much of the time they incubate normally, their feathers providing insulation properties against both nocturnal cold and considerable daytime heat. When the adult leaves the nest the eggs are in greater danger, and most open-nest desert birds are extremely reluctant to leave their eggs uncovered during the day unless the nest is in a patch of shade. If forced to leave, the female will often use her feet hastily to scrape a covering of sand over her eggs as a short-term protective measure.

Once the eggs have hatched, the chicks face considerable problems. These include the continuing need for protection from sun and soil heat, sometimes resolved by hiding in crevices or burrows or by seeking some shade, but often demanding parental protection, again in the fashion of a sunshade. This effectively limits the capacity of one parent to hunt for food, in circumstances where food is often scarce enough anyway. Nestlings, and even the young of species that leave the nest as soon as their down is dry and wander about under their parents' watchful eyes, lack mobility, which makes them heavily dependent on the moisture within the food brought by their parents. The sandgrouse have evolved an extraordinary solution to this problem (see p. 84).

SMALLER GROUND BIRDS OF THE DESERT
In the Old World, the first group of small birds to catch the eye as the terrain becomes increasingly arid and stony is that family of small thrushes known as chats because of their distinctive 'chack' or 'chat' call, reminiscent of two pebbles being struck sharply together. Prime amongst these are the wheatears, upright and perky, with longish, slender legs. Most wheatears show the distinctive white patch on the upper tail and rump from which the group gets its name – 'wheat' being derived from the Anglo-Saxon word for white, and 'ear' being a corruption of 'earse' or 'arse' in the same language, meaning (politely) rump or rear. Most wheatears spend much of their time on the ground, and many are confidingly tame. Distinctive though the males usually are in breeding plumage, the duller females of many species are so similar as to pose considerable problems of identification even to the experienced ornithologist.

Even the common wheatear, a migrant summer visitor to temperate and cool-temperate Eurasia, Iceland and Greenland, favours stony, comparatively dry ground. Its relationship to wheatear species that remain year-round in arid parts of Africa is the subject of debate: experts differ in their views on whether the Somali wheatear and the West African mountain wheatear are simply non-migratory races of the common wheatear with slightly different plumage, or separate species in their own right. In Asia, the common wheatear's place is taken by the rather drabber Isabelline wheatear, named (as are a number of other drab or 'dirty'-coloured birds) after Isabella of Spain, Queen of that country in Columbus's time, who was reputed never to take a bath!

More typical of the semi-deserts of the Mediterranean basin is the black-eared wheatear, which has an 'ecological substitute' to the east in the central Palaearctic region, the pied wheatear. The rocky, arid uplands of southern Europe and the Atlas Mountains of North Africa, up to altitudes often in excess of 2500 m (over 8000 ft), are home to the very distinctive black wheatear, its strikingly handsome velvet-black plumage relieved only by the white rump patch in the shape of an inverted 'U'. Rocky screes and crags are its home, where it behaves much like a smaller version of the more colourful rock thrushes.

Most arid of all in its choice of habitat is the appropriately named desert wheatear, although even this species does not penetrate the desert heartland, preferring the fringes where at least some vegetation survives for much of the year. It is sandier in plumage than the common wheatear, and its tail pattern separates it from all other wheatears, which have varying amounts of white on the base and particularly sides of the tail. In the desert wheatear only the rump and undertail coverts are pale – buff rather than pure white – and the comparatively long tail is quite black. This makes a ready identification aid, especially as first views are often of the bird flying away, showing its rump and tail pattern to best effect.

Desert wheatear races occupy suitable terrain from North Africa and the Arabian peninsula east to the high (4000 m or over 13,000 ft) plateaux of Tibet. The more northerly and higher-altitude populations are migratory, forced to be so by winter snows and food scarcity. During the hot summer breeding season, desert wheatears build their grassy nests either in the shelter of a stunted bush or clump of grass, or commonly below ground in a natural cavity among the rocks or in a deserted rodent burrow. Here there is a considerable measure of protection from predators, with the added

benefits of a stable microclimate of moderate warmth and humidity contrasting markedly with the extremes of daytime heat and night-time cold outside. Where food is concerned the desert wheatear and the black wheatear seem to concentrate their attentions on terrestrial invertebrates, and this diet produces much of the water they need. Insects such as beetles, small grasshoppers and ants will doubtless predominate, but spiders and other arthropods will be eaten avidly when the opportunity arises.

The starts are closely related to the wheatears, with similar behaviour and harsh calls, and a similarly scratchy but still melodious song. They too derive their name from Anglo-Saxon roots, 'staert' meaning tail. Most familiar are the woodland redstart of temperate Europe and the black redstart. The latter, traditionally a bird of mountain screes that has adapted well to life on the rooftops of southern European towns and villages, extended its range dramatically at the close of the Second World War: amazingly it colonized the heaps of rubble created by the blanket bombing raids on European cities.

The redstart species are comparatively brightly coloured compared with the two desert species in this group. One, the brown rock chat, has penetrated eastwards from the African homeland of the group and colonized the arid areas of India; interestingly, like the black redstart it also frequently ventures into towns and cities. A mixture of dull sooty browns, the brown rock chat must be one of the least colourfully plumaged of the world's birds. The other desert species, the blackstart, ranges along the southern part of the Sahara, through the Ethiopian deserts to the western half of the Arabian peninsula. Although sombre in plumage, the dull grey-browns of the blackstart are relieved by chestnut patches on the ear coverts, and by the pure black rump and tail from which it derives its name.

Blackstarts are birds of rocky outcrops in the desert, often in areas almost devoid of vegetation – a contrast to the wheatears and to the brown rock chat. Usually tame, and often surprisingly numerous considering the harshness of their habitat, blackstarts seem to live in pairs throughout the year. Like all chats they are restless birds, forever on the move and always fanning or flicking their wings. Instead of flicking their tail up and down and bobbing their head, as do the wheatears,

A male mourning wheatear in its rocky habitat in the Negev Desert of Israel.

blackstarts half-open their wings and tail in a tempo of metronomic regularity. This display features all through the year: pairs of blackstarts defend their territory year-round, not only against others of their kind but also against both resident and migrant wheatears. This is a clear indication both of the close relationship between the two and of the constant importance of the territory as a food-providing zone for this species – perhaps not surprisingly, considering the terrain.

Blackstarts feed on insects and other small terrestrial invertebrates; like wheatears, from this diet they very largely satisfy their moisture needs. The nest, again in parallel to the wheatears, is usually underground or at least sheltered from sun, hot air and predators deep in a rocky crevice.

The small family of Australian chats (more properly called 'chat-warblers', endemic to Australia and not closely related to the Old World chats proper) are in striking contrast, so far as plumage is concerned, with these two sombre Afro-Indian species. Best known of the five is the white-faced chat, to European eyes startlingly reminiscent in its grey, black and white plumage to a short-tailed version of the white wagtail with rather brown wings. This is essentially a coastal or marshland bird, but three of its relatives – the orange, crimson, and gibber chats – are all desert birds. Australian chats spend most of their time on the ground, running athletically to catch insects and other invertebrates but also feeding to a considerable extent on seeds when they are available. In addition, when the erratic climate has favoured the desert with rain chats are well able to take advantage of the glorious display of blossom that follows.

One unusual anatomical feature they possess is the brush or feathery tip to their tongue. Covered in microscopic fleshy 'bristles', the tongue can be dipped into a flower's nectary and a watery, sugar-rich meal withdrawn. The two most spectacularly beautiful chats, the orange and crimson, particularly favour this feeding technique. Each is highly nomadic, following the spasmodic rains and exploiting the flushes of flowers and nectar they produce as an aid to survival.

The gibber chat – sandy brown above, yellowish below – is named after the pebbly rock desert gibber plains of central Australia. It appears not to be so nomadic as the other species: some at least spend their life spans in one small area, regardless of the length of the drought or the seasonal severity of the temperatures. Like the other Australian chat-warblers, gibber chats have brush-tipped tongues and so can feed on nectar on the extremely rare occasions when the desert blooms, but much of their food is thought to consist of terrestrial invertebrates. During the heat of the day, gibber chats seek shelter under rocky piles or down burrows – despite the fact that on occasion this must be a risky business, since the original burrow digger (also escaping the fierce heat) may turn out to be a hungry predator like a snake or one of the larger lizards.

Although they are apparently not as nomadic as the orange and crimson chats, gibber chat breeding does seem to be dictated to some degree by the climate. There is no strict season, but clutch sizes are determined by how favourable a season it is – prolonged drought possibly inhibits breeding altogether, while sudden rains provoke the instant response of nest-making and large clutches of eggs typical also of nomadic birds.

At all times gibber chats are confiding birds, reluctant to fly, but when they have a nest the adults will employ the 'broken-wing trick' display to draw potential predators away from it. When danger, in the shape of a crow or lizard, threatens, a parent gibber chat will run towards it, turning at what seems to be a suicidally close range. With one wing trailing along the ground as if broken, the parent bird staggers ahead of the predator on a rambling path, but always away from the nest. Should the predator attempt to strike, then of course the gibber chat will either run swiftly away from harm, or fly off – but by then the predator's attention has been well and truly diverted. This ruse usually works well.

Another generally colourful and peculiarly Australian family also has desert-dwelling representatives – the malurid wrens. As with the Australian chats, these wrens are unrelated to the wren family ranging widely over both the Old World and the New. All of the fairy wren group are tiny, with an overall length of 12–15 cm (5–6 in.) of which much consists of the long tail, usually held cocked. Of the thirteen species, most are brightly coloured with glossy black and various shades of electric blue, so iridescent as to put a kingfisher to shame, predominating. They live in scrub country; several species venture into semi-arid habitats, but one, the white-winged wren (as its name suggests, with strikingly white wings contrasting with a body and tail in various shades of iridescent cobalt blue) ranges right across the great dry heartland of central and western Australia.

These tiny birds are insectivorous, and their disproportionately long, strong legs indicate that they spend much of their lives on the ground, darting about seeking prey beneath clumps of spinifex grass and other desert vegetation. There is some debate over the relationships between the Australian wrens: in some ways they appear to be a specialized group of warblers, while in others they show affinities to the babbler family, both anatomically and in behaviour. One striking social characteristic of most if not all babblers, shared by the white-winged wrens, is that they live and roam in cohesive small parties. Usually each group consists of a dominant pair of adults in prime condition, with up to a dozen 'hangers-on'. These may be adult or immature birds, and some may be offspring of the dominant pair from a previous breeding season. Those other adults in the group are never in such excellent plumage as the dominant birds.

It is the dominant pair that will mate and the female which will lay a clutch of eggs – but in a nest built with the assistance of the whole party. Once the clutch of eggs is complete, others will share with the dominant female the tedious tasks of incubation and later brooding the growing young, which normally entails shading them from the sun. The territory over which the group ranges will be defended by them all, and when there are young in the nest all will assist in gathering food for them. This communal nesting strategy seems to have evolved to help ensure that a brood of young is reared successfully even when conditions are hostile. Should tragedy intervene and one or other of the breeding adults perish, then the next in line in the group's well-established social hierarchy swiftly assumes the lead role.

Closely related to the fairy wrens are the three emu wrens. They are similar in size, with spherical bodies and heads; long, slim cocked tails; and the oversize legs and feet indicative of a terrestrial lifestyle. But emu wrens are far less colourful than their cousins: buff underparts and dark-streaked brownish upperparts are relieved only by a chestnut crown and blue bib in the male of the rufous-crowned emu wren, the desert specialist of the three. The female lacks the blue bib. So secretive are they, and so well camouflaged, that brief glimpses are the most that can be hoped for as rufous-crowned emu wrens scuttle about hunting their insect prey beneath – and through – the apparently impenetrable spinifex clumps.

That brief glimpse may well be enough to reveal the strange feathers that give the emu wrens their name. The first impression is of a bird with plumage in very poor condition – the tail feathers especially appear to be worn down almost to the central quills. This rather hairy look – similar to that produced by the feathers of the massive flightless emu – is caused by the complete lack of microscopic hooks on the feather barbules. In a normal bird these hooks hold the barbules together to give the smoothly knit, immaculate surface typical of a well-preened feather.

So elusive are rufous-crowned emu wrens, and so hostile their desert habitat, that comparatively little is known of their breeding habits or social organization. What has been discovered is that nesting often follows rains whenever they occur, and that the nest is a domed structure often built into the heart of a spinifex tussock – this is perhaps not surprising. What seems quite astonishing is that the normal clutch size appears to be of only two eggs. Even in kinder, temperate climates, similar-sized birds would be expected to lay at least three times this number of eggs. The implications are that either emu wrens are very long-lived (and thus do not 'need' to lay many eggs during each year of their life), or that egg and nestling losses are very low (so that most eggs would give rise to an adult successor). Both of these suppositions fly in the face of what would be expected for such tiny birds in such an extremely harsh environment. An intriguing mystery remains here.

The New World provides the home for the vast majority of the world's species of true wren. Largest of them all – most fall in the 10–15 cm (4–6 in.) size range – is the cactus wren at around 20 cm (8 in.) long. The colloquial name indicates that this is a desert specialist of the family, and it occurs throughout the desert areas of California, Arizona, New Mexico and western Texas. Cactus wrens, perhaps because of the harshness of their environment, are rather more catholic in their choice of food than most other wrens, which seem restricted to insects and other small invertebrate animals. Insects and other arthropods certainly feature prominently in the cactus wren's diet, but this species has the size and muscle to tackle larger animal prey including small lizards. In addition it seems frequently to eat soft, pulpy fruit and seeds when they are available. Soft fruits and insects should provide for much if not all of their water needs.

Cactus wrens spend much of their time in and around various cacti, yuccas and other prickly desert plants. Surprisingly for their size, they move nimbly and with considerable speed through cactus branches, even preferring the cholla, which more than any other positively bristles with dense clusters of very sharp spines. Their nest – a neat, usually domed structure of soft, dry grasses – is built deep in the protection of these spines. It is an interesting reflection on the cactus wren's ability to live amongst these spines, and human ornithologists' failure to cope with them, that relatively little is known of the cactus wren's nesting habits and biology!

But it is known that both parents share the tasks of incubation and feeding the young, and that both in and out of the breeding season the nests are also used as shelters for roosting – protection against the sharp chill of the desert night. For some time after fledging, the young return with their parents to roost overnight in the nest. But within a few weeks they gain independence, not just in finding food in a hostile climate and in an immediate environment physically dangerous by the presence of cactus spines, but also by building their own roosting 'nests'. Initially crude structures, these must provide valuable training for building the real thing when the cactus wren reaches maturity.

Most of the smaller desert birds described so far have been predominantly insect-eaters, though several have demonstrated adaptability by including seasonal or sporadic fruit and seeds within their diets. In general terms, where free-standing water is extremely scarce, smaller birds with only a short-haul foraging range probably find it easier to extract their water needs from a diet of animal matter than from a diet composed largely of seeds. So it is not surprising that 'carnivorous' small birds tend to outnumber vegetarians in deserts. But one group of small, predominantly vegetarian, birds has effectively colonized and exploited the desert areas of the Old World – the larks.

Even in temperate regions, most members of the lark family tend to be found in more open, often stony and certainly drier habitats, verging in many cases on semi-desert. But there are also real desert specialists, and indeed it may well be that the lark family as a whole arose in the major desert areas of North Africa, Arabia and Asia, the heart of the Old World. The various desert species would then be the typical larks, with those that frequent gentler climates only more familiar because these places are more accessible to human beings. These better-known larks would represent divergence from the 'norm', and would be better seen as indicators of diversification than of traditional habits and habitats.

One of the larger members of the family is the thick-billed lark of the northern Sahara and Arabian deserts. Bulky in flight, and conspicuous because of the white trailing edges to its wings and its black-tipped white tail, the thick-billed lark is distinguished by its huge bill

– finch-like and powerful. The comparatively large head with its bulging cheeks is a sign of the powerful musculature that enables the beak to crush the toughest of drought-resistant seed cases produced by desert plants. To give additional purchase, the edge of the upper mandible has a notch that allows the seed to be held fast while maximum pressure is applied. Though their favourite food is large seeds, often plucked from the plant, thick-billed larks will sometimes dig for plant tubers, and are not averse to tackling any unwary ground-dwelling invertebrate animals they may encounter. They deal with these as with tough desert seeds and few small arthropods or snails have a shell strong enough to resist that massive beak.

Typical thick-billed lark habitat is the stony desert known locally as hamada – gently undulating limestone plains copiously covered in flints and rock flakes. Much of the time they feed on the ground, walking, running and occasionally hopping as they search. Outside the breeding season they may range about the hamada in small groups. During the breeding season the male outlines and defends his territory in typical lark fashion, singing high over the desert so near-stationary as to appear to be attached to the early morning and evening sky by a length of elastic. Below him, the female sits on her eggs in a simple scrape; normally sheltered from the fiercest heat of the sun by an overhanging rock or stunted plant, the scrape will be lined with a few dry grass stems and sometimes animal hair or plant down. Often the pair will have ringed the nest rim with a miniature pebble wall. She will usually have a clutch of three to five handsomely marked pinkish eggs.

As a demonstration of the versatility of the shapes and sizes of lark beaks, the similar-sized bifasciated or hoopoe lark offers an admirable example. The bifasciated lark has a wider range than the thick-billed, covering all of the Sahara, the desert areas of Ethiopia and the Horn of Africa, northwards through Israel to Syria, the entire Arabian peninsula and eastwards into Iran, Afghanistan and north-western India, ascending to altitudes of at least 1500 m (5000 ft). Interestingly, males are appreciably larger than females: one possible reason is that this reduces competition for food between the members of a pair. Although there would obviously be a considerable area of 'common ground', females would hunt invertebrates too small to be of value to males, while males would be able to tackle prey too large for females to handle. With food and moisture supplies so limited and critical, every evolutionary stratagem to maximize feeding efficiency is worth bringing into play.

The bifasciated lark gets its alternative colloquial name from the prominent black and white barring on its wings, conspicuous only in flight but reminiscent (as is its long, slightly downcurved beak) of the hoopoe that is widespread across the warmer regions of the Old World. Otherwise the plumage is what might be expected of a desert-dwelling, largely terrestrial bird, with overall sandy-buff to sandy-grey upper parts (depending on region). White underparts help obliterate the counter-shading to be expected of a bird standing in the open in bright sunlight.

This combination of excellent plumage camouflage on the ground, especially when stationary, with striking black and white patterns visible when flying, is a feature of many desert birds including several wheatears, larks, coursers and the much larger houbara bustard. It is shared by some mammals such as rabbits, hares and sand rats, which flaunt the white or black areas of their tails during some forms of movement. It is thought that in most cases these are signals – sometimes for others to escape, sometimes for territorial display. Often there is no reason why the same plumage patterns could not serve both purposes in appropriate circumstances. In the case of the hoopoe lark, so loath is the bird to fly, preferring to sprint away on its long, strong legs if danger threatens, that the principal purpose seems most likely to be display.

Males may defend a territory exceeding 2 sq km (0·8 sq mile) in extent – an indication of the scarcity of long-term suitable food, for these are sedentary birds. Some display chases occur on the ground, but the male also spirals upwards for hundreds of metres, parachuting down slowly in song flight before plummeting the final few metres to earth, wings closed. As in many larks, the song is a complex one. In the case of the hoopoe lark it is composed of various musical pipings and fluting whistles, and lacks the chirrups of some other species.

The nest is made of grass, often in a shallow depression with some shade from a rock or plant, but exposed to tremendous heat even so. In the hottest areas of Arabia, including Kuwait, nests have been reported in desert vegetation several centimetres above ground and thus enjoying some cooling effect from any breeze that may be blowing. Like the emu wren from Australia, the hoopoe lark lays an astonishingly small clutch of eggs, normally just two.

The long, slightly downcurved beak of the hoopoe

Rufous-naped lark: excellent camouflage and long strong legs indicate a largely terrestrial lifestyle.

lark is both longer and more robust than that of a thrush of comparable size. Certainly the beak is able to deal with many of the seeds that the hoopoe lark encounters, but its prime use seems to be for digging – reportedly even in soil sun-baked almost to rock – for insects, including the ferocious ant-lion, and their larvae. Other small terrestrial invertebrates are eaten, as are any small or young lizards or scorpions unable to escape the hunting hoopoe lark's speedy dash in pursuit.

Last of the larks under consideration is the aptly named desert lark. It is one of a sub-group of three so-called sand larks (the others are Dunn's lark and the bar-tailed desert lark). Desert larks have a distribution only slightly less widespread than the hoopoe lark: they are sedentary, and perhaps because of this have developed many geographical races or sub-species which sometimes differ quite appreciably in colour, but normally match the colours of the rocky desert substrate on which each lives. At all ages, and in all races, about the best that can be said of desert lark plumage is that it is nondescript. That said, a drab mixture of sandy buffs, browns or greys may clearly be of excellent camouflage value for a bird that spends much of its life on the ground.

At about 15 cm (6 in.) long, with a shortish beak, pointed but of medium strength, the desert lark is perhaps more typical of the entire range of larks than the ones previously discussed. It is also more typical in that seeds are the most important component of its diet, though insects, spiders and other invertebrates are taken if the opportunity offers. The song is comparatively simple, with a few fluting and twittering notes, often produced from the ground but sometimes in a low-level undulating song flight – far from typically lark-like.

The nest is a grass-lined scrape, beside or beneath a plant or stone, sometimes within a burrow. It is frequently recorded as having a characteristic small bank of pebbles round the rim – the remarkable adaptation described earlier, which acts as a soakaway, or protective dam, during sudden, shallow flash floods following a desert storm.

One-third of the circumference of the world away, across the Indian Ocean and the Malay archipelago in the red heart of Australia, lives one of the best known of all desert birds. Best known not because of its desert-living adaptations but because it is one of the most popular of all cage birds, the budgerigar is so linked with humans and domesticity that its real origins are often obscured. In its natural habitat, the vast desert interior of Australia, its way of life is reasonably well understood considering the difficulties of conducting field studies in such an unrelenting environment.

Budgerigars in the wild, as in the aviary, are flock birds, gregarious in the extreme, which makes their frequent solitary confinement as cage birds seem less acceptable. To see a tight-packed flock, often tens of thousands strong, twisting and turning in flight as one – bright green against red earth or shining steel-blue sky – is a stunning sight.

Superb eyesight and reflexes enable them to move with extraordinary precision, and there are no mid-air collisions among these chattering, warbling flocks. On occasion, in good years or in favoured locations after rain, flocks may reach millions strong, quite literally darkening the sky. It is equally fascinating to see a smaller flock, so bright and obvious in flight,

apparently vanish totally as it plunges into the eucalyptus trees to seek shade.

Budgerigars are vegetarian, with seeds of spinifex and Mitchell grass predominating in their diet. Unlike the larks, they rarely seem to take animal matter, though sometimes freshly emerged succulent greenery embellishes their dry diet. They are nomads, and the flocks will head with unerring accuracy (using often unknown or imperfectly understood signs) for areas often hundreds of kilometres distant where recent rains have caused the billabongs or waterways to fill up and produced a flush of fast-maturing plant growth. The flocks feed avidly on the seeds produced, and frequently breeding will occur following lightning-fast courtship – stimulated no doubt by the collective enthusiasm and participation typical of flock birds that breed at the same time. The typical nest site is in a tree hole or hollow log, often in the fragmented strip of woodland along the seasonal watercourses. Not only is the breeding season often opportunist, governed by the unpredictable occurrence of rains, but so too may the clutch size vary from three to four eggs up to eight, depending on how much grass seed has been set after the rains.

Though nomadic birds get opportunities to drink from waterways replenished by rains, and from permanent waterholes – either natural or artesian well-derived to water grazing stock – there may be intervals of months or even years in some parts when no rain falls within the birds' range. In these circumstances budgerigars are well able to survive on the very small quantities of water remaining in sun-baked, long-ripened seeds. Budgerigars are among the best adapted of all desert vegetarians in their ability to exist well on a diet with so little moisture content.

Rather larger in size at 19 cm (8 in.), more sombre in plumage (but still beautiful), and just as confiding if not even tamer than a budgerigar, is Bourke's parrot. Their habit of continuing to feed even though an observer is only a few metres away, coupled with the soft blues, greens, pinks and browns of their plumage, makes Bourke's parrots easily overlooked – not least because these colours blend strangely well with their surroundings. Most Bourke's parrots over the uninhabited vastness of the interior are nomadic, but unlike budgerigars they usually go about in pairs or small groups. Where boreholes have created permanent water sources, even deep in the desert, stable populations establish themselves in the neighbourhood and develop regular flighting patterns. The timing is unusual – the birds come in to drink in the semi-darkness just before dawn, and just after dusk. Bourke's parrots are vegetarians, eating a mixture of seeds and green plant material, especially fresh leaves emerging after the rains.

More tantalizing is the third desert dweller, the night parrot. Only one specimen has been collected this century, back in 1912, and that is now lost; most of the albeit sparse information was obtained in the nineteenth century. The last sighting is usually given as sixty or seventy years ago, but reputable records continue to turn up – few in number, but enough to suggest that considering the night parrot to be extinct may be premature.

Old records indicate that the night parrot, larger again than Bourke's parrot at 23 cm (9 in.), feeds extensively on spinifex seeds but eats fresh green matter in quantity when it appears after the rains. The old records are sometimes less helpful, even conflicting with one another, when it comes to nomadic habits. Some observers rate their flight as feeble, stating that night parrots could easily be caught by running after them as they scuttled off on the ground; while others report a strong but erratic flight to waterholes some kilometres distant.

The excitement when some lucky ornithologist returns with a photograph is easy to imagine, but neither the night parrot's habits, nor its preferred habitat, help in the search. They are greenish birds, mottled with yellow and dark brown, with seemingly oversize heads and eyes and a strangely loose, pheasant-like tail. The large eyes, of course, relate to its nocturnal habits: during the day, when it could be more easily seen, the old reports suggest that it either hides or more likely shelters from the heat in a tunnel burrowed beneath a spinifex clump or in a hollow log or mammal burrow. To make finding them even more difficult, their favourite habitat is dense spinifex grassland. As they are both quiet and secretive, and normally terrestrial in their habits, the challenge of relocating the night parrot and confirming its continued survival is a difficult one.

Another largely terrestrial desert bird, this time a carnivore dwelling in the desert areas of the south-western United States, is far from extinct. This is the roadrunner, a pheasant-sized (50 cm or 20 in.) member of the ground-cuckoo subfamily. The great majority of the Old World cuckoos are brood parasites, laying their eggs singly or in groups in the nests of other birds. The parent cuckoos then cease to have any part in the raising of their offspring, leaving this often substantial task to hapless 'foster parents', sometimes diminutive compared with their unwanted parasite. Typically their own clutch of eggs or brood of tiny young is quickly ousted from the nest by the precociously muscular young cuckoo, although in some cuckoo species the young are raised together with their foster siblings.

Not so the ground-cuckoos and the roadrunner, which builds a substantial nest for itself in thorny scrub or in a cactus. The basic structure of twigs and leaves contains a compact cup, often made of dried cattle, horse, deer or antelope dung, sometimes embellished with a cast snake skin or two. Typical clutches range from three to six eggs, although occasionally two or more females may be attached to the same male and lay in the same nest, raising the clutch size to a dozen eggs or more. Both sexes share the tasks of incubation, brooding and feeding the young. Since incubation starts as soon as the first egg is laid (unlike with most smaller birds, where it begins when the clutch is complete), the young hatch at intervals of one or two days. If the brood is large, then at a couple of weeks old there are substantial size differences between the oldest and the most recently hatched. Should feeding conditions deteriorate or if the climate become even harsher it is the smaller chicks that perish first, unable to compete with their larger, stronger siblings in grabbing a meal from a returning parent. The parents make no attempt to give preferential treatment to their weaker offspring. Cruel though this may seem to human eyes, this strategy (which has evolved in a number of other species, including owls, whose food supplies may fail) does maximize the chances of at least one, or some, of the brood fledging successfully.

The roadrunner has been described as a tireless and energetic predator, with great adaptive capacity and resourcefulness. They have been known to lie in wait behind a suitable rock, positioning themselves to catch swallows and swifts skimming low over a rainstorm puddle to snatch a drink, just as a cat would. Any noise of a creature in distress will bring roadrunners at the gallop – making squeaking noises through pursed lips is an ideal way for birdwatchers to tempt roadrunners out of dense desert scrub for a clearer view. 'Runner' is appropriate, as roadrunners do most of their hunting on foot, and are capable of sustained speeds of 20 kph (13 mph), with dashes to secure prey timed at almost 40 kph (25 mph)!

Though most pairs (they appear to remain mated, and to live in pairs – sometimes trios – together for life) hunt the desert soils, whenever a tarmac road crosses the desert local roadrunners will use it for ease of access to fresh hunting grounds. Passing traffic will also cause casualties among all sorts of wildlife: roadrunners are interested in feeding from the carrion so readily provided, from large insects up to jack rabbits or even deer. So where these rare roads cross roadrunner deserts the motorist stands a high chance of sighting a roadrunner or 'chaparral cock', running ahead on its long, strong legs.

Besides their speed, roadrunners are equipped with lightning-fast reflexes and a longish, stout beak. They use the latter to tear apart carrion and to attack even tough-skinned or prickly fruit. Their main prey items, small snakes and lizards, are caught and swiftly subdued, if not killed, by pounding them with the powerful beak on a rock or on the hard soil before they are swallowed head-first. Small mammals like mice and gophers, their young and the eggs or young of any ground-nesting birds are eaten enthusiastically too. Also listed amongst roadrunner food are many large insects, together with scorpions, centipedes and spiders, including tarantulas. Add to this the occasional verified

record of them eating young rattlesnakes, and it is not surprising that roadrunners feature at the centre of many local folk tales, particularly amongst American Indian tribes. Prime among the folklore is the idea that roadrunners build corrals of sharp cactus spines round rattlesnakes, then wait for the rattler to sustain a mortal wound by impaling itself on the spines in its attempt to escape. The roadrunner then moves in for its meal.

Also the subject of American Indian folklore, but for centuries disbelieved, is the poorwill. Named from its 'poor-will' call, this bird, little larger than a thrush, is a comparatively short-tailed member of the nightjar family. Flying silently on velvet-soft wings, nightjars are insect catchers active at dusk and night. Large eyes give the clue to their low-light lifestyle. On close examination, what appears to be a small, insignificant beak turns out to be just the horny tip of a mouth that opens literally from ear to ear. With this huge gape, fringed with strong bristles to give an even greater

Often seen as almost a cartoon character, the roadrunner is one of the most skilful and adaptable exploiters of desert conditions.

catching area, nightjars sweep through the insect-rich evening air, mouths agape like aerial plankton nets.

Poorwills inhabit North American 'cold' deserts, where, although the summer days are unbearably hot, the winter days and nights are cold – often extremely so. As a result insect food is just not available during the winter months, and migration southwards to warmer climates would seem to be the only solution. But perhaps not. . . .

Over a century and a half ago, the Navajo Indians of Arizona told stories of birds that slept away the winter, tucked securely into crevices in the desert rocks. Little attention was paid to these 'folk tales'. But between 1917 and the 1930s various ornithologists noted the ability of hummingbirds to become torpid overnight, with temperature, heartbeat and respiration rates all dropping substantially. For birds living such hyper-active lives, with a rapid turnover of food and energy, this was a major survival strategy at the colder fringes of their range. The more far-sighted of these scientists also postulated that related bird families, including the swifts and the nightjars, might share this ability. But although torpid white-throated swifts were found in cold weather clustered together in a rocky crevice in California, no evidence was forthcoming to support the ability of nightjars to do the same.

Then, in December 1946, a poorwill was found in a rock crevice in the Chuckwalla Mountains in the Californian Colorado Desert. Jaeger, the ornithologist discoverer, found that the bird was to all intents inert, with respiration and heartbeat undetectable. Fortunately he ringed the bird before replacing it, because on visits in subsequent winters he found the same bird in the same niche. Although not many poorwills have been found hibernating in this torpid or dormant state, field and laboratory experiments have confirmed that genuine hibernation (rather than brief overnight torpidity as in the hummingbirds) can and does occur in birds.

In the poorwill, body temperatures drop from a norm of around 40°C (104°F) to something near 18°C (64°F). Respiration and digestion are both reduced to 'tick-over' levels, with a resultant dramatic saving in energy. The normal levels of body fat accumulated by a poorwill during the late summer and early autumn should, it has been calculated, allow it to survive in hibernation for a hundred days, corresponding closely with the three months that would seem to be required by the desert winter. So this is the overwinter sleeper of the Navajo campfire stories.

One of the jewels of the bird world, a male ruby-topaz hummingbird feeds on nectar from a cactus flower.

The third medium-sized carnivorous bird of the American deserts may not be the subject of Indian folklore, but has all the qualifications for such a role. It is the gila woodpecker, which is associated throughout western Mexico, Baja California and southern Arizona with various species of massive cacti, particularly the yucca or Joshua tree and the largest of all cacti, the giant saguaro. A conspicuous creature with its zebra striping of black and white on back, wings and tail, contrasting with its sandy grey body and red crown patch, the gila woodpecker makes little attempt at concealment, and advertises its presence with abrupt, noisy calls. Like the smaller, duller cactus wren, it has mastered the skills of moving about on the surface of these large cacti, despite their defensive barrier of ferocious thorns.

Like other woodpeckers, gila woodpeckers have their toes arranged two pointing forward, two back, a condition called zygodactyl – in contrast, most perching birds have their toes arranged in a three-forward, one-back format. Their legs and toes are comparatively long and strong, and well protected from cactus spines by horny plates or scales of tough keratin. As with all woodpeckers their claws are long, curved and very sharp-pointed, ensuring (with their toe arrangement) maximum grip between the spines. The beak is long, strong and sharp – well able to probe between clusters of spines without endangering the bird's eyes.

The gila woodpecker is perhaps better described as an omnivore, for although it concentrates on animal matter, should suitable seeds or ripe fruit become available then it will exploit this fresh food source. The animal matter in the diet will include any nestfuls of young birds that the woodpecker may encounter, together with any unwary large insects. Their major hunting technique centres on extremely sensitive hearing, aided perhaps by a sense of touch. Combining these two senses, gila woodpeckers can detect the activities of insect grubs burrowing within the flesh of saguaro cacti. Holding on with sharp claws, and using its tail as a prop, the bird begins to excavate. As in many other woodpeckers, the central pair of tail feathers are longest, and have specially strengthened shafts to fulfil this valuable role. This means of support accounts for the woodpeckers' habit of always working head-uppermost on a trunk or branch – unlike, for example, the nuthatches, whose tail feathers are soft and not employed in this way, allowing them to move about head-up or head-down with equal facility.

Using its beak as a combined hammer and chisel, the gila woodpecker swiftly reaches the cactus-boring insect's tunnel. Then its immensely long (about 5 cm or 2 in.) tongue comes into play like a harpoon. The tip is horny with backward-pointing barbs – just like a whaler's harpoon in miniature – and is poked along the tunnel until the larva is encountered, stabbed and withdrawn on the barbed tip to be eaten. When not in use, this oversize tongue is 'stored' – not cluttering up the mouth, but in a special tube running from the floor of the mouth down the front of the neck, then performing a U-turn and running up the back of the neck to finish in a coil on top of the woodpecker's skull. During the excavation process, headaches are avoided by a shock-absorbing pad of cartilage between the woodpecker's beak and its skull.

The comparatively soft flesh of the cactus makes an ideal site for the excavation of a typical flask-shaped woodpecker nest cavity, entered through a tight-fitting hole. In subsequent years these second-hand gila woodpecker cavities are of great value to other desert birds, providing sheltered and protected nest sites for species as varied as purple martins and elf owls, for which nest sites would otherwise be in very short supply. The cactus reacts to this invasion of its tissue by surrounding the nest cavity with tough scar tissue, and because of this the nest may outlast the plant. At the end of the cactus's life the soft flesh swiftly rots away, leaving only the fibrous skeleton – and the gila woodpecker nest flask – which was then often used by the local Indian tribes as a drinking vessel.

It seems that, far from damaging the cactus by these excavations, gila woodpeckers often function in the role of tree surgeons. One of the insects that attack saguaros, the larva of a moth called *Cactobrosis fernaldialis*, not only burrows through the cactus tissue but introduces a bacterial disease which causes a very damaging rot. As they excavate to find the moth caterpillars and the larvae of a fly that breeds prolifically in the rotting tissues, the woodpeckers usually clear the entire rotten area of the lesion. The cactus then quickly surrounds and isolates the area with a wall of scar tissue. Here is a remarkable example of biological control of a problem that sometimes threatens to deface the striking desert landscape.

One of the most spectacular of all adaptations to desert life that occurs among birds is found in members of the sandgrouse family from the Old World. Sandgrouse are fast-flying birds, often found in flocks, which look and behave rather like pigeons. They are placed in a small uniform order of their own by taxonomists, but are thought to have links with the shorebirds or waders, and, however strange the combination may seem, with the pigeons and doves. Sandgrouse have short legs with feathered tarsi (the normally unfeathered part of a bird's leg, just above the foot) and feet – providing insulation from the heat of the sand – and powerful but short and rather pointed wings. Their speed in the air, habit of flying in flocks and waterfowl-like tendency to 'flight' morning and evening over well-used routes to food or water made them a popular quarry during the colonial expansionist phase of British history. Thus they were comparatively well-known birds, even in Victorian times, despite their remote habitat.

Towards the end of the nineteenth century the British ornithologist and (importantly) aviculturalist Meade-Waldo reported an astonishing behavioural feature of the sandgrouse breeding in his aviaries. Though the distances involved were obviously short, the male sandgrouse carried water to their young in the nest. This they did by wading into their drinking water bowls and allowing water to be absorbed into their belly feathers. Then the young drank by pushing their beaks up into the wet feathers and squeezing out the absorbed water.

Although soon afterwards other observers confirmed this behaviour, over the years these reports were viewed with increasing incredulity and scepticism. They were even discounted – strangely enough – by ornithologists of unquestioned ability and particular interest in the desert birds of Africa and Asia. The local tribespeople were, it seems, familiar with this water-carrying habit from their own hunting exploits, but it was not until the 1960s that Stephen Marchant, working in the desert near Baghdad in Iraq, reported having seen this behaviour in the field. He was at the time unaware of Meade-Waldo's account, published more than half a century earlier.

There is now no doubt that male sandgrouse can and do transport water at least 35 km (22 miles) from desert waterholes to their nestlings in the heart of arid areas. Best studied are Lichtenstein's sandgrouse in equatorial Africa, the Namaqua sandgrouse from the Kalahari Desert in southern Africa, the pin-tailed sandgrouse from Iraq (all in the genus *Pterocles*) and Pallas's sandgrouse (in the related genus *Syrrhaptes*), which breeds in the Desert Corridor between the Caspian Sea and Mongolia.

Nor is it a simple matter of soaking the belly feathers in water. In 1967 Cade and Maclean made a detailed study of the whole operation, showing that male sandgrouse belly feathers have a microscopic structure

Lichtenstein's sandgrouse prepare to drink – and collect water for their chicks – from a waterhole.

unique among birds, which gives them a far greater absorptive capacity than man-made or natural sponges or absorptive tissues. Their belly feathers, fringed with spirally coiled threads of down, can take up between fifteen and twenty times their own weight of water, giving the average male sandgrouse a carrying capacity of 40 g (about 1½ oz) or more.

Although the pigeon-like sandgrouse may have some distant affinities with the shorebirds or waders, desert areas would seem to be the last place where true waders could be expected to live and breed, so strongly associated are they with water, fresh or coastal, and with marshes and swamps. It is perhaps a reflection of the versatility of this large family that several species have evolved strategies that allow them to survive successfully for all or part of the year in the driest of the world's habitats.

By far the best-adapted group to desert life are the coursers. Confined to the Old World, four species are involved: the cream-coloured and Temminck's from Africa, Arabia and the Middle East; the Indian, from the desert areas of India and Pakistan; and Jerdon's, from a group of remote hill valleys in northern India. Until very recently Jerdon's courser – the only courser with white on its wing tips – was considered extinct, the last authenticated sighting being in 1900. Enthusiastic Indian ornithologists were determined to prove these reports premature, and in 1981 their dedicated efforts in country extremely hostile to fieldwork were rewarded when a small, but evidently quite stable, breeding population was rediscovered.

The coursers are a most attractive group, little larger than a starling in body size. Their plumages cover the full range of sandy-buff colours, with some form of black and white eyestripe patterning, and a brown or chestnut crown to add a touch of elegance. For much of their time they are terrestrial, running swiftly on long legs. They have three-toed feet like the plovers but, unusually, the claw on the central toe is broad, with a serrated, comb-like edge. This comb, presumably used in preening to keep the feathers in prime condition, occurs in two other families, the herons and the nightjars. With their slimy frog, fish and eel diet it is easy to see the benefits of such a claw to the herons, but quite how it evolved in two other groups quite so disparate is difficult to understand. Certainly this is no classic example of 'parallel evolution', where similar features evolve in quite unrelated families as an adaptation, for example, to living in the same habitat (the long, curved wings of the swifts and the unrelated

swallows are a case in point). Coursers usually run away from threatening situations, head held low, giving them a very short-necked appearance. Once at a safe distance they pause and, like a submarine's periscope, a long neck is gradually extended so that the bird can achieve a better view of the action – often from behind a concealing rock. If need be, they will even stand on tiptoe. Against the stony or sandy background of the desert their plumage provides excellent camouflage, particularly for the incubating parent on the nest; at this time the adult will normally rely on its cryptic plumage colours for defence, remaining motionless even when danger comes within a couple of metres. Overnight, in the chill air, the incubating bird will closely cover the clutch of two or three equally well-camouflaged eggs – sandy with brown and black speckling.

During the heat of the desert day the parent on duty will often crouch over the eggs, not in contact with them but acting more as a sunshade, keeping the eggs in shadow. Panting to help lose heat, the bird may turn its tail into any breeze that is blowing, raising the feathers on its back like ventilator slots to deflect the breeze down on to its skin. The nest itself is a rudimentary scrape, often with a rim of small pebbles or pieces of dry vegetation brought by the male to his incubating female.

The short, slightly downcurved beak is used to catch insects and any other soil invertebrates available, usually taken by surprise since coursers feed on the run. Unwary small lizards are eaten, and there are some records of coursers feeding on grain. Though this is probably unusual a number of other waders, especially on or prior to migration, will also turn their attention to energy-rich vegetable foods.

During the breeding season, food shortage determines a thinly scattered distribution pattern across the desert, but these birds are so well camouflaged and so secretive that they are often overlooked. Some populations migrate, and gather into small flocks before moving off in search of fresh feeding grounds. Long-winged, they demonstrate considerable powers of flight, especially when under attack from falcons. Although they have a fair turn of speed, they are no match for a hunting falcon. Instead, coursers show a remarkable ability to climb at speed. This is the perfect counter to the falcon, which itself seeks to gain height (but in a much slower and more laboured fashion) before launching another high-speed diving attack.

The pratincoles are another close-knit group of waders, but far from the popular concept of what a wader should look like. Where long legs, neck and beak might be expected, to all intents most pratincoles resemble super-size swallows. They have a short-legged, long-winged stance on the ground, where they spend relatively little time compared with most waders, and in flight their slim, sickle-shaped wings, deeply forked tail, swooping flight and aerial feeding habits give added weight to the 'swallow' illusion.

Pratincoles are generally birds of semi-arid habitats in Africa, southern Europe, Asia and Australasia; and it is the last of these, *Stiltia isabella*, that is the odd one out. A bird of the blacksoil desert plains of central Australia, always appreciably drier than the habitats of any of its cousins, it is a genuine desert specialist. Structurally, too, it is distinctly different from others of its group, with a comparatively short rounded tail and much longer legs than the norm. Only in plumage, with black underwings and a dark chestnut breast, does it resemble its fellows. In flight it is less agile than its relatives – more like a marsh tern than an oversize swallow – and its feet can be seen projecting well beyond the tail tip. These structural differences are related to its habits, which astonishingly more closely resemble those of a courser than a pratincole. Doubtless this is a genuine example of parallel evolution to suit the desert habitat.

Unlike the other pratincoles (including the oriental pratincole, which also occurs in Australia), this parallel evolution leads to a largely terrestrial lifestyle rather than an aerial one, with insect food caught on the run in a short, swallow-like beak. Typical of birds of the dry heart of Australia, where rainfall is sporadic and unpredictable, many Australian pratincoles are nomads, moving and breeding when the conditions are appropriate. One of its breeding stratagems seems to be unique among waders: once the chicks have hatched from the two or three eggs laid in a simple scrape nest they seek out a rodent burrow nearby and establish it as their refuge, both if danger threatens and to escape the fiercest heat of the day. They emerge only when a parent returns and gives a summoning call indicating that the coast is clear.

Perhaps not unique, but certainly unusual in their habits, are the stone curlews. Like the coursers they are a widely distributed group, all favouring semi-arid habitats although often ones that have permanent water-courses or lakes within them. Even at the north of their range in temperate Europe stone curlews favour stony, dry, open fields and grassland, often over free-draining limestone or chalk soils. There are several genuine desert subspecies, adapted to life far from water. They derive their moisture from the insects and other soil invertebrates, small lizards and even the young of ground-nesting small birds that constitute their diet.

Streaked buff and brown plumage provides admirable camouflage during the day, when the stone curlew moves around relatively little, stalking in slow motion on long legs (showing the bulky 'knee' joint – actually the ankle – that gave rise to the colloquial name 'thick-knee'). Apart from its stealthy, even secretive gait, the stone curlew's most conspicuous feature is its eyes. Set on the sides of its head and giving a useful 360° of all-round vision, these are huge and made more obvious by the bright golden irises. They give a clear pointer to the stone curlew's nocturnal lifestyle. Resting by day, often in the scant shade cast by a rock or some dry vegetation, the stone curlew becomes active during the brief tropical evening, continuing to hunt well after dark for those terrestrial creatures that also save their active lives for the cooler period between sundown and sunrise. These birds' blood-curdling shrieking calls strike chill into the heart of an unwary desert traveller. Like sandgrouse, the adults may flight several kilometres to water but the chicks must survive on water derived from their animal food.

The final desert-specialist member of the wader family is the Australian or inland dotterel, a small member of the plover subfamily (which contains familiar sandy-shore birds such as the ringed, snowy and semi-palmated plovers). It is an uncommon wader from the dry interior of Australia, as its names imply. Little bigger than a thrush, the Australian dotterel has a strikingly attractive plumage. Like its Northern Hemisphere counterpart, its back is a richly mottled mixture of buff, gold, chestnut and brown – excellent camouflage against stony soils. In contrast, its head and underparts are as striking as those of any wader. The whitish head is marked with a black bar running across the crown and extending into a vertical bar down through each eye, a plumage character unique amongst waders. The buff breast and dotterel-chestnut belly show another unique mark, a bold black Y; its arms extend to meet behind the neck in a black collar, the stem running down the centre of the belly. Though not anxious to fly, in flight Australian dotterels lack a wingbar and show warm chestnut-buff undersides to their wings.

Australian dotterels appear to be nomadic over much of their range, settling and breeding wherever adequate food is available. For them food appears to comprise at least as much vegetable matter in the form of seeds as it does insects and other small terrestrial invertebrates. Because these birds are seen more often by desert travellers after dark than during the day, it has been suggested that seeds are eaten during the day, and that insects emerging once the heat has left the desert soil surface are eaten during the night.

As would be expected of a nomad, with a food supply so much at the mercy of the climate, there is little evidence of a fixed breeding season. The nest is a simple scrape, in which the clutch of eggs is as often sheltered from the heat of the sun as it is actually incubated by the sitting bird. Should the nest be left, then the parent in charge at the time will use its feet to scrape a layer of earth over the eggs as it departs, protecting them both from the eyes of predators and, to an extent, from the sun.

LARGER GROUND BIRDS OF THE DESERT

Most of the birds considered in this chapter so far have been largely terrestrial in lifestyle, perhaps quite appropriately considering their habitat and the lack of vegetation. Some have been plant feeders, others predominantly insectivorous, and yet others able to mix their diet with ease as conditions, and thus food type and abundance, change. Before looking at the desert birds which spend much of their lives on the wing – and are essentially hunters or scavengers – the larger terrestrial desert birds merit a mention. Largest of all is the ostrich, but today no desert-specialist races survive and it is best considered as a dry plains bird that occasionally penetrates semi-arid or even arid habitats. The ostrich, the biggest and, at 1500 kg ($1\frac{1}{2}$ tons), heaviest of all the world's birds, is flightless, but the world's heaviest birds retaining the capability of flight are in the bustard family.

Various bustards range the Old World, most of them favouring huge expanses of open, dry grassland such as the Asian steppes, or dry scrub country like the plains or veldt of Africa. The houbara bustard is the desert specialist, occurring from the western extremes of the Sahara – and even further west, on the Canary Islands – right across Africa and Arabia, penetrating just into Europe in southern Armenia, and along the Desert Corridor to the north-east to the Kirghiz steppes and the Altai and Mongolian deserts. While the African birds are year-round residents, sedentary by nature, the more easterly races, facing extremely harsh winter cold, are nomadic if not migratory, wandering southwards to warmer climates.

Houbaras favour stony desert areas where the low-growing shrub *Artemesia* occurs, dotted sporadically about. Their diet is thought to consist primarily of green plant material, particularly *Artemesia* stems, plus the seasonal berries or seeds of other desert plants and the bulbs of various wild onions. From these they also derive their moisture. Their beaks are quite stout and powerful, and doubtless any available terrestrial invertebrates and small lizards are eaten, as are fly maggots from the rotting carcasses of animals that have perished in drought conditions.

Medium-sized for a bustard, the houbara stands about 60 cm (24 in.) tall, with a long neck and long, strong legs, and weighs up to 3 kg (nearly 7 lb). In common with many birds of open habitats, including the desert species so far discussed, visual signals play a major role in communication and in various behaviour patterns. To birds of woodland, where the dense cover restricts visibility and thus the useful range of visual signals, voice or song signals are of paramount importance.

The houbara bustard has two kinds of visual signals. The first is negative, in that the finely marked plumage of its back and flanks, predominantly sandy with brown, black and white smudges, streaks and wavy lines, provides unbelievably good camouflage for so large a bird in such apparently poor country for concealment. Since its large flight muscles provide good breast meat, houbara bustards have long been a target for human hunters – certainly for thousands of years before the comparatively modern falconers and game shooters appeared on the scene. But their extensive shyness indicates that natural predators have also traditionally been concerned with this rich potential food supply.

When danger threatens, the houbara first freezes and then sinks slowly to the ground – or rather its body does, leaving the neck and head erect and alert. Gradually the head and neck too are lowered, ultimately lying stretched out in front of the crouched bird, which by now has become almost invisible. Even birds which have been shot and fallen to earth with their plumage in some disarray are notoriously difficult to discern against the desert soil backdrop. Danger past, the crouched bird keeps a bright yellow-irised eye on the intruder before rising and stalking off in a stately manner, not breaking into a run for some time. Running, houbaras clock up to 40 kph (25 mph). Rarely do they fly unnecessarily, but if they do, a thrust of the powerful legs launches them into the air at the end of a short take-off run, and deep flaps of its broad wings carry it swiftly away, usually low over the ground.

In the air, the transformation is startling. The sombre, well-camouflaged bird reveals huge white patches in black wings, a pattern that could hardly be more eye-catching. This is the second component of the visual signalling, seen at its best during courtship display when the male struts back and forth in front of his potential partner, neck feathers fluffed out into a ruff, tail fanned and wings spread wide for maximum effect.

Largest of all birds, the ostrich is now only an occasional visitor to true desert habitats.

BIRDS OF PREY

The houbara is one of the favourite quarry birds for falconers from India and Arabia, two countries where this ancient sport is still enthusiastically pursued by rich devotees. The falconers choose their prime hunting birds, sakers, cherrugs and peregrines, but even so their task is not easy. Houbaras are strong, heavy prey for these falcons, and have also evolved an upward-spiralling defence flight to escape attack. Houbaras are on record as voiding the contents of their rectum at pursuing falcons, clogging their feathers and forcing them to give up the chase – but this may be more accidental than deliberate. In addition, the bustards tend to stay in a small flock, and should one of their number be brought to the ground the others may attack and drive off the falcon as it attempts to bind on to its prey.

These are the hired assassins of the desert ecosystem, imported by falconers to exploit the wide-open spaces of the desert, an admirable location to demonstrate their flight and hunting prowess in a spectacular fashion. But not for these mercenaries are the perils of desert existence – at the end of the day they return with their masters to a secure shelter, and to the certainty of a nutritious meal no matter whether their hunting was successful or not. But what of the real desert birds of prey: how do they compare?

Although peregrines and laggar falcons can exploit the semi-arid desert margins successfully, a specialized 'desert falcon' group has been identified whose prime habitat is genuinely arid. Paramount amongst these as a hunter, and perhaps because of this and other tractable features of its behaviour a favourite for training by falconers, is the prairie falcon from North America. Perhaps as a reflection of their desert habitat, prairie falcons are overall brownish in plumage, only an old male showing any shade of blue in its mantle – a marked contrast from the magnificent steel-blue mantle of an adult peregrine.

Prairie falcons are on average rather smaller than many peregrine races, and (as in the peregrine and most other falcons) there are striking size differences between male and female. Female prairie falcons have a wingspan of over one metre (say, over 40 in.) and weigh up to 1 kg ($2\frac{1}{2}$ lb), while males have wingspans up to 95 cm (37 in.) and weigh around 600 g (21 oz). This one-third less weight in the male is the origin of English-speaking falconers' term 'tiercel' for the male, tiercel being a modification of the old term 'tercel', meaning a third part. The origins of this size difference are thought to lie in an evolutionary strategy designed to reduce competition for food, on the basis that different-sized predators will select different-sized prey. This is of particular value in habitats such as deserts where food is almost perpetually in short supply.

Though they are not averse to large insects and reptiles if they can take them, prairie falcons hunt mostly birds and mammals up to the size of jack rabbits. Featuring most often amongst their mammal targets – obviously taken by surprise on the ground – are ground squirrels and prairie dogs, but as the desert conditions become harsher hunting for them becomes an evening or early morning task. It is tempting to speculate that the prairie falcon's rather angular, owl-like head and oversize eyes may relate to hunting in poor light: no other reason has been advanced. Deep in these desert areas, reptiles up to the size of a large chuckwalla lizard are attacked, and reports suggest that lizards weighing up to and even in excess of 1 kg ($2\frac{1}{2}$ lb) are taken. Such prey are attacked in a series of dives or 'stoops', from no great height but carried home with considerable determination and ferocity. The target is the victim's head, the weapons the falcon's formidable talons. Often these attacks are accompanied by persistent harsh screams.

A wide variety of desert birds feature in the prairie falcon's diet, ranging in size from horned larks through desert quail and doves to sharp-tailed grouse. Usually these birds, which are largely ground-dwelling as would be expected in a desert habitat, are surprised and flushed on the ground. Flying fast and low, the falcon usually secures its prey after a very short dash as it rises from the ground in alarm. Only rarely will prairie falcons adopt the hunting tactic that makes the peregrine so famous, climbing in flight to a considerable height, then soaring in the eye of the sun until suitable prey flies past far below. Then the peregrine dives, gathering speed in powerful flight that some estimates suggest reaches 200 or even 250 kph (125–155 mph). The impact of hunter on prey at the bottom of this stoop can be heard several hundred metres away: the prey is often killed instantly.

As with all falcons (but not buzzards, eagles and hawks), prairie falcons build no nest of their own. Either they will use a suitable hollow on a rocky ledge, often with a sheltering overhang, or they will take over the disused nest of some other bird – in the desert often that of a raven. Egg laying usually takes place in late winter, and seems to be timed to match the appearance above ground of the first young ground squirrels of the year: this means that the number, and size, of ground squirrels is at a peak when the growing brood of young falcons is at its most demanding for food; and when they are freshly fledged from the nest there are plenty of 'targets' which the parents can use to teach the young some hunting skills.

The aplomado falcon is much smaller, the heaviest females reaching only 400 g (14 oz), and rather more catholic in its choice of habitats – its range extends well into South America. It is one of the typical birds of prey of Mexican deserts where yucca and saguaro cactus prevail. In recent years its northern limits have contracted appreciably – it was once a familiar bird as far north as Texas and Arizona. It is thought that the intrusion of farming activities into its traditional habitats, often supported by irrigation schemes, may have had a part to play in this.

After the Second World War, DDT and other chlorinated hydrocarbon pesticides were widely used in farming because of their efficiency, cheapness and long effective life. DDT had been developed during the war particularly to cope with body lice and malaria-carrying mosquitoes, which were responsible for discomfort and disease among troops fighting in tropical regions. It proved to be a life-saver on a major scale, and naturally enough was converted to peacetime use as an agricultural insecticide. What was not realized at the time was the sinister nature of its amazing persistence. This was brought to light following detailed observations on peregrine falcons in Britain.

For some years, ornithologists had experienced growing concern at the rapid fall in the peregrine population, attributable to the mortality of some adults but more particularly to the regular failure of breeding pairs to produce young. Inspection of failed nests revealed infertile eggs, often broken. A comparison of eggshell thickness with that of eggs taken by collectors several decades earlier showed that peregrines were laying very thin-shelled eggs. Piece by piece the jigsaw pattern of cause and effect was put together, showing that the persistent chlorinated hydrocarbon pesticides steadily accumulated in the body fats, particularly of birds like falcons, predators at the top of the food pyramid and therefore acquiring 'at second hand' the pesticide doses carried by their prey. When the stored fat was brought into use at time of high energy expenditure the toxic residues were released into the blood at dangerous, sometimes lethal, levels, causing severe behavioural disturbances and upsetting the peregrines' reproductive physiology – hence the fragile and infertile eggs.

A growing realization of the severity and extent of the problem in a wide variety of habitats across the globe, and of its cause, led eventually to the banning of this group of pesticides in many countries. It may well be that the same problem has hit the aplomado falcon in the north of its range. But it is to be hoped that, as with the peregrine in Europe, after a period of years its numbers will increase and the United States will again have a flourishing population of this elegant and colourful falcon.

Though the aplomado falcon *is* a falcon, in many ways its hunting techniques are reminiscent of the hawks, and indeed the aplomado is quite blunt (or rounded) in wing shape – not pointed, as are most falcons. This, and the aplomado's smaller size, must help when it comes to sharing out the scarce food resources of the desert. Falconers would consider it a sluggish bird, far too prone to seek a perch on a nearby cactus and wait for prey, be it bird, small mammal or reptile, or large insect. Rather like one of the African goshawks, it will pounce from its perch, often securing a kill immediately. If the prey is a bird and escapes, then the chase is relentless and agile – the aplomado follows every twist and turn of its target around and even into the vegetation, just like a sparrowhawk. To judge from the number of fast-flying prey, either the aplomado is a master of surprise or more probably it possesses a falcon-like turn of speed, ready to be tapped on demand. When prey is reasonably abundant, pairs of aplomado falcons have been reported hunting as a team, one acting as a beater or driver, the other lying in ambush. Records suggest that team work gives on average a better, heavier catch than solo hunting.

In Africa and Asia, the desert falcon group is represented respectively by the lanner and laggar. These two are similar in build, plumage and hunting strategies, and most authorities consider the laggar to be just another race of the lanner. Lanners are slightly smaller and lighter than peregrines, and more buoyant in flight. True desert birds are pale sandy brown above, paler below, with a reddish-brown cap. Those from semi-arid habitats on the desert margins often have strikingly bolder plumage colours, with greater contrast than their drab but effectively camouflaged desert cousins.

Like other desert falcons, the lanner has a broadly catholic diet largely determined by its opportunist approach and by the seasonal abundance of prey. Those in the Sahara often occur close to wadis or waterholes, preying substantially on the doves and sandgrouse that flight in from the surrounding desert to drink, often in large flocks. The hunting lanner leaves its vantage point – often a sheltered, rocky ledge some distance from the water – once the flock of drinking birds has settled and makes a stealthy, low-level approach, aiming to take its prey by surprise either on the ground or immediately after take-off. Male sandgrouse, their belly feathers heavy with drinking water to be taken back to their chicks, make the easiest targets as their take-off is impeded. The lanner is not the fastest of falcons, and once either pigeons or sandgrouse are in the air and up to maximum flight speed it has little chance of catching them. Only occasionally will a lanner circle at any height and then stoop on prey like a peregrine.

Nesting begins strikingly early for the lanner – often in what are the late winter months in northern temperate latitudes. This timing ensures that lanner young will be at their most demanding for food when massive flocks of spring migrants, flying north to their temperate breeding grounds, must cross the Sahara. Here, early spring and late autumn are perhaps the only times of real seasonal abundance of prey in bird form. To use this short-lived food source for the critical period of raising a brood of young successfully is yet another example of the range of behavioural adaptations employed by desert birds.

Nor is it just the spring migration that falcon populations exploit. So conditioned are we to the idea of breeding being a springtime feature of bird populations that, quite illogically, breeding at any other time is considered to be dramatically abnormal. It would seem logical that the migration south in autumn should also be made use of – particularly so because on autumn passage the young raised during the season accompany their surviving parents to their wintering grounds, so overall the number of birds moving is far greater than in spring. In the Mediterranean, Eleanora's falcons breed in late summer, often on uninhabited and arid rocky islets, and feed their young on southbound migrants.

Closely related to Eleanora's falcon is the sooty falcon – so closely related that some experts suggest that the two species separated from a common ancestor only fifteen thousand years ago, which in evolutionary terms is very recently. Uniformly slate grey, the sooty falcon is slightly smaller than Eleanora's but shares its hobby-like flight silhouette, with long, sickle-shaped wings and a comparatively long tail. Interestingly, in neither species is there much evidence of the sexual dimorphism found in most birds of prey. The males, though slimmer, are only slightly smaller than the females, whose weights are around the 300–350 g (11–13 oz) mark.

Sooty falcons breed in the heartland of the Egyptian, Libyan and Arabian deserts, and on waterless islands in the Red Sea and Arabian Gulf. Their usual nest site is a cavity under sheltering rocks, or on the ground underneath the branches of a dense desert bush like *Euphorbia*. In this, the most severe of desert habitats, available food would not sustain a family raised during the summer months, especially as sooty falcons feed to a large extent on small birds caught on the wing. Only occasionally do they supplement their diet with large insects or small rodents – both of which are comparatively scarce here anyway. So sooty falcons, too, are late summer breeders, raising their young on the rich food supply of autumn migrant birds. Once the young are on the wing they too migrate: they fly with the adults to overwintering grounds on Madagascar and the adjacent African coast. Here, intriguingly, they are frequently seen in small flocks with Eleanora's falcons – both species often feed not just on small birds but also on large insects and bats. In winter quarters sooty falcons outnumber Eleanora's very considerably, and the numbers of birds counted greatly exceeds the known total of breeding pairs. It seems that substantial populations of sooty falcons have desert breeding grounds yet to be discovered.

The Australian desert is not without a falcon – in this case the strikingly handsome black falcon. The almost totally uniform sooty black – or sometimes very dark brown – plumage of the adult is relieved only by a whitish chin and ear coverts, and by some white under the tail and towards the bases of the wing feathers, usually visible only in flight. Black falcons appear substantial in size, in part perhaps because of their colour. In reality they are longer overall than prairie falcons, with much the same wingspan of just over 1 m (40 in.). But as their weight is only about two-thirds that of the prairie falcon, they seem much more manoeuvrable and buoyant in flight – almost like one of the smaller kites. As with the sooty falcon, sexual dimorphism is not striking, with males only around 10 per cent smaller than females.

Although the black falcon will take prey on the ground if opportunity offers, including small marsupials, lizards and large insects, its main quarry is small birds, normally caught in the air. It is a nomad, moving about the dry heartland of Australia in association with concentrations of likely prey. The most numerous of the black falcon's prey, and perhaps offering the best meal for a relatively short chase, are quail; but other flocking desert birds including various doves, and parrots also feature. It hunts close to the ground, periods of apparently lazy flapping flight alternating with glides. Should prey be taken by surprise and startled into flight, then the black falcon accelerates to top speed very swiftly.

It is a persistent and aggressive hunter, normally pursuing its target from behind and screaming constantly, which some experts suggest adds to the terror and confusion in the victim and makes capture easier. Should the prey seek refuge in a bush, then the falcon will dive repeatedly at the bush until the creature is flushed from cover – a technique similar to that sometimes used by aplomado falcons. Also like the aplomado, the black falcon sometimes soars high above the desert, stooping rather like a peregrine on larger quarry such as galahs, ducks and doves.

On occasion, black falcons will use their commanding size and strength to take food by piratical attacks on other birds of prey like the letter-winged kite. This bird is another nomad, following the rains in small flocks. The black falcon's nest site, too, is usually taken over at second hand from birds ranging from crows to wedge-tailed eagles. The nesting season, like the distribution pattern, is what would be expected of a nomad – geared to take advantage of prey becoming available after irregular rains.

Around the globe, three features stand out as characteristic of the desert falcons. Two appear as logical adaptations to survival in their habitat, but one is more difficult to explain. This is the lack of the striking sexual dimorphism so characteristic of other birds of prey.

Of the adaptive features, the flexibility of the desert falcons' breeding season just about covers the range of options available. The lanner breeds early, to capitalize on the food supply afforded by summer migrants crossing the desert northwards in spring. The sooty falcon and the similar Eleanora's have followed the other evolutionary pathway and breed in the autumn, feeding on southbound migrants. The black falcon follows the breeding pattern typical of nomads, exploiting the short-lived and irregular food resources made available following the occasional rains – in the case of falcons the 'crop' of young small birds raised on the seeds of desert plants or on the flush of insect life accompanying plant growth.

The second of the clearly adaptive hunting stratagems is the widespread habit of hunting at dusk and dawn. This has obvious value as a tool to aid survival; it allows the falcons to 'sit out' the fiercest heat of the day, and lets them feed when many of their quarry are also moving about, feeding and drinking.

This behaviour is a case of the desert falcons trespassing on the province of another well-known group of predators, the owls. In common with several other groups of birds, races of a number of owl species penetrate into semi-arid and arid habitats round the desert margin. Amongst these are the largest and most powerful of all owls, the eagle owl, some of which have the hunting power to tackle prey as big as hares or small deer. Desert-edge races from both Africa and Arabia tend to be slightly smaller than the largest, from North America and Europe, and appreciably paler in plumage. At the other end of the size scale are various semi-desert races of the little owl from Europe and Asia, and the long-legged, largely terrestrial burrowing owl from the dry grasslands of America. Both these species take prey ranging from small insects and other invertebrates to reptiles, mammals and birds up to much the same weight as the owls themselves.

Though some owls, including both the little and burrowing owls, hunt during daylight hours, most are renowned for their prowess in hunting after dark, or at least in the very low light levels after sunset. They have various specialist adaptations for this lifestyle, of which by far the best known is their phenomenal power of sight. All birds have large eyes – even the starling has eyes which, relative to its body size, are several times larger than human eyes. Comparatively speaking, owls' eyes are much larger still, and are very advanced in their anatomy. Large though their eyes appear from the front, this is only the tip of the iceberg, as the bulk of the eyes occupy a substantial proportion of the skull.

The eye is shaped rather like a pear. The wide 'base' holds the retina which is rich in rods, the vision receptor cells that are most sensitive at low light intensities. Cones, the cells responsible for colour vision, are less numerous, so in daylight owls have poorer colour vision and detail resolution than do birds that are normally active during the day. The cornea and lens are large, ensuring that maximum light falls on the retina. Since both eyes face forwards owls have excellent binocular vision, which allows the precise judgement of distances that is so important in striking their prey. Thus in the very poor light after sunset – a time when many desert animals venture forth after sheltering from the heat of the day – the eyesight of desert owls is vastly more efficient than a human's. But there is a disadvantage attached to this super-sensitive sight: so large are the eyes, and so oddly shaped, that they cannot swivel in their sockets. To change its field of view the owl must rotate its head, and this movement could alert potential prey to the nearness of danger.

Even more startling than its power of sight is the sensitivity of an owl's hearing, which may often play a greater part in nocturnal hunting. A superficial view of an owl's head gives no indication of the presence of ears, even in those species called long-eared or short-eared. In these and some other owls, including the eagle owl, tufts of feathers above or beside the eyes have no connection with hearing at all, but are simply plumage features probably connected with display. Behind the disc of facial feathers that give the entire owl family its characteristic appearance, and beneath the feathers of the side of the head, lie the external openings of the ears. Unlike most mammals, including mankind, these do not have the sound-gathering flaps of skin, supported by cartilage, properly called the pinnae, that we recognize as 'ears'. And there is another striking difference: whereas the ears of most creatures are paired, and symmetrically located on either side of the head, those of the owls are not. Huge and shaped like a trumpet bell, the external openings are located one low and nearer the front of the skull, the other almost on top of the skull and set towards the back of the head.

This asymmetry considerably improves the range-finding ability of the ears, allowing the development of hearing so precise that, even in total darkness, a long-eared owl can locate and strike successfully a scuffling mouse 30 m (nearly 100 ft) away. A similarly accurate visual-distance judgement is achieved by an old range-finder camera, where the two observation lenses are set at different distances from the viewfinder.

Owls' hearing is also enhanced greatly by the disc of facial feathers. Unlike most birds' feathers these are stiff and almost bristle-like, and so hard that they form a sound reflector similar to the receiver 'dish' used to collect and focus television signals from satellite transmitters a vast distance away.

Like the eyes, the ears occupy around one-third of the skull volume, which leaves rather little space, the cynic might comment, to accommodate the legendary wisdom of the owls. Indeed there is no evidence of unusual cerebral capability save for enlargements of those parts of the brain devoted to interpreting sound and visual signals. So the attribution of the scientific name *Athene* to the little owls, after the Greek goddess of wisdom, is probably misplaced.

As with their eyes, owls' superb hearing also poses problems, there is a considerable risk that the sound signal that the owl seeks to locate and identify will be swamped by background noise – not least by the rustling movements of its feathers rubbing against each other as it turns its head to scan its habitat, or by the swoosh of its beating wings. In both cases, evolution has minimized the problems. The barbs of owls' body and wing feathers have soft, filamentous appendages which give both the appearance and the feel of velvet. They effectively silence body movements, and to some extent also the noise of wingbeats. Most wing noise is caused by the hard edge of the flight feathers cutting through the air. A close-up view of the leading edge of an owl's wing shows that the flight feathers have a comb-like fringe, often only a millimetre or two (less than one-tenth of an inch) long, but sufficient to break the airflow and eliminate almost totally any swish of air over a fast-moving hard edge.

These features are exploited by the two genuinely desert owls, one from southern North America, the other from north-east Africa and Arabia. The latter is one of the least known of the world's birds – certainly of the world's owls. Until recently, about all that was known was derived from a single specimen, shot and preserved in 1878 in Baluchistan. Hume's tawny owl is a pale sandy-coloured version of the tawny owl familiar to European ornithologists. But however similar it may be in its habits and superficial appearance, this is far from simply being a desert-adapted race or subspecies of the tawny owl. In the last decade there have been several sightings of this elusive bird in various desert areas across the Middle East, and even a little information on its breeding habits has been gleaned.

Slightly larger than a tawny, Hume's owl is much paler in overall colour, with buff upper parts mottled in grey and brown, a pale collar, and underparts of dirty white with faint darker markings. The facial disc resembles that of the tawny owl in shape and function, but the eyes are strikingly different, having bright orange irises rather than black. The feet, too, are different: not in the four powerful talons set square, each toe at right-angles to the next, but in the lack of feathers on the toes. Tawnys have feathers on their feet, and otherwise only the fishing owls have featherless toes. This is unexpected in Hume's owl, and its adaptive significance remains a matter of intrigue, awaiting resolution.

Obviously much remains to be discovered about Hume's owl, not least the full extent of its distribution. Though several recently fledged young have been seen, only one nest is on record – in an underground hollow, an ancient man-made cistern. It seems likely that most nests will be in rock crevices or caves, sheltered to some degree from the sun. Hume's owl does seem to be as vociferous as the tawny, with a distinctive *hoooo, huhu-huhu* call, sometimes performed in duet mode by the pair. As yet, an equivalent to the young tawny food call, *ku-wick*, has not been heard.

Most prey items so far recorded are terrestrial creatures ranging from gerbils and jerboas down to small desert mice and even smaller lizards, insects and other invertebrates. Hunting seems to be strictly nocturnal, with the prey usually located from a prominent vantage point perch, from which the owl descends in a silent glide or near-vertical parachute drop to secure its victim – much the same approach as the hunting tawny owl. Owls, in common with other birds of prey and insect-eaters, produce castings or pellets of the indigestible remains of their prey. These are coughed up at regular sites, which makes prey analysis comparatively straightforward, though there are some shortcomings with prey like worms that leave few traces in the pellets.

The other characteristic desert owl is far smaller. It may in fact be the smallest of owls, with a total length (or height, as it usually perches in a vertical posture) of about 14 cm (6 in.), or little more than a tit. It carries the scientific generic name *Micrathene* – *micra* to suit its stature, coupled once again with *Athene*, goddess of wisdom. Its common name, too, reflects its size – elf owl. It has a restricted distribution, confined to arid areas in the southern United States and Mexico, and is best known for its association with the giant saguaro cactus because it is small enough to use old gila woodpecker or flicker holes for its nest or to roost during the day. Characteristically, if and when found it is to be seen dwarfed by the mighty cactus, its pale 'eyebrows' peering out prominently from the dark, circular hole which seems a perfect fit for its tiny body.

Dull in buff plumage streaked with brown, the elf owl has a rounded head with a comparatively poorly emphasized facial disc. This characteristic is common among the various little owls and their relatives, and in the burrowing owl, where it may reflect the fact that these species often hunt in daytime, relying more on their eyes than their ears to locate prey. But this interpretation would be misleading in the case of the elf owl, which is strictly nocturnal – during daylight hours it remains infuriatingly well concealed so far as bird-watchers, anxious for a glimpse of this tiny specialist bird, are concerned. After dark elf owls are more often heard than seen, as they have for their size an extremely loud voice and a striking call – a rapid run of high-pitched notes, accelerating and descending in pitch towards the end. Their food is predominantly the larger insect life that emerges once the heat is out of the sand, together with spiders, scorpions, small lizards and the like.

Depending on food availability, elf owl clutches can comprise up to five chalky white, almost spherical eggs. In common with many other owls, they have another survival strategy concerning eggs when food is scarce. Despite their small size, the female lays her eggs at two-day intervals – not daily, as might be expected – and she starts to incubate as soon as the first is laid. Again, this is a contrast to most similar-sized birds. So the eggs hatch at two-day intervals, and for much of the time they spend developing in the nest the owlets are in staggered sizes. If food is plentiful all will be reared, but should the food supply fail then the smallest and weakest owlet receives less food and will probably be eaten by its starving oldest sibling. This process may be repeated with the next smallest and so on. Repulsive cannibalism though this may seem to human eyes, it does at least maximize the chances of at least one young owl fledging successfully.

To human eyes desert life is all about survival, and the one group of birds most closely associated with deserts – and with failure to survive in them – is the vultures. Essentially, they are two groups of birds, as the Old World vultures are not closely related to those from the New World – the structural and behavioural similarities between the two provide yet another case of parallel evolution. As a general rule, both groups share long, broad wings with deeply 'fingered' tips, ideal for energy-conserving soaring flight on the currents of hot air rising from sun-heated desert sand and rock. Both groups have heavy, sharply hooked beaks, ideal for tearing open thick hide to reach the flesh within. But both groups have strangely ineffectual-looking feet, with comparatively weak toes tipped by short, blunt nails, rather than the formidable killing claws and long, sharp talons of the true birds of prey. This conforms to the vulture lifestyle, predominantly scavenging on dead or at the very least moribund creatures: for this the strong beak remains a necessity, but powerful talons are superfluous. Similar, too, are the largely naked head and neck in both groups. When feeding, vultures often have their heads buried deep within a carcass: feathers here would perhaps be an impediment. Certainly it is the most difficult part of the body for any bird to keep in good condition by preening, and the problems that a

95

vulture would face after feeding in this way defy description.

Perhaps most of the world's vultures do not fully qualify as desert birds, despite popular conceptions of their lives. Though many can – and do – spend considerable time over desert areas, for much of the time avoiding the furnace-like heat of the ground by soaring thousands of metres above it amidst cooling air currents, they also spend much time in adjacent habitats. This is particularly the case where pastoral tribes or ranchers are grazing stock in the dry grasslands and stunted scrub fringing the desert proper. This arid to semi-arid landscape offers a precarious livelihood, subject to sudden and sometimes prolonged failure of the food and water supply. In such drought conditions, mortality among the artificially high numbers of sheep, goats and cattle, none of them adapted for desert survival, can be calamitous for the herdsman – but a bonanza for the vultures.

Vultures are late risers, roosting in dead trees or on rocky crags until the sun has warmed the desert enough to create vital thermals. Once these hot-air upcurrents are established the vultures flap lazily into life, climbing to their soaring positions in a slow, wide spiral, taking as much help from the lift of the air as they are able. Once on high they patrol endlessly, ever on the alert, their phenomenally good eyesight allowing them to spot and identify even motionless carrion far below.

Often, though, their attention will be drawn to a potential food source by the movement of other desert creatures around it – jackals or hyenas, for example. In flight, a patrolling vulture will carry its head steady, long neck folded so that the head appears to sprout directly from the wings. Occasionally the head will be raised or lowered, neck extended, to inspect areas below and behind that have been masked by the long, broad wings. There may be an additional benefit in soaring at this height, as the temperature is appreciably lower anyway, and there are bonuses in the form of cooling breezes. So only when they descend to feed do vultures have to cope with the full heat of the desert day.

Just as important as scanning the desert beneath is keeping an eye on other vultures, soaring often hundreds of metres or more away. With many pairs of eyes on the lookout, once potential food is located the nearest vulture will swiftly spiral down to investigate. Its neighbours in the aerial surveillance network will notice its descent and follow – and so too will their neighbours. So, very swiftly, a descending spiral of vultures, often dozens strong, gathers over the carcass, to land and begin feeding in an unruly and revolting scrum, operating in a silence broken only by the occasional hiss that is the limit of a vulture's vocabulary.

Best-known and most numerous of the New World vultures are the black and the turkey, widely distributed from the northern United States well down into South America. Though both can and do carry out their scavenger existence in desert areas – or at least over the desert fringes – so widespread are they, and so catholic in their habitat choice, that it would be misleading to class them amongst desert-specialist birds.

Not so, perhaps, the two condors. With wingspans of around 3 m (10 ft), they are amongst the world's largest flying birds – but not the heaviest, as they weigh only around 10 kg (22 lb). The California condor can certainly be classified as a desert bird, its natural habitat being the arid valleys among the foothills of the southern Rockies. Recently, it has been restricted to remote rocky gorges and canyons from Monterey through the Sierra Nevada foothills to Fresno. It also has the unhappy distinction of being one of the world's rarest birds. The residual population is just dozens, now held in captivity as a carefully planned captive-breeding programme was judged to be the only way of stopping the California condor's otherwise inexorable slide into extinction.

As is so often the case, man seems to be to blame. Requiring a vast territory to provide sufficient food, this was probably never a common bird. When the first settlers came, equipped with firearms, these huge birds were an obvious target. Then, to provide food for the settlers, the deer herds were slaughtered, depriving the condors of their main source of carrion. After that came the cattle ranchers, anxious to maximize the success of their herds. So they set poison baits in carcasses to eliminate predatory wolves and coyotes. These carcasses were naturally attractive to hungry condors, which also perished. Increasingly, scarcity gave the condor a 'rarity value' among collectors of stuffed birds and of birds' eggs, so a new form of persecution further depressed the population.

Finally – far too late – special legal protection was afforded to the remnants of the California condor population. Its survival now depends on the success of captive-breeding, which has now been accomplished, and on the development of strategies for releasing captive birds back into the wild. This is beset with many problems, and researchers are only at the

beginning of a long and hard struggle.

To the south, the very similar Andean condor is in a much stronger position. Although the local Indian tribes do trap some birds, the human pressures in their remote Andean highland strongholds are far less than in California. So remote are their breeding grounds, and so inhospitable to field studies are feeding areas like the Atacama Desert of the west coast, that this is a comparatively little-known bird.

It is not just the sheer size of the condor's outspread wings as it soars (they have been likened to two doors placed end to end) that is spectacular: the display too is remarkable. With massive wings spread to emphasize his size and to show the silvery white patches on the secondary feathers to best effect, the male holds himself with body almost vertical before his female on a rocky crag. Turkey-like, he bends his beak down to touch his chest, inflating the naked skin of his head and neck which becomes inflamed with red and yellow. At the

Specialist snake-eater, the long-legged secretary bird exploits high desert snake populations.

same time he produces a staccato *tok-tok-tok* by clicking his tongue, rotating slowly about his vertical axis as he does so.

Nesting follows much the same pattern as that of the California condor. Breeding occurs only every second year, so far as is known. The pair select a secluded ledge or cave high in the Andes on which to lay the single large egg, which is chalky white to start with but soon becomes discoloured as it is laid directly on the ground: there is no nest as such. Probably each pair have a number of suitable sites in their territory, which may often cover hundreds of square kilometres, and may use different but still ancestral sites in successive years. This pattern is reasonably common among the larger birds of prey, but the full explanation of its purpose remains to be discovered. The sexes share the incubation, which lasts for over fifty days, each bird sometimes sitting for twenty-four hours at a stretch. The youngster remains for several more months on the nesting ledge before it makes its maiden flight, and as with the California condor is fed and cared for by its parents for at least a year. Although it should be able to care for itself well before this, such an extended period of parental care is another feature indicative of the difficulties of finding food, and of survival generally, in this terrain.

The Old World vultures are in many ways very close counterparts to those in the New. As might be expected, because of the much wider geographical area covered there are rather more species – but there are no equivalents to the condors. Most Old World vultures are also birds that exploit desert habitats and the food supplies in the form of carrion that these provide, but as with the New World vultures the desert is often only one of the habitats they use. Some are mountain birds, others more birds of the grassy plains than of true deserts, and yet others have taken readily to the increasing food supply provided by man on the fringes of major towns and cities in the form of refuse tips.

Such man-made food sources provide comparatively easy and rich pickings, but one of the smaller 'generalist' vultures merits attention for the means with which it obtains food in the much more difficult circumstances of the desert. This is the Egyptian vulture, which is unusual in a number of ways.

Vultures normally have long, broad wings and short, rounded tails. But the Egyptian vulture has long, comparatively slender wings, almost pointed at their tips in contrast to the usual heavily 'fingered' pattern of soaring birds. Although the adults have rounded tails of medium length, the immature birds have long, diamond-shaped tails. Such tails may possibly give these less experienced birds the benefits of better flight control in their novice stages. Again, most vultures are black, brownish or greyish in plumage, with colour restricted to the fleshy parts of the head. The adult Egyptian vulture is white with black wing tips almost like a gannet, and, like the gannet, in the breeding season its feathered head has a golden cast. And of course the feathered head is not the norm, although the Egyptian vulture is not unique in having the naked fleshy area confined to its face.

But what is particularly worthy of attention in the Egyptian vulture is its way of tackling the eggs of ostriches and other large desert or desert fringe birds. Small eggs it can pick up and crush, but larger ones are

beyond the powers of its comparatively slender beak. When confronted with a very substantial meal – some 2 litres ($3\frac{1}{2}$ pints) or more of moist, nutritious food – in the shape of an unattended ostrich egg, the Egyptian vulture seeks a nearby rock or stone which it picks up in its beak and uses as a hammer, delivering repeated blows until the tough shell cracks open. The contents are then swiftly consumed.

Egyptian vultures are adaptable birds, which may explain why they are one of just a handful of birds the world over to have developed any form of tool-using technique to help them obtain food. They are one of the vultures commonly to be found scavenging on town refuse dumps, and equally frequently are in attendance at carcasses, be they on the plains or in the desert. Normally, there will only be one or two at a carcass, unlike the morbid scrum, often dozens strong, of squabbling griffon or white-backed vultures. Egyptians are one of the smallest of vultures, and so must defer to their larger relatives should an argument develop over a tasty morsel of rotting flesh. They tend to keep to the fringes of the action, darting in and out (though perhaps this implies a nimbleness that they do not really portray) to seize scraps as they become available.

Much less of a generalist, much larger, but strangely sharing much the same flight silhouette as the considerably smaller Egyptian vulture, is the lammergeyer. Long, slim, almost pointed wings with a 2·5 m (8 ft) span and a very long diamond-shaped tail make the lammergeyer's outline unmistakeable far overhead. A closer view of the perched bird shows a dark brown vulture, long-necked, with a paler golden to ginger head made the more distinctive by black eye patches and two drooping tufts of feathers – the 'beard' of its colloquial name, bearded vulture. Unlike that of most vultures, the iris of the eye is bright yellow, standing out against the black cheeks. So long are its wings that when folded they extend beyond the tip of the long tail. The extremely distinctive flight silhouette and the feathered head (which is almost loosely crested on the nape) are argued to be the features that make lammergeyers some form of link between the vultures proper and the eagles.

Lammergeyers are birds of intensely arid, spectacularly precipitous desert crags and gorges, widely scattered in desert areas of northern and southern Africa, Arabia, the Middle East and Asia as well as the drier parts of the Mediterranean basin. Nowhere are they common, and sadly in many regions their numbers seem to be declining, so rarely will more than two or three be seen in any one day. They choose nest sites high on precipitous cliffs, often beneath an overhang or actually inside a cave. Though small compared with some eagle and vulture nests, lammergeyers do build their own nest, largely of twigs and branches which are obviously collected some considerable distance away; this they ornament with more macabre but locally gleaned debris such as old bones, horns and leathery pieces of aged skin. Though there may be more than one egg, it is most unusual for more than a single youngster to be reared. Rather on the pattern of the condors, incubation periods are of the order of two months, while after hatching it may be three more months before the young bird finally leaves the nest. It can be five years or more before the drab brown immature bird attains adult plumage, and some years after that before it breeds successfully. So these are long-lived birds, probably surviving for two or three decades even in their rugged habitat.

At carrion or carcasses, despite its size the lammergeyer is a poor competitor. It stands well back from the fray and has to subsist on what is left when other vultures and ravens have eaten their fill. This usually is little more than fragments of skin, hooves, horns, skulls and other major bones. In its capacity and in the strength of its walls the lammergeyer gut is adapted to this uncomfortable diet, and it contains powerfully acidic digestive juices. The Spanish colloquial name for the lammergeyer is *quebrantahuesos*, meaning 'bone breaker', and this gives the clue to its most extraordinary adaptation in relation to diet.

Just as the Egyptian vulture is very unusual in being a tool-user, so too does the lammergeyer have to adopt uncommon tactics to maximize the benefits to be obtained from its limited and robust food source. The skulls and longest bones are picked up in its feet and carried up into the air perhaps 30 or 40 m (100–130 ft) above a favoured rocky outcrop. Flying into the wind, the lammergeyer judges, with accuracy derived from much practice, the correct point at which to release its load, which plummets down on to the rocks. If it does not shatter at the first attempt, then the process is repeated until the bone fragments, no matter how dangerously sharp they may appear, are small enough to be eaten. The largest long bones, once fractured, are subjected to a different technique. The lammergeyer carefully extracts the highly nutritious marrow from the central cavity using its tough tongue, which is long, narrow and concave like a gouge – or better, shaped precisely in the form of the metal marrow-scoops used by cooks in nineteenth-century kitchens!

So, in their wide-ranging and often fascinating ways, do desert birds cope with the extreme harshness of the climate in which they live. Drawn worldwide from an astonishingly large number of families, all manage one way or another to make a success of life where food and water are in perpetually short supply, or available in unpredictable gluts irregularly spaced in time. Some migrate, some are nomads, some are year-round residents in the desert: all must overcome, for at least a substantial part of their lives, aridity and searing heat.

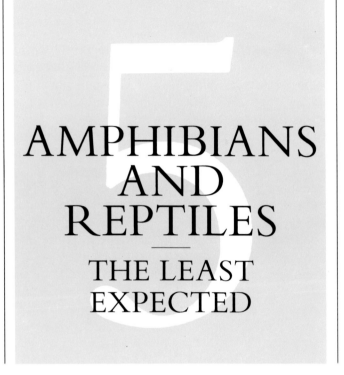

AMPHIBIANS AND REPTILES
THE LEAST EXPECTED

Of all the vertebrate animals – those with an internal skeleton of cartilage or bone, based on a backbone composed, for flexibility, of many segments called vertebrae – it is the amphibians that seem least likely to be found in deserts. Far back in evolutionary time, amphibians were the first group of vertebrates to venture out of fresh water and on to land, but as their name implies they retain a strong attachment to water for at least part of their lives, and often the greater part. For the most part their skins are soft and moist. This moistness often allows the skin to play some part in respiration, absorbing oxygen from either the air or the water around them. Mating, egg-laying and the subsequent development of the eggs through larval stages into small young adult forms are closely linked with a wetland habitat. The eggs, for example, are fertilized by free-swimming sperm in the water; they are thin-shelled, and though gelatinous they would rapidly dry out on land. The larval stages that hatch from these eggs often have gills and a finned tail – adaptations to a free-swimming aquatic life.

A sidewinder scales a dune in the California desert.

FROGS AND TOADS

The major groups within the amphibians are the frogs and toads, and the newts and salamanders. Of these, it is some of the frogs and toads that have managed, despite all the odds, to evolve lifestyles that allow them to establish and maintain populations in the very heart of the desert. To do so they must be opportunist, responding very swiftly to the rains, seasonal or sporadic: they must complete their life cycles before the short-lived desert wetlands evaporate under the powerful sun. Clearly this is a high-risk situation, particularly if the first showers or storms are not followed by sufficient further rain to establish lakes or pools.

In the Arizona desert rains soften the soil enough in some areas to allow an amazing emergence of spadefoot toads. Using their powerful hind feet, at the end of the last rains they will have dug themselves 30 cm (12 in.) or more deep into the ground, where they will have remained securely encapsulated in a mucus-lined chamber ever since. After they buried themselves, their skins hardened to a leather-like waterproofness, with only the tiny nostrils remaining open to allow life-supporting respiration to continue at the lowest possible level. In this state of aestivation all metabolic processes are reduced to the minimum for survival. In this kind of tick-over phase food and oxygen requirements are negligible, and so water loss due to respiratory and digestive processes is minimized.

But within hours of the first rainfall the spadefoots' skins have softened and they are on the move, first up to the surface and then to the nearest substantial pool where the males begin their croaking chorus. Within a day or so of the arrival of rain the females will have joined them, and after a brief but frenzied courtship – often indiscriminately communal – batches of eggs, jelly-like blobs of spawn with a dark embryo at the centre, have been laid in the pool and fertilized by whichever male has the securest grip on the female's back. This essential task complete, the adult spadefoots feed avidly, replenishing their depleted body reserves prior to digging themselves in again in the hope of surviving for yet another reproductive season when the next rains fall.

Even allowing for the high temperature of the desert pools, the spawn develops with extraordinary speed – far faster than most tropical swampland frogspawn. Hatching has often started within twenty-four hours and within a couple of days the pool is swarming with large-headed, long-tailed tadpoles – at this stage they look like their kind the world over. They are not the only wildlife in the pools. Resting stages of algae and freshwater crustaceans, some microscopic, some larger, either present since the last rains or having blown in as

dust subsequently, have also sprung to life, forming the basis of a short-lived food chain based on the algae.

The tadpoles can survive readily on the algae alone, but in many of these pools there will also be abundant small crustaceans, particularly fairy shrimps. These too develop from resistant eggs with phenomenal speed, and once they have done so some of the tadpoles may turn carnivorous and start feeding on them. The immediate effect is that they develop much larger heads than their siblings, with the larger mouth necessitated by their new predatory lifestyle. As they grow bigger and more powerful their carnivorous habits begin to include cannibalism, as they attack and feed on their smaller and weaker algal-feeding relatives. So the pool now contains two quite difference types of tadpole – an 'insurance policy' evolved by the spadefoot toad to protect itself against most eventualities.

If there was just a single spell of rain, then a couple of weeks later the pool will have shrunk considerably and become shallow, warm and low on oxygen. In these circumstances, the tadpoles need to reach toadlet stage quickly and hop away to bury themselves for

Bright-eyed, plump and active after the drought has broken, a spadefoot toad sets off in search of a mate.

protection. The larger, carnivorous type is the more successful of the two in these conditions: as the pool shrinks, weakened herbivorous tadpoles are overwhelmed and eaten by the carnivores. The carnivores also eat each other, but at least some may survive and move away to safety.

Conversely, if the rains continue, life for the hunting carnivores becomes much more difficult. The water is high in oxygen, and frequently stirred up by fresh rainfall. The hunters cannot see their prey in the murky water, but the algal feeders, their foodstock continually replenished in the fresh water, have no such difficulty and continue to grow steadily, soon becoming too big for the carnivorous type to tackle. In this situation, toadlets should leave the pool in considerable numbers.

Although predators such as lizards, snakes and birds may take their toll, a reasonable number of survivors will reach the safety of cracks in the mud or hiding places under rocks or plants. Here they will spend a brief few weeks of terrestrial life, feeding on both plant and animal matter, before digging themselves deep burial chambers in which to ride out the oncoming dry season. Those that fail, together with the residual algae, shrimps and tadpoles – many caught in gluey mud as the pool dries – will perish under the heat of the sun. The algae and shrimps will have formed some drought-resistant spores or eggs, but any residue will contribute to the reserve of nitrogenous waste. This is the fertilizer required for fresh generations of plants and subsequently animals, and it is a scarce and valuable commodity in the desert.

LIZARDS

The problems of amphibians in desert surroundings, where their continued existence is threatened by the action of heat and desiccation on their thin, essentially moist skins and on their unprotected eggs, are not carried forward into the reptiles. In evolutionary terms, the amphibians established a foothold on land for vertebrate animals; in the reptiles, the essential link that amphibians must maintain with water is finally severed.

It can be argued that the reptiles are the most characteristic animal group in desert habitats, with numerous representatives particularly of the lizards and snakes. Certainly in many ways they are pre-adapted (see p. 111) for a desert existence – water loss, for instance, is reduced to a minimum by their hard, impervious scaly skin, and transparent scales even cover the eyes of snakes. Reptile eggs have tough, leathery shells – not as rigid as a bird's egg, but equally resistant

to drying out. Although some female reptiles may remain with their clutch of eggs, the great majority simply excavate a pit, often in soft sand or soil, lay their eggs, refill the pit and leave the eggs to hatch alone. Once the youngsters emerge, as miniature versions of the adult, they struggle to the surface and immediately begin an independent life.

Reptiles' main excretory product is solid or near-solid uric acid; so, like the birds, they minimize water loss in this function. It may well be that their 'cold-blooded' nature is overall of benefit to them, at least in terms of conserving energy and water. With a water-proof skin, an animal whose bodily processes are speeded up or slowed down under the influence of the external temperature tends to lapse into torpor overnight when the temperature falls. A warm-blooded creature – a bird or mammal – would need to consume energy, either as food or from its bodily fat reserves, to maintain its high body temperature overnight. Although most birds and mammals are well insulated by feathers or fur, this metabolic process has to continue; and in continuing it makes further demands on bodily water resources.

The converse occurs during the heat of the day, when reptiles are physiologically incapable of lowering their own temprature by metabolic means. Once the external temperature is reached at which destruction of body tissue begins (40–50°C or 104–122°F), their only resort is to seek shelter. In reality, of course, most reptiles will have sought refuge beneath the sand, in rock crevices or in burrows dug by themselves or another animal, long before this.

During the day, most lizards seek to keep their body temperature close to their own particular norm by selecting the most appropriate microclimate for their needs. Early in the morning, with temperatures low, this will involve exposing as much of the body as possible broadside-on to the sun's rays, to gather maximum warmth. As the ambient temperature increases, so the lizard will turn more head (or tail) to the sun, gradually reducing to a minimum the skin surface being warmed. Eventually, the heat may become too much, and shaded shelter will be found. Besides direct solar radiation, reptiles will also have to exploit, or avoid, the coolness or heat of the rocks or sand on which they move about.

Some lizards are able to influence the heat they receive from sunlight by changing the colour of their skin. Amongst these are various chameleon species, often more typical of semi-arid areas and perhaps the best known of all lizards. They achieve their colour changes by means of sac-like cells in their skin which contain dark pigments like melanin, which is derived from the breakdown products of spent blood corpuscles. The amount of melanin in the cells exposed to light is controlled by slender muscles which are operated like purse strings by a part of the chameleon's nervous system which functions automatically in response to both sunlight and the chameleon's background.

When hunting, chameleons are aided not just by the slow-motion stealth which is their trademark as they approach potential prey, nor simply by their powers of camouflage achieved by skin-colour changes. Unlike many reptiles, which have poor sight and relatively immobile eyes, their vision is good, and each eye swivels independently over a very considerable field of view. Also, while many lizards lurch or jump forward to snap up prey between their horny jaws, chameleons have a very long tongue. Normally held folded in the mouth, the tongue is flicked rapidly forward, often over a few centimetres' range, striking and securing prey on its extremely sticky tip – a hunting stratagem with a much greater chance of success.

The horned lizard from America also has dark blotches on its skin that can change in size and darkness. This flattened, almost disc-shaped lizard is small – rarely more than 10 cm (4 in.) long – and covered in spines, resembling a small, herbivorous dinosaur. This desert lizard manipulates its skin colour mainly to provide camouflage against the soil. Its spines also make it an unpopular meal, despite its tempting size, to larger lizards and snakes.

A further defensive tactic is the horned lizard's ability to breathe in deeply and swell, jumping forward with a hiss of escaping breath sufficient to frighten most intending predators. Its ultimate defence is strange, and has yet to be fully explained: this lizard is known to be able to eject blood from its eyes, perhaps for some distance. It is an expensive means of salvation but, if effective, worthwhile.

Startlingly similar in shape and size, and in its thorny skin and blotchy coloration, is the moloch or thorny devil, a lizard from half a world away in the Australian desert. The thorny devil enjoys the far from delightful

Throat and collar scales erected in a threat display, the Australian bearded dragon Amphibolurus *demonstrates why it got its name.*

scientific name *Molochus horridus*. Moloch was the name of a devil god to whom human children were sacrificed, and *horridus* is an obvious reference to the creature's bizarre appearance. It, too, is far less aggressive than its appearance indicates – a timid lizard, it hides its head between its legs if danger threatens.

Thorny devils show two unusual adaptations to desert life. One is their favourite food, ants, which are often numerous in the desert, usually in an almost endless supply as the workers trek to and from food sources. The slow-moving thorny devil just collapses on the ground nearby, picking off the ants one by one with its sticky tongue; the record books say it can catch and consume up to seven thousand in a day. The other adaptation is this lizard's means of taking in water. Its tough skin cools swiftly at night, and attracts condensing dew. Hundreds of grooves and folds in the skin channel much of this water towards the thorny devil's lips and mouth, where it is eagerly sipped.

Rather larger than these two prickly miniature

Distended and thorny-scaled, the horned lizard is too much of a mouthful for most predators.

monsters, and with a different defence strategy, is the gila monster from the south-western states of the USA. When full grown it reaches 50–60 cm (20–24 in.) in length, and it can weigh almost 2 kg (4½ lb) when well fed. Gila monsters are also called beaded lizards because of the corn-on-the-cob appearance of their scales. But the real beaded lizard is a closely related species from Mexico. The gila monster's scales are strongly patterned in yellowish orange and black – typical of warning coloration in many parts of the animal kingdom, alerting potential predators to the poisonous or strongly distasteful nature of their prey.

Slow-moving and long-lived, gila monsters prowl the desert after dark seeking their prey: nests of birds' or reptile eggs, or broods of young rodents, are particular favourites. Though these lizards possess venom glands above their jaws, they are probably rarely used and are only simple in form: the poison is chewed into the prey rather than injected through specialized fangs as in the snakes. The gila monster's feeding strategy is a very straightforward one: it gorges as much as it can whenever possible, storing any surplus as fat in the tail, which at times of plenty swells to twice its normal size. Over the next few lean weeks – or even months – the

lizard can survive by slowly metabolizing these reserves.

The horned lizard, the thorny devil and the gila monster dwell in mostly stony desert: true sand deserts and dune systems present problems of movement as well as of survival. Once the day is under way the sand becomes extremely hot as well as slippery, so securing a foothold becomes a problem. The geckos, more familiar as 'house guests' feeding on insects in the tropics, rely on tiny but very effective suckers on the ends of their toes to secure a foothold against the pull of gravity on ceilings and even on panes of glass. In the Namib Desert of southern Africa, one gecko has evolved webbing between its toes – reflected in its name, *Palmatogecko*. Another spreads the load of its weight on soft sand, and gains extra purchase on the slippery, moving surface by means of the broad, feather-like fringes to its toes. From another lizard group, the agamids, one slimly built species holds its body well clear of the hot sand on long legs, and raises its feet in a

rota with metronome-like timing so that at any one time only three feet are on the sand while one is cooling off.

This lizard, along with many others, can swiftly vanish into the sand if danger threatens, or when the time comes to escape the severest heat of the day. Only a few centimetres below the surface, the insulating blanket of air trapped between the sand grains above reduces the temperature appreciably, as well as intercepting all the direct radiant heat from the sun. Some, like various members of the skink family, establish more or less permanent burrows or occupy those deserted by other creatures like rodents or large spiders. The stump-tailed skink from Australia uses the same tactics as the beaded lizards, storing fat in its short, bulbous tail against harder times. Another Australian lizard, *Diplodactylus*, stores fat in a similar manner but in

Warning colours on the beaded scales alert potential predators to the noxious nature of the gila monster.

addition uses its heavily armoured tail to block the entrance to its burrow, excluding predators and maintaining favourable humidity levels during the heat of the day.

When lizards wish to submerge in the sand, they use an eel-like swimming movement which quickly buries them. Many spend most of their daily (or nightly) lives in this subterranean manner hunting subterranean prey, rather than just diving to escape heat or predators. Some of these (for example *Meroles* of the Namib) have 'normal' lizard limbs and dimensions, and seem modified for their unusual way of life only in having rather pointed or wedge-like heads, streamlined for pushing their way through the sand.

Some lizards carry this adaptive evolution much further. There are several skinks with greatly reduced limbs – sometimes just the fore-limbs, sometimes all four. One, aptly called the legless skink, from the Namib lacks detectable limbs – but X-ray examination reveals the vestiges of limb girdles on the skeleton. This small, shiny lizard closely resembles the slow-worm (*Anguis fragilis*) of temperate climates, and has evolved snake-like transparent scales over its eyes, as additional protection against sand grains. Other sand-swimming lizards have developed a form of eyelashes. True eyelashes, made of hair and evident in most mammals as eye protection, are absent in the reptiles. These 'false

Webbed feet support the web-footed gecko as it speeds across the soft sands of the Namib Desert during the night.

eyelashes' are comb-like fringes to the scales above and below the eye.

This evolutionary process of limb reduction is seen at its extreme in the flap-footed lizard, whose limbs are reduced to larger scales on its flanks – the flaps. So snake-like is it that an expert eye is needed to identify it correctly as a highly modified lizard. This is one of the most expert of the below-surface sand dune dwellers, moving with ease and speed and striking with snake-like speed at the geckos and skinks that share its habitat and form the major items of prey.

SNAKES

The genuine snakes also manage to flourish in the desert. All snakes' eyes are permanently open, without eyelids and protected by a single transparent scale. Although their near vision is reasonable, a snake's eyes are best at detecting movement, so prey that remains rigidly still might escape detection. Hearing, too, is poorly developed in snakes. The eardrum is on the surface of the head, unprotected by any form of fleshy external 'ear' as in mammals; so, particularly for those that live, or frequently hunt, underground or down burrows and rodent runs, eardrums of the conventional

Almost legless, the skink Chalcides sepsoides *moves snake-like over and through the Saharan sand.*

form could be easily and irreparably damaged. Instead, the eardrum is tough and horny, and more effective at detecting ground vibrations than actually hearing – indeed, sound travels relatively poorly below ground anyway.

Snakes share with many of the lizards a forked tongue. This is the outward evidence of their prime sensory system, as well as being one of the main reasons for human dislike of their kind. The forked tongue flicks continually in and out, kept moist by saliva within the mouth. Sometimes it flicks apparently aimlessly into the air just in front of the reptile's nose, while at other times the slender tips touch the ground. Using their tongues, snakes combine some parts of the human senses of taste and smell. But the combination they use is a far more sensitive indicator of what is going on – and what has gone on – in their environment than any of the rather dulled senses that evolution has left to our present high-technology, supposedly sophisticated state of development.

Particles, often molecule-sized, of scent, of debris, of the passage of potential prey or danger, are collected on the forked tongue, withdrawn into the mouth, and analysed in two shallow pits (known as Jacobson's

organs) in the roof of the mouth. Once the scent or taste is identified, the resulting information is relayed to the brain for appropriate action. As it glides along, the snake continually monitors its surroundings in this way.

Efficient scenting of prey (all snakes are carnivorous) is obviously of paramount importance to the hunting snake. Different hunting strategies are employed by desert-dwelling snakes, and one of these probably exclusive to them. A number of vipers bury themselves in loose sand, leaving exposed only the eyes and the invaluable notch in the upper lip through which the tongue flicks in and out. Concealed in this way, the viper waits for prey to come within range before striking. Horned, Gaboon and other desert vipers of this type are appreciably more portly for their length than most other snakes. This may well be a reflection of their passive hunting technique, as most other snakes must either move with speed or be able to penetrate rodent tunnels or the hiding places of any prey animal beneath rocks or in crevices.

Most zoologists consider that the pythons and boa constrictors, which sometimes flourish in arid or semi-arid habitats, are the most primitive of the snakes. An examination of a python skeleton will show vestiges of limbs, indicating that in times long past these snakes had ancestors with legs. Externally, all that is now visible are two horny spurs, one on each side of the vent.

The python and boa hunting strategy is also thought to be primitive. A lightning-fast strike with the wide-open mouth, equipped with a fearsome array of backward-pointing teeth, secures the prey. In a trice two or three coils of the long body are thrown around the victim, and then begins the long, inexorable process of squeezing the life out of it by suffocation. When the meal is limp and lifeless, the python releases its grip and begins to swallow it whole. Small prey are consumed with ease, but creatures of larger girth than the snake itself – not infrequently the case – can just as readily be accommodated. All snakes can do this, because they have relatively large mouths and flexible jaw bones. In addition, they can dislocate their jaws at the hinges, allowing a much wider gape than would otherwise be possible. After slowly swallowing their victim, the jaws snap naturally back into place.

The more evolutionarily advanced snakes kill their prey with poison. Some venoms act on the nervous system, speedily paralysing the prey, while others destroy the structure of the blood. There are two types of venom-carrying snakes. In one, the more primitive, poison flows from modified salivary glands down grooves in teeth at the back of the mouth – these snakes are known as the back-fanged species. In the more advanced, front-fanged snakes, the poison glands consist of pouches above lengthened hollow front teeth. The venom is injected by the force of the bite just as an injection penetrates the flesh from a hypodermic syringe and needle.

In some of these front-fanged species – like the vipers – in order to improve their killing efficiency evolution has lengthened the fangs to such an extent that the mouth cannot close satisfactorily with them erect. They are fixed to the gums and jaw by strong but elastic cartilage that allows them to fold back when not in use. As the viper opens its mouth to its fullest extent in order to strike, so they snap out like a flick-knife, locking into position as the head lunges forward and delivering their lethal dose of venom to maximum effect.

A single substantial meal will satisfy the food and water needs of a snake for days, and often for weeks. Their waterproof skin and much reduced metabolism when resting in the comparative cool of an underground lair helps them survive without water over this period.

Probably the peak of evolution among snakes is reached by various members of the rattlesnake family. The true rattlesnakes are by far the best known – even notorious – of these. Though they specialize in hunting small birds, reptiles and mammals they have a lot of highly potent venom, and if provoked can kill much larger mammals including deer, cattle and human beings.

The rattlesnake's rattle is a series of rings of dry skin, left at the extreme tip of the tail from previous moults when the snake has shed or sloughed its skin. When the snake is disturbed or alarmed, and wishes to give warning of its presence, it shakes the tail to produce an ominous dry rattling noise. But except when they are hunting, most snakes seek to avoid confrontation, and given adequate warning they normally slip away unseen and unheard.

Rattlesnakes, and other snakes of a group called the pit vipers, hunt after dark. They rely not just on the information picked up by the tongue, but on a longer-range 'secret weapon'. This is a device closely parallel in its principle, if not in its purpose or mode of action, to the most sophisticated technology now used by human beings in heat-seeking missiles and, more constructively, for locating people buried by rubble after earthquakes.

These snakes have a small pit on either side of their face which is sensitive to the body heat of their prey. It is an extremely sensitive infra-red detector, capable of locating not just warm-blooded creatures like mammals and birds, but also cold-blooded reptiles. In some way as yet imperfectly understood by humans, it transmits an image of the prey and its surroundings that allows the snake to approach silently and strike accurately. Even blindfolded snakes used in experimental tests are successful.

Much conjecture surrounds the techniques that snakes use to move: many can swim, some can climb smooth-barked trees – the near-vertical trunk, as well as along the branches – while one or two can even glide from tree to tree or from tree to ground on extended flaps of skin along their sides. Yet put any snake in the centre of a sheet of absolutely smooth glass, and it writhes helplessly about. Evolutionary pressures gradually removed limbs from the ancestors of today's snakes: what did they substitute as a means of getting about?

Snakes move forward by passing a sinuous wave right along their bodies, flexing to one side and then the other, using special muscle blocks to do so in a coordinated manner. The scales on the underside of a snake's body are ridged, and from the head to the vent each scale is attached beneath a pair of ribs. The ribs are open-ended, like croquet hoops – not joined in front as they are in mammals and birds. The scales – and the ribs – are moved in sequence, each a little way forward at a time, by waves of muscle movement (known as sinusoidal waves) passing along the snake's body. The ridges on the scales get a grip on the ground, just as if they were tiny claws, and the scales then pull the body forward just a little. Very shortly afterwards another sinusoidal wave passes, and the snake moves a little further, essentially walking on its ribs.

Some of the desert rattlesnakes, however, move differently. To cope with having to move about on shifting sand, and to minimize the contact made by their bodies with the burning hot ground underneath them, they coil their bodies almost into an open spiral and move diagonally, and at amazing speed, across their desert home. This leaves a series of tracks in the form of parallel lines up to 1 m (3 ft) long and maybe 20–30 cm (8–12 in.) apart, each not connected to the next – a very puzzling sight until the snake so expert in crossing sand dunes is seen making them. These snakes are called sidewinders – for obvious reasons – and typify the superb adaptation present in the snakes.

INVERTEBRATES

SURVIVAL STRATEGIES FOR THE SMALLEST

For most small animals like insects and arachnids — spiders, scorpions and similar creatures — the problems posed by living in deserts are rather less than those faced by larger animals. This is because, like many desert plants, insects and arachnids are built with a waterproof cuticle or 'shell'. As the name 'invertebrate' implies, these arthropod (jointed-limbed) small animals lack an internal backbone or bony skeleton. Instead they have an external skeleton called an exoskeleton. This hard cuticle is largely composed of a substance called chitin, which is not only strong but impervious to many gases and liquids — an effective 'suit of armour' provided during the processes of evolution.

The possession of such a protective skin to prevent insects, arachnids and the like from drying out in the heat of the sun is an example of pre-adaptation: arthropod life cycles, which are complex, provide another. Most have a life cycle which includes several stages. First comes the egg; then the larva (often with several growth periods separated by moults, when the cuticle is shed and replaced by a larger version); then the

pupa; and ultimately the adult, reproductive phase. These stages may vary enormously in length, and may be physically very different from one another — as different as the moth egg is from the caterpillar, or the caterpillar from the free-flying adult moth. This situation creates tremendous flexibility in desert-adapted species.

The various stages of all invertebrates, not just the insects, may have varying ability to resist drying out. Often it is the egg that has a toughened shell, impervious to drought and able to last for months or even years before rainfall and an accompanying flush of plant and subsequently animal growth stimulate it to hatch. This is often the most persistent drought-resistant stage, but in many cases there may be a prolonged larval life, carried out not in the glare and heat above ground, but in the comparatively equable temperatures some distance below the surface. In many cases, too, the pupal stage may be almost as well protected as the egg — the moth within its protective cocoon or chrysalis, for example. The adult invertebrate may, as in the beetles, centipedes and scorpions, be well protected within the armour of its chitinous exoskeleton, and live a long, productive life in the desert. Or it may be short-lived in the extreme — it may survive on fat, stored in its body while a larva, for just long enough to mate and lay eggs before expiring. Or again, if the invertebrate is an insect, and a winged one, the flying adult may be as

The Namib Desert's strangest plant, Welwitschia, *showing the female cones.*
Inset   *The sap-sucking bug* Probergrothius sexpunctatus *is found nowhere except on female* Welwitschia *cones.*

111

nomadic as the birds, seeking out fresh feeding grounds where rain has recently fallen.

Generally speaking, those groups of invertebrates which require a marine environment are absent from deserts – but not entirely, as in the case of the several species of brine shrimps like the Australian *Triops*. This almost perfect miniature mimic of the much larger king crab, is a 'living fossil' species, alive today but of great antiquity. They can survive in the extreme salinity of desert salt lakes, and produce tiny but tough eggs that can blow in the dust from one drying salt pan to colonize newly created salt lakes, often a considerable distance away and sometimes years later.

Similarly, most invertebrates whose life stages at some time are dependent on permanent fresh water are absent from the world's deserts, except at permanent waterholes or oases. Here a surprisingly rich fauna of worms, leeches, midges and flies survives, with their attendant insect-hunters like dragonflies: but they are absolutely dependant on their water source. This is essentially a microcosm of another habitat, set within the desert, and falls outside the context of this book.

SMALL PARASITES

Let's now take a look at the major invertebrate groups occurring in desert areas. Other than in water, most of the protozoans, the single-celled microbial animals, are absent, except for those that are parasitic in other animals and thus divorced from true desert existence. But even so all of them must have evolved strategies, often extremely complex ones, demanding – as do various tropical diseases including malaria and trypanosomiasis – an intermediate host and vector, often a blood-sucking insect like a mosquito or tsetse fly.

Flatworms, tapeworms and roundworms (or nematodes) are also largely confined to a parasitic existence. The nematode roundworm *Dracunculus*, usually called the Guinea worm, shows a pattern of life that is complex even for a parasite. It is ultimately a parasite of humans in tropical regions, particularly in arid zones. People get infected when, after a long hot journey across the desert, they stop to slake their thirst at a wadi or waterhole. Often the wadi will be large enough to support an enormous population of tiny copepods or water fleas, and inevitably some will be swallowed. Of these, the occasional individual will have been infected as an intermediate host by the microscopic larval stage of the roundworm.

Once accidentally swallowed, the *Dracunculus* leave the dead copepod and migrate through the human gut wall into connective tissue, often settling in the legs. Here they mature, lengthening greatly. As she matures, which may take more than a year, the female becomes packed with thousands of eggs which hatch while still inside her body. At this stage the nematode moves towards the skin, her probing head causing a large blister, often near the ankle. The blister is accompanied by a powerful burning sensation, hence the reference to 'fiery serpents' sent by God in the Bible. The logical way to relieve this pain, particularly after a long hot day crossing the desert, is to plunge the affected areas into the nearest cool water – the wadi. The sudden chilling causes the blister to burst and the head of the Guinea worm to rupture, liberating the larvae into the water. Here they are swallowed by copepods, and so the cycle starts again.

The only way of extracting Guinea worms is to pull them out slowly from the blister. This must be done over several days as the nematode may be 1 m (3 ft) long. The area surrounding the nematode is naturally inflamed and susceptible to secondary bacterial infection, which can cause severe problems. Even worse, should the *Dracunculus* break during the extraction process, the formation of scar tissue or even some rigid calcification around what is left may cripple the unfortunate person involved. In the past the nematode used to be wound round a small stick, which was then fixed close to the wound, ready for more winding the next day. It has been argued that this is the likely origin of the first symbol of medicine, and that currently of the British Medical Association – a branch with supposed 'serpents' twined around it.

The annelids, or segmented worms, are rare in genuine desert surroundings. But some occur around oases, where occasional blood-sucking leeches, members of the same group, occur to plague man and animals alike.

MOLLUSCS

Most molluscs and shellfish are marine or freshwater creatures, with free-swimming, unprotected larvae. The only group really well adapted to terrestrial life are the snails, which, protected within a thick insulating spiral shell, are sealed off from the outside world by the horny disc of their operculum, a kind of 'safety door' with which they plug the entrance to their shells. Several snails have adapted to desert habitats, exploiting plant material in season and at the cooler, dewier times of day and night. They are able to extract a vegetarian meal even from tough desert plants, their tongues working like microscopic rasps with multiple rows of teeth, replaced as they wear out, scraping tiny fragments from the tissue beneath them.

Some desert snails graze largely on the lichens encrusting rock surfaces. These slow-growing and long-lived plant cooperatives, a mutually beneficial combine of single-celled algae embedded in a tangled mat of fine, hair-like fungal threads or hyphae, are by their nature tough and inaccessible to almost any other herbivore. It has been argued recently that these snail grazers make a material contribution to the turn-around of nitrogenous materials in the starved desert soil, as well as helping to speed the fragmentation of the limestone rock on which the lichens grow and so turn it into soil.

For its size, a snail has the biggest and perhaps the most powerful 'foot' in the animal kingdom. Many desert plants are extremely spiny, none more so than the cacti of the Americas, but even these can be scaled by a determined snail. The sole of the foot is tough but flexible, allowing it to function as an elongated suction cup, shaping itself to every irregularity beneath in order to maximize its grip. Cells in the sole secrete a thick mucus; the 'slime' glints silver in the light of the desert dawn and indicates where the snail has been. On rough or prickly surfaces this substance serves as a protective lubricant, while on smooth ones (like vertical surfaces of rock, made glass-smooth by their coating of desert varnish) it acts as a semi-fluid adhesive, supporting the whole weight of the snail and its substantial shell. Being water-based, the slime is a potentially costly asset to the snail in the desert, to be used only when adequate dew or mist is available. For much of the rest of the year the snail aestivates, its metabolism running at only a tick-over rate, secure in the enclosed humidity behind the closed operculum and tucked into the shadiest spot it can find.

ARTHROPODS

Paramount among the successful invertebrates of the desert are the Arthropoda, particularly the insects, spiders and their relatives. Other arthropod groups are also represented, including the brine shrimps and their terrestrial relatives, the so-called woodlice or pea-bugs. With even more legs, but similarly armoured and well adapted to cope with the problems of drying out, are the millipedes (which are vegetarians) and their fast-moving carnivorous relatives, the centipedes, some of which carry potent venom.

Most of the varied groups of arachnids (spiders, scorpions and their allies) are reasonably well represented in desert habitats, and some – for example the scorpions and the sun-spiders – seem to be more at home in such conditions than elsewhere. These eight-legged creatures range in size from soil mites less than 1 mm (twenty-five to the inch) in length, and dwelling largely underground, to comparative giants like scorpions reaching 20 cm (8 in.) or more in length or sun-spiders whose outstretched legs may span 15 cm (6 in.).

Although some of the smaller mites may be omnivorous, most arachnids are carnivores. This poses something of a fundamental question, because the scant plant life of the desert appears to support relatively few herbivores; the essence of life in any habitat is the 'pyramid' built up on a broad base of herbivorous animals consuming plant matter, in their turn preyed upon by various predatory groups, with the tip of the pyramid being occupied by the dominant carnivore. However, in many desert areas there are more plant foods than meet the eye. Especially beneath the surface, where there are vestiges of a soil structure with some humus, detritus-feeding arthropods like collembolas (springtails) gather, as do myriad nematodes as well as a few larger earthworms and insect larvae. These form the herbivore base for several tiers of predators.

Even where there is little evidence of plant life, such as among dune systems, detailed examination reveals wind-borne seeds and fragments of decaying plant and animal matter that can be trapped by invertebrate creatures and eaten. This goes a long way towards resolving the apparent enigma of how such a wealth and range of invertebrates survive in desert conditions. There is, even here, a food chain based on vegetarians, although in many groups the predatory life prevails, and many must eat considerable numbers of their own kind in order to survive. The benefit is that predators derive most of their moisture from the body fluids of their prey.

Among the more voracious of the predators are scorpions and spiders, many of them small but some large enough to tackle victims as large as lizards and occasional small birds and rodents. Not surprisingly perhaps, most of the spiders are ground-dwelling, often lurking beneath stones and leaping out on to unsuspecting prey passing by. It would be pointless to spin webs in windy conditions where there is little flying prey, and generating the silk to make the web would probably in any case represent a dangerously wasteful expenditure of precious body fluids.

The sun-spiders of the order Solifugida (which

ironically means 'fleeing from the sun') are often called camel spiders by desert travellers, in whom they instil considerable fear because of their size, hairiness and speed. The concern is to a degree misplaced, because camel spiders are not actually dangerous to humans – nevertheless, their bite is painful. Most are large – larger than the majority of true spiders, to which they are only distantly related. There are about eight hundred species, occurring in the hot desert zones of all continents except Australia. Most shelter from the heat of the day and are nocturnal hunters.

Sun-spiders are renowned for their speed across the sand, reputedly achieving 16 kph (10 mph) in sustained dashes, which would place them among the fastest of all land-dwelling invertebrates, and, size-for-size, high on the land speed record charts. Speed is obviously of assistance as they hunt, sprints being interrupted by pauses when they use their senses (perhaps 'hearing', but more probably mostly smelling) to locate or track potential prey. The 'head-end' of a sun-spider is disproportionately large, and once the prey has been overtaken by surprise and sheer speed the reason becomes apparent. Again for their size, the sun-spiders have the largest and most powerful, pincer-shaped hollow jaws (called chelicerae) of any small animal. Once seized, their prey has little or no chance of escape as its body fluids – containing both nourishment and vital water – are sucked out.

Scorpions have been feared by humans for millennia – quite validly, as they have a potent sting which can be dangerous and is always extremely painful. They have often been used to symbolize evil, and the ancient Greeks signalled their respect by immortalizing them in the Zodiacal sign Scorpio applied to one of the major star constellations. They are in fact amongst the most antique of all land animals. Fossil records show perfectly recognizable members of the scorpion family dating back to Devonian or even Silurian times, in rock strata laid down between 350 and 400 million years ago. So little has their fundamental structure changed over this time that today's scorpions can fairly be described as 'living fossils'.

There are also about eight hundred members of the scorpion family, mostly tropical but with a few in subtropical or warm-temperate climates, such as that surrounding the Mediterranean Sea. Most of the desert species are yellowish or brownish, with the occasional black species like the Emperor – one of the biggest at 20 cm (8 in.).

Scorpion structure is reasonably uniform between species and comparatively well known, with a 'head-end' or cephalothorax carrying the pair of conspicuous pincers (pedipalps) used to capture prey. Also on the cephalothorax are various small mouth parts and four pairs of walking legs, as well as a cluster of inconspicuous and probably not very effective or useful primitive eyes. Behind is the abdomen, with twelve armoured segments of which the last five form the arching tail, ending in the conspicuous sting. This has a rose thorn-shaped stinger linked to a bulbous sac of venom, which is produced by a pair of glands nearby and injected by powerful muscles as the sting stabs home. The venom is usually a nerve toxin that quickly paralyses small prey. Some American species possess venom capable of killing larger animals, including humans, within hours if a suitable antidote is not injected. The muscles paralysed include the vital ones associated with breathing and the heart.

Scorpions are essentially nocturnal animals (which is why they have little need for effective eyes), and often lead solitary lives except during the mating season. Much of the heat of the day is avoided, resting quietly under the shelter of a rock or deep in a crevice. Some Australian and American species actually dig a spirally descending burrow deep into the cool and, usually, moister sand 1 m (3 ft) or more below the surface. Others simply bury themselves a few centimetres below the surface in the loose sand or gravel. A thick cuticle protects them from water loss; and, as they are carnivores, much of their water requirements come from the prey on which they feed.

Moisture loss during respiration is minimized by the intriguing construction of their lungs: four spiracles, or small pores, lead through the body wall to a series of 'book lungs', in which the respiratory surfaces are neatly arranged, like the pages of a part-open book. Each spiracle has a flap covering it, which is movable and can speed respiration at times of high exertion, or reduce it to a minimum (saving evaporative moisture loss) during resting periods when the temperature is at its highest.

Courtship display and the mating process are fascinating, if slightly bizarre, to watch. Male and female scorpions differ little in external appearance – the male is slightly the more slender of the two – and each sex has a genital opening (protected by plates called opercula) at the base of the abdomen. Ideally for desert-dwellers, the mating processes have evolved to minimize any drying out of either eggs or spermatozoa. The male produces a ball of spermatozoa protected within a

tough gelatinous capsule known as the spermatophore, which he ultimately transfers into the female's genital pore.

But first comes an extended courtship 'dance' perhaps best likened to the lobster quadrille of Lewis Carroll's story. Clasping pincers, male and female face one another, tails arched high over their backs and twining together – with some caution so as to prevent stinging each other. Still clasping pincers the two will sway, shuffling from side to side and back and forth with precision timing (considering the number of feet involved) that would be the envy of any dancer. As courtship progresses, the male extrudes his spermatophore which becomes attached to the ground beneath them by a short stalk stuck to the surface. His subsequent dance manoeuvres guide the female so that her genital opening covers the spermatophore, whereupon the sperm within are liberated into her genital tract. As with some spiders, once the mating ritual is complete it behoves the male to move swiftly away – otherwise he runs the risk of being killed and eaten by his mate.

Venomous sting poised at the tip of its arched tail, the scorpion Opisthophthalmus *of the Namib is ready for defence or attack.*

The next stage is equally fascinating. Once her eggs have been fertilized the female retains them within her body for up to a year and more, perhaps in some way yet unknown assessing the most favourable season in which to 'give birth'. Inside the female, the eggs develop until what she 'lays' is a thin membrane containing a fully developed young scorpion – a miniaturized version of the adult. This process, unusual in animal groups, is called ovo-viviparity.

Once in the outside world, the young scorpion cuts itself free from the eggshell and then retreats with its siblings, of which there may be dozens, to the protection of its mother's back. Here it will stay for some days, probably surviving on its body reserves, before descending to the ground and beginning its independent existence. Subsequent development to adulthood is slow, interrupted by seven or eight moults as the old rigid cuticle, now too small, is shed and the growing scorpion stretches the new elastic exoskeleton (formed within the old one before it splits and is shed) before it hardens. It is no surprise, therefore, that scorpion life-cycles take several years to reach completion.

Scorpions are carnivores, sensing the presence of their prey by means of hairs on their pincers and legs that provide senses of both touch and 'smell', and possibly taste also. Their technique is not that of pursuit, although they can be fast-moving: rather they lie in wait in semi-concealment, motionless, grabbing suitable prey with their pincers as it passes. Once the victim is held, the arched tail is quickly brought forward over the head to deliver a paralysing dose of venom, capable of quickly incapacitating the insects, lizards and occasional small rodents that are caught. Scorpions are messy feeders; around and outside the mouth they have a series of small toothed appendages which macerate the tissue of prey with the assistance of digestive salivary fluids. As the soft parts are broken down and the victim's body fluids are released, this semi-liquid mush is sucked in. Eating is a slow process, and at the end the indigestible hard parts of the prey are left as a kind of pellet. Having fed well, the scorpion may go for weeks without further food.

Though seemingly very well protected, scorpions are not themselves immune to attack, and cannibalism is common at any time – not just after mating. Their defensive technique of standing their ground, sting poised for action, renders them vulnerable to predators that can handle this situation. They may be simply overwhelmed by masses of ants, while praying mantids and some beetles have the necessary body armour to protect themselves from scorpions, usually smaller than themselves. Some birds and mammals (including monkey, baboons and the mongoose tribe) have speeds of reaction that allow them to tear or knock off the sting, rendering the scorpion defenceless.

INSECTS

Although insects are remarkably abundant in the desert, those with aquatic stages in their life-cycle (for example dragonflies) tend to remain close to permanent water sources. Wherever there is a vestige of plant material herbivorous insects are found, and wherever there are herbivores, nature is bound to provide an array of carnivorous predators to feed upon them.

Sometimes, as in the case of the yucca moth of the North American deserts, a close association has evolved between the insect and its host plant which is to their mutual advantage. After mating, the female moth visits the yucca flowers and collects pollen from the plant's anthers, the male part. She then rolls the pollen into a ball and carries it off to another plant where she places it securely on the stigma, the female part of the flower. In the pollen ball she lays an egg, and her emerging larvae feed on the developing seeds within the ovaries beneath them. Although this process destroys some ovaries and their contents, as the larvae move around the flower head they also distribute pollen from floret to floret, effectively pollinating more than they destroy.

Once full-grown, the larva falls to the ground and buries itself deeply, remaining in pupal form for a year. It then wriggles to the surface, using miniature hooks on its pupal case to ease its way through the sunbaked soil and showing a mobility unusual and unexpected in a pupal stage. Here the adult moth emerges to fly free, after a journey through hardened soil that, as an adult, it would have found difficult if not impossible to perform.

So successful is the ant family that it would be strange not to find some members exploiting the arid regions of the world. Some of the oddest of these, from the deserts and semi-deserts of America, Africa and Australia, come from different genera but have evolved similar lifestyles. These are the honeypot ants.

Their colonial structure is similar to that of most other ant species, with an army of workers foraging for food to support the colony and its queen. Her main function in life is to produce, deep within the nest, eggs which will provide yet more workers. Amongst the food collected by the workers is honeydew, the watery, sugar-rich excretion of aphid colonies which feed by sucking plant sap. The aphids' intake, through tubular mouthparts embedded in the plant's vascular system – similar to mammalian blood vessels – in which sap is moving under pressure, far exceeds their needs. The substantial excess is excreted as honeydew. The ants protect these 'aphid herds' and regularly collect honeydew from them to take back to their nest. In arid regions, when there is a flush of growth following the rains aphids are quick to exploit the sudden abundance of plant sap.

Honeypot ants are equally quick to exploit the aphids, and as a reflection of their dry habitat have developed a most unusual means of storing this fluid bonanza, which contains water, readily digested sugars and other nutrients. Within the nest, certain workers are selected as special recipients of honeydew. They receive more and more, becoming almost immobile as their abdomens swell until translucent and golden with the honeydew they contain. They hang from the roof of the nest, living food stores, waiting to regurgitate the honeydew later as food for the workers when conditions outside make normal food difficult to obtain. Such food stores are also of value at all times, not just in conditions of maximum stress, to the native peoples of desert areas and to bands of nomads passing through. They recognize the nests and open them to remove the 'honeypot' storage workers, biting off and eating their swollen abdomens with relish.

Perhaps because of their colloquial name, white ants, the termites are commonly regarded as being near-relatives of the ants. But in fact they form their own insect order Isoptera, while the ants are grouped with the bees, wasps, sawflies and their allies in the order Hymenoptera. Oddly, the termites' closest relatives are probably the cockroaches and mantids – although only one of these, a wood-feeding American cockroach, shares the termites' ability to digest cellulose, the basic chemical of which plant cell walls are constructed.

The termites owe their ability to digest cellulose – and their resultant reputation as one of the most destructive insects, both domestically and agriculturally, that are known to humans – to protozoans which live symbiotically (that is, to the mutual benefit of themselves and their host) in the termites' gut. Vast numbers of these microscopic, single-celled animals possess the digestive enzymes that higher animals lack, and can break down cellulose into readily absorbed and nutritious components.

Termite mounds are a conspicuous feature of many arid and semi-arid landscapes. Rock-like in appearance and texture, they are far from being simple mounds of earth. Considering the size of the workers that build them, their construction is on a colossal scale. The fabric is essentially sand and soil particles, a little decaying vegetable matter and copious secretions from the termites themselves – all set like concrete by the desert sun, and often standing taller than a man. Like an iceberg, only a fraction of the termite citadel is visible above ground. Tunnels and chambers penetrate deep into the subsoil often for several metres, so that the water table is reached and a water supply ensured. The mounds themselves are hollow, with numerous flues leading down into a subterranean chamber often large enough to house a human being. The above-ground

Harvester ants taking seeds to store in their nest in the desert of New Mexico.

portion heats in the sun and, like a warmed chimney, draws air upwards and out through the various flues. Ground-level air inlets draw air into the mound, and carefully constructed dried mud louvres and fins direct its passage so that a cooling 'air-conditioning' draught passes right through the colony.

One Australian termite builds mounds flattened from side to side, like the tip of a dagger protruding through the desert soil. The thinnest edge points to the midday sun, to minimize the load on the 'air-conditioning system' during the heat of the day. The longer sides point north–south (so the two sides actually face east and west) so accurately that desert travellers call these insects compass termites. This exposure of the larger walls towards sunrise and sunset ensures that, at these chill times of day, maximum sun strikes the colony and speedily warms it up to working temperature for the inmates.

At the heart of the colony the female lies in comfort, surrounded by attentive workers which feed her and remove the hundreds of eggs she lays each day from her greatly distended abdomen – really little more than an ovary. She, and the entrances to the mound, are guarded by soldier termites, a larger, specialist caste of worker with a huge, heavily armoured head bearing fearsome jaws whose sole task is defence. Unable to feed for themselves, they, like the queen, are nurtured by workers with high-energy liquid food secretions.

Though the worker termites superficially resemble ants a few millimetres long, they have a far less robust cuticle and are a pallid grey in colour (hence 'white ants'). Since they lack ants' body armour, which protects them against dessication as well as predators, termites feed during the cool of the night. They often construct tunnels of sand above soil level, and even up tall vegetation, so that they may travel undisturbed to their prime feeding grounds. Most of their food is taken back to the nest, and all of it is plant material – unlike ants, which can be carnivores when occasion arises, they do not adapt their diet to whatever food supply is currently plentiful. Calculations made in the Australian outback suggest that the termite population from below ground consumes a greater weight of the scanty grass supplies than all the sheep, cattle and kangaroos grazing above ground put together!

The grazing pressure exerted by the termites is a

Often taller than a man, termite mounds are ventilator shafts, the visible evidence of an underground air-conditioned insect metropolis.

119

steady one, and in natural circumstances they and the sparse desert vegetation on which they depend would co-exist in a reasonable balance – prolonged droughts would reduce the available plant growth and cause parallel falls in termite numbers. Only when pastoral peoples introduce domestic grazing stock, particularly at pressurized twentieth-century levels, is the competition from termites perceived as a pest problem.

Not so with the locust, identified even in the Old Testament as one of the major plagues of mankind. The desert locust, which ranges over the desert and sub-desert areas of northern Africa, the Middle East and the Indian subcontinent, is probably the most destructive insect in the world so far as the human race's crops and natural vegetation are concerned.

Unlike termites, which exert steady pressure, for many years locusts will cause little detectable damage. Then, suddenly, their numbers explode and enormous destruction of plant life follows. For generation after generation, the desert locust will live a solitary life just like any other largish (about 5 cm or 2 in. long) grasshopper in a dry habitat. After mating the females lay eggs, well spaced out to ensure that each emerging miniature grasshopper has adequate plant food. While the adults have wings and can fly competently – as well as leaping prodigiously, powered by their long, folded back legs, to escape predators – the larvae can only walk and hop. As with the scorpions, a series of moults into larger exoskeleton cuticles, coupled with the internal development of sex organs, takes the locusts to adulthood over a period of a year or more.

However, sometimes this pattern changes, suddenly and completely. The reasons are not fully understood, but one at least seems to relate to sudden torrential rains, when the ground is softened and plant growth is, for the desert, unusually luxuriant. Locusts lay their eggs in this softened ground, and in these circumstances egg production may rise dramatically and many females will lay in the same area. The immatures which hatch from these eggs, called 'hoppers', are not solitary but congregate in ever-expanding groups. This is the gregarious phase referred to in the desert locust's scientific name, *Schistocerca gregaria*.

These bands of hoppers are darker in colour than the solitary phase, absorbing heat better and therefore more active earlier in the day. Devastating all in their path, the expanding groups of hoppers move about, coalescing with other groups, feeding voraciously and growing rapidly towards maturity. The adults of the gregarious phase are longer-winged than the solitary

forms, and better long-distance fliers. Dreadful though the damage caused by hoppers can be, it is nothing to that inflicted by swarms of millions of flying adults. Close proximity to others of their kind induces additional hyperactivity and excitement, and the swarms may travel thousands of kilometres, destroying every form of plant life in their path. Local scorpion populations will have a bonanza, exploiting this sudden but short-lived abundance of one of their favoured prey items. But they, and other predators that may gather from miles around, particularly the highly mobile birds of prey, can exert little or no controlling pressure on overall locust numbers.

Control with insecticides is feasible when the hopper bands are small – but the time and place of their occurrence are difficult to predict and the area that needs to be kept under surveillance is impossibly large. Once the locusts are winged and on the move, any attempt to control them by aerial spraying is usually futile and may result in additional environmental damage in the form of agrochemical pollution. Eventually, the problem subsides: locust swarms run out of food and to some extent the internal 'steam' that led them to form in the first place. Swarms break up and shrink; possibly influenced by changing weather patterns, they rapidly return to the solitary phase. But it may be some time before normality returns to the vegetation of arid landscapes, and the pastoralists and cereal-farming tribespeople of the marginal lands can resume their traditional way of life.

If the desert locust is the most damaging of the desert invertebrates, then a group of darkling beetles from the Namib Desert in southern Africa probably takes the title of 'best adapted to desert life'. These species of tenebrionid beetles are comparatively long-legged, with bodies some 20–30 mm (about 1 in.) long. They are active, searching for food during the daylight hours and sheltering only from the most extreme heat. Since they are vegetarians, the scanty plant life offers them comparatively little in the way of moisture. But they solve this problem in an amazing way, exploiting the principles of physics and the frequent nocturnal fogs that sweep across the Namib.

One, the head-standing beetle, emerges on foggy nights from its hiding places beneath the sand and clambers to the crest of the dunes. There, it faces into the wind and tucks its head down into the sand, raising its long back legs high into the air. The sea mist condenses on its hardened body, chilled as it is after a few hours in the sand after dark, and runs down the legs and grooves on the elytra or wing cases. Ultimately this tiny trickle of moisture is channelled into the beetle's mouth and eagerly drunk. On a particularly favourable night, when relative humidities, air and beetle-body temperatures combine to give maximum condensation, lines of darkling beetles assemble on the crest, each capable of taking on board some 40 per cent of its own body weight as water.

This is astonishing enough, but other darkling beetles use tactics similar to those employed by desert travellers either lost or low on water. The beetles emerge from the dunes on foggy nights, and on the windward side of a dune drag their bodies along its flank. This ploughing action creates a miniature trench between two parallel ridges of sand. The laws of physics then come into play, as droplets of condensed water from the fog are attracted to the ridges, which collect two or three times as much water as the surrounding flat sand. Reaching the end of its furrow, the beetle turns and moves back along the same line, sipping the condensation as it goes. There can be few better examples of diversity of approach in overcoming the desert's main challenge – obtaining water.

The darkling beetle, Coelocnemis, *from Mexico. Other darkling or head-standing beetles are among the more amazing of Namibian insects.*

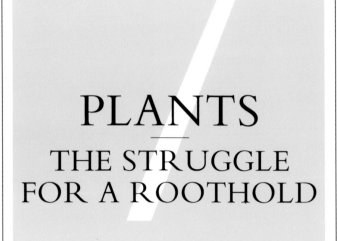

7

PLANTS
THE STRUGGLE
FOR A ROOTHOLD

Heat and drought threaten desert plants in exactly the same way as they do desert animals. Plants will 'die of thirst' in much the same way as animals if too much water is lost through evaporation, and plants too must achieve a water balance that allows them to continue to grow towards maturity, quickly or slowly depending on which evolutionary track they are following.

In deserts, as in all of the world's habitats, plants are the basis of all life. Alongside their beauty and fascinating diversity of shape, lifestyle and colour, plants are important because they recycle the atmospheric gases vital to life on earth. In particular they liberate the oxygen which is vital to animals and utilize in their own nutrition and growth carbon dioxide, effectively 'locking up' a gas that would otherwise be contributing to global warming through the greenhouse effect.

Green tissue, usually leaves but sometimes the stems, is the plant's main food-producing system. Leaves and stems occur in a multitude of shapes and sizes, formed by evolution to suit particular lifestyles and habitats. Within are the fundamental units of plant anatomy, the cells. Boxed in by a rigid cellulose wall, each green cell contains a jelly-like cytoplasm in which are the nucleus

(containing genetic information coded on to chromosomes), mitochondria (controlling energy production) and chloroplasts.

The chloroplasts contain the green pigment chlorophyll, perhaps the most important chemical catalyst of all. It is responsible for activating the harnessing of the sun's energy (in abundant supply in the desert) to manufacture the plant's carbohydrate food in the process called photosynthesis. Using sunlight as the energy source and chlorophyll as the catalyst, the green cells of the leaf take in carbon dioxide from the air and combine it with water from the roots to form sugar or starch. Oxygen is liberated as a by-product and enriches the atmosphere.

Larger plants need some form of skeletal structure or reinforcement to hold themselves up, usually found as strong fibres or woody thickening to cell walls. Vascular cells are the 'plumbing' essential to transport food and water around the plant. Xylem vessels carry water usually up from the roots, while the phloem carries foodstuffs manufactured in the leaves to all parts of the plant. These tubular vessels occur in bundles, with reinforcing fibres, and look rather like veins.

Clearly, the leaves are of major importance in the everyday life of the plant. Not only are they the food-producing organs, but they are in effect the 'lungs' too. For photosynthesis the plant must take in carbon dioxide and give out oxygen: this is termed

A Joshua tree silhouetted against the Mojave Desert sunset.

transipration. In desert conditions (just as for animals in respiration) this process must be carried out with minimum water loss.

Viewed microscopically, all leaves are constructed on the basis of a sandwich. The core consists of thin-walled, spongy cells called palisade tissue, heavily laden with chloroplasts which have plentiful spaces between them to allow gases to circulate. These are protected from damage and drying out by the upper and lower parts of the sandwich, the leaf surfaces or epidermis. This epidermal layer is composed of smaller, stouter cells, close-packed like cobblestones, with their outward surfaces or cuticle often waxy or slimy and almost totally impervious to water.

The plant takes in carbon dioxide from the air, through special pores called stomata in this epidermis. Air input, and oxygen emission, is controlled by special guard cells, shaped like microscopic lips, which open and close as required. However they remain tightly sealed at times of stress when the plant is attempting to minimize water loss. In the leaves of desert plants, the stomata are much fewer and further between than in the leaves on plants from moister habitats, and they usually open at night to 'breathe in' when temperatures are lower and humidities higher than during the day.

BASIC DESERT ADAPTATIONS

Leaves of plants adapted to desert conditions are termed xeromorphic and, irrespective of the type of plant or which desert it comes from, they share several characteristic features. The most obvious is that they have a high ratio of volume to surface area: the leaves are small, comparatively thick and compact. This parallels the situation in desert mammals, where the best adapted also have a high weight (or volume)-to-surface ratio. The camel and the addax find survival under desert conditions much less difficult than do tiny rodents like the pocket mouse and kangaroo rat. Additionally, small leaves dissipate heat more effectively than large ones.

Within these stout leaves there is more palisade tissue than normal, increasing the efficiency of transpiration. As desert leaves are naturally more prone to wilting when water is in short supply, evolution has endowed them with an unusually high proportion of strengthening cells to support their tissues mechanically and prevent structural and cell damage. The leaf may be rolled or grooved, with the stomata sheltered within the roll or deep in the grooves. Winds are frequent in the desert and have a pronounced drying effect, particularly on plant life. This is minimized by protecting

A tussock of Mammillaria *cactus in bloom in the Mexican Desert.*

the stomata from the passage of hot, dry air. In plants whose leaves are not rolled or grooved, or whose surfaces are not waxy, a dense covering of tiny hairs (which under the microscope appear star- or bladder-shaped) protects the leaf surface. These trap a layer of still air that acts both as thermal insulation and as an effective wind shield over the stomata.

SOIL PROBLEMS

Desert soils do not help in plant survival. In some ways soils are almost as important as water to plant growth, but in the desert they are impoverished, lacking humus and vital minor nutrients. This problem, added to the heat and drought, prevents all but a comparative handful of the world's plants from colonizing desert habitats. In structure, too, desert soils present plants with huge difficulties. Sands are mobile and dry, and long-rooted perennials are usually the only plants to succeed. Once they mature, it is easy to see how they manage to survive, but how do they get through the earlier stages? To this question there is at present no full answer.

Rock is little better, though the cracks do provide moisture and soil traps into which deep-rooted plants can penetrate. Sand, however, can act as a sponge, absorbing whatever rain falls and allowing briefly favourable conditions. In these situations it is mostly the short-lived annuals — the desert ephemerals — that flourish.

NON-FLOWERING SEED PLANTS

The so-called higher plants are those clearly visible to the naked eye and obviously recognizable as plants, shrubs or trees. Surprisingly, in several desert areas there is an astonishing diversity in the microflora – those plants with just one or only a few cells, normally best observed under a microscope. They include soil bacteria, vital in the process of breakdown and decay of organic matter, and even blue-green algae – single-celled plant forms more usually aquatic and, if not, closely associated with damp conditions. In their surface layers these algae form drought-resistant resting spores to tide them over the long, dry intervals between the rains; but they swiftly return to life as soon as there is adequate moisture.

The plant kingdom is divided by botanists into two major groupings, the gymnospermae (or non-flowering seed plants) and the angiospermae (the flowering seed plants). The gymnospermae include the various mosses, liverworts and other plants that still show close links with their early ancestry, though are by no means necessarily 'primitive'.

Mosses and liverworts – larger plants with more complex structures than the algae, but demanding a watery environment for their reproductive cycle (which is far more complex than that of the algae) – are, not surprisingly, scarce or absent from desert habitats. Fungi, however, are often widespread.

These lowly plant forms do not have the ability to photosynthesize their own food – all are active parasites or saprophytes. The saprophytes derive their nourishment from a network of thread-like hyphae running through dead, decaying matter, and they play an important part in its decomposition. The parasites invade living tissue – normally that of other plants but some (like ringworm) active on the skins of animals. Wherever there are green plants, there are parasitic fungi: often they are only minimally harmful to their host, and sometimes they may actually be beneficial, helping its root system to absorb soil nutrients better (for example, the mycorrhizal fungi). Some, though, may eventually be lethal to their host, weakening it so that under the stress of desert conditions it swiftly succumbs to water shortage.

Lichens flourish in the desert. Though thought to be a feature of rocky coasts, tundra and woodland, crustose lichens (like miniature, roughly circular piecrusts coloured in greys, greens and oranges) frequently cover rock faces and dry soils. They take swift advantage of any rain to photosynthesize and grow, then endure the

Although classed as 'lower' plants, lichens are actually a sophisticated co-operative of algal cells enmeshed in a fungal mat.

subsequent drought in a near-dry resting condition. Lichens are amongst the hardiest of all plants and, though slow-growing, may be among the longest-lived. Arctic species are estimated to be at least four thousand years old.

At their most advanced the gymnosperms are represented by the various conifers. This extensive group would seem to be well adapted, with their needle-like, hardened leaves and with protected stomata, for survival in arid conditions. But though they flourish in the semi-aridity of temperate sandy heathland, the conifers have few representatives in the genuine deserts of the world. Even the best-known examples, those antique cypresses growing in remote high gorges in the mountainous regions of the Sahara, may actually be survivors, hanging on to life in the desert after establishing their roothold some thousands of years ago when the climate was milder and the terrain more hospitable.

The most striking example of a successful desert gymnosperm comes from the extraordinary conditions of the Namib Desert in southern Africa. Like so many living things from the Namib it is unique and endemic – only to be found in that desert. Like the conifers in the Sahara to the north, most specimens are aged, perhaps one thousand years old or even more. Welwitschia, when well grown, has a massive, turnip-like root, sometimes 1 m (3 ft) in diameter. It serves as a food and water storage organ, and sends a tap root deep into the subsoil in search of water as well as spreading a network of tough, fibrous roots nearer the surface but under the overhang of its extraordinary leaves.

At first sight, welwitschia could easily be mistaken for dead, or at least in the last stages of an unsuccessful struggle for survival. An untidy heap of browning, frayed leaves lie in a contorted tangle on the ground, blowing fitfully and rustling in the wind. These strap-like leaves, traced back to their origin in the crown of the plant, turn out to be the split, weathered sections of just two massive leaves, which are green and completely encircle the crown. The worn appearance of their tips is hardly surprising as the wind constantly pushes them back and forth over the abrasive, rocky soil. These two leaves were those that the plant started with, perhaps hundreds or – according to some estimates for larger specimens – maybe two thousand or more years ago. They grow continuously: tissue that wears away is soon replaced. If it were not, the leaves would be hundreds of metres long.

So few and far between are Welwitschia *plants that it is astonishing that cross-fertilization is necessary between male (below) and female (p. 110) cone-bearing plants.*

The leaves are actually much shorter, perhaps 1 m (3 ft) or a little longer. But for desert plants this is massive, and a striking contradiction of one of the first principles of survival for desert plants – that small leaves lose least water. Nor are the leaves succulent or waxy or fleshy in any way – rather they are dry and fibrous. This is an important survival feature, for welwitschia is a plant of the Namib. Here, rains are exceedingly sporadic, and although they are readily absorbed first by the superficial root network, and later by the deep tap root, this opportunity arises but rarely. The major weather feature in that desert is the nocturnal mist sweeping in off the South Atlantic, and in this situation the large size and fibrous nature of the leaves are used to good effect. The mist condenses on the leaves. Some drops on to the ground, to be absorbed by the fibrous roots, but some is absorbed into the fibrous tissue of the leaves from where it is conducted back to the crown to be used by the actively photosynthesizing green tissue of the fresh leaf bases.

FLOWERING SEED PLANTS

The second great grouping of plants, the angiosperms, is subdivided into the monocotyledons (with just a single seedling leaf, and normally with parallel veins in their leaves) and the dicotyledons (with two seedling leaves, and usually with a branching network of leaf veins). To these two groups belong the majority of desert plants, and between them they show an amazing range of adaptations to aridity, heat and unstable soils.

Generally speaking, in arid climates most of the plant life consists of perennials that are resistant to the stress of drought. Sometimes they are bulbous but usually they are woody, with the particular exception of the fleshy cactus family. However, where the soil is slightly richer and more stable, and enjoys either a regular wet season or sporadic rains, far more favourable conditions may occur. But there is a strictly limiting factor: they occur for only a short time. This situation can enable rapid growth to take place, and allows an annual (as distinct from perennial, but better called 'ephemeral') plant life to develop.

Most desert ephemerals have seeds that are extremely drought-tolerant, but spring to life from dormancy with great speed when adequate moisture is available. Under the favourable – if short lived – growth period, these ephemerals are very productive. This allows their swift life-cycle to progress to the provision of seeds that are well stocked with a nutrient store for the embryo when it is able to develop in the future, all within a

Cordia Oaxacana, part of the borage family and one of the most spectacular Mexican desert flowers outside the cactus family.

well-made, robust seed coat set up to endure prolonged drought and abrasion as it blows about in the wind. All of this is vital for the long-term survival of these ephemerals in the desert ecosystem.

Herbaceous perennials, non-woody plants, are not normally common in 'hot' deserts except in areas where salt water is available in some form. Many saline desert swamps retain their moisture for long periods: here a range of specialized plants has developed, able to cope with extracting the water from the soil and excreting the excess salt it contains. Some of these are woody shrubs, but many are herbaceous, with fleshy or glabrous leaves. One plant family is outstanding in its ability to flourish in saline conditions: the Chenopodiaceae, a herbaceous group with inconspicuously coloured but prolific flowers. In 'cold' deserts some herbaceous perennials do find conditions to their liking, particularly those with well-developed underground stolons or tap roots. Here a real winter occurs, and the habit of herbaceous plants of temperate and cold climates is adopted. The above ground parts are lost to the first frosts, but the plant itself survives by means of its underground organs, often protected from extremes of cold by an insulating layer of snow. Many widespread families are represented, including the Cruciferae (the cabbage family), the Compositae (the various thistles and daisies), the Leguminosae (the clovers or vetches) and the Ranunculaceae (the buttercups).

EVOLUTIONARY ROUTES TO SURVIVAL: PERENNIALS

Two clear evolutionary pathways have enabled the higher plants to survive in 'hot' deserts. One is that of the long-lived woody perennials, which display a wide range of survival stratagems derived from thousands upon thousands of years of evolution. The other is that of the short-lived annual, with its fantastic growth rate and ability to endure the worst rigours of the desert climate in its best-protected form, the seed.

First, let's look at the long-lived perennials. There is a problem right at the outset. Although it is easy to marvel at the adaptations that allow the mature plant to survive in the desert, in many cases it is far from easy to see how the seedling could possibly have survived long enough to reach adulthood. This is particularly so in those species where a slender root reaches deep into the desert soil to tap water resources several metres below the surface.

In all probability, these species lead two-phase lives. In the early years, the first phase, the plant depends heavily on a superficial network of fibrous roots, trapping whatever dew and rainfall occur. This allows slow growth, much of it devoted to below-ground root development, including that of the tap root that will one day, in the second phase, become the plant's mainstay. In all these bushy plants, growth and the weight of plant tissue are heavily biased towards the roots and away from the shoots. True, the leaves must photosynthesize to create food, but in the desert sunlight and air (containing carbon dioxide) are abundant, making life easy for the green cells with their chlorophyll. Water is the limiting factor, and so the major share of resources is dedicated to root formation. Not only does this maximize the potential water intake, but it secures the plant more firmly in soil that is often excessively loose, pebbly or friable, in conditions where frequent strong winds could cause havoc.

Many desert shrubs – the sagebrush, salt-brush and mesquite, for example – are small and often some metres apart on the desert surface. This, too, is a reflection of the size of the root system compared with the above-ground parts of the plant. All the soil between these scattered bushes is explored and exploited by roots desperately competing to extract sufficient water from it. The plant needs a block of soil that size full of roots to provide enough water to support it – but it can only afford to produce a comparatively small, compact structure above ground.

The creosote bush of the south-western deserts of the

United States grows in a similar manner. Within its own root zone, it collects water so efficiently that no competitor can glean enough to survive more than briefly. Creosote bushes expand not by setting seed but by the development of suckers – new shoots sprouting skywards from a root were it comes near the soil surface. In this way, with almost infinite slowness, the bush expands in diameter.

As it grows larger, the original stems at the centre tend to die off (but leaving roots to continue the water-collecting purpose) and the bush assumes the shape of a hollow ring. Some of these rings have a diameter of 25 m (over 80 ft) or more. They are of course part of, not descendants of, the original clump of shoots, developing in a plant continuum that botanists believe is between ten and twelve thousand years old. This is appreciably older even than the Arctic lichens, and if the idea is accepted that the present-day shoots belong to the original, founding plant, it makes the creosote bush the oldest living thing on this planet: something of an achievement in one of the planet's most hostile environments.

Shedding the above-ground parts – the stem and leaves – can be identified as a winter survival strategy in 'cold' deserts and in temperate-climate winters. But in a modified form it also has a place in the ranks of 'hot' desert plant survival strategies. Perhaps the best desert examples are among various bulbous plants including some tulips, the autumn crocus and particularly various onions or *Allium* species.

The bulb below ground is essentially a compacted stem, surrounded by the thick, fleshy bases of the leaves. In the wet season the leaves emerge, flourish and photosynthesize above ground, feeding the products of their photosynthesis back down to fatten the leaf-base food store still more. As the dry season takes a grip, the green leaves of the *Allium* wither and a spectacular flower emerges. On a stout stalk, it is often a spherical mass of star-like florets, each on a long stalk. Many are so desirable to gardeners that even in their desert habitat they are threatened with extinction at the hands of plant

Despite structural similarities, these Euphorbia *trees from Central Asia are quite unrelated to the cactus family.*

Far more spectacular than garden Crocus *cultivars are these* Crocus sieberi *from the arid mountainsides of the Asian Desert Corridor.*

Many desert plants have evolved spines – up to 6 cm (2½ in.) long in this Acacia *– to protect themselves from grazing animals.*

collectors. These flowers quickly set seed, some of which may eventually germinate. The *Allium* has other means of multiplying at its disposal, though, since small bulbils grow at its base and eventually break off to form new plants. During the worst of the hot season the leafless bulb survives, its metabolism reduced to an absolute minimum some centimetres beneath the desert surface.

Most of the desert shrubs are physically tough, and resilient in their physiology. The various desert *Acacia* species, and the mulga and mallee bush of Australia, survive in areas where bush fires are often ignited by lightning from thunderstorms that produce no rain. Leaves, if present, are swiftly burnt, and if the fire is severe little may remain above ground but charcoal and charred twigs. Yet in due course, especially if rains follow, fresh shoots will emerge from the blackened stem bases and growth will be resumed.

Over the course of time many desert shrubs have evolved protective measures to defend themselves against grazing herbivores. In the desert, grazing wildlife may be scarce compared with that on grassy plains. But plant food is comparatively even scarcer, so effective deterrent mechanisms have a clear evolutionary benefit.

Such protective stratagems can be either physical or chemical. Sometimes the physical deterrents are obvious – painfully obvious in the form of massive spines over 6 cm (2½ in.) long and as stout as a nail. The spines may be arranged in complex clusters, or branched in 'crows' feet' to provide a more effective shield. At times the physical side is less obvious but no less effective: the silica-based, razor-sharp edges to the leaves of some grasses, for example. Other leaves, such as those of conifers, have needle-sharp tips. Again these are often silica-based, and they frequently cause an allergic reaction as well as wounding the skin. Yet others, like welwitschia, have a leathery or sandpaper-like surface that is difficult to bite.

In many spine-protected plants, particularly cacti, the spines are arranged so that the highly desirable succulent leaves or stem behind them are almost totally protected. But not always: in Africa the oryx can cope with some spines; while on the semi-desert margins antelopes like the gerenuk – with its very slender snout and ability to stand on its hind legs and reach the tender, less-protected topmost shoots – can nibble between the acacia spines.

Desert scrub plants have been shown to provide ample evidence that they are consumed more slowly and with less relish than temperate plants. The two researchers involved were both aptly named Chew! Much of the low palatability they identified was due to various chemicals occurring naturally within the plants. These include materials which may be irritant or toxic, like white latex saps; alternatively they may be highly aromatic, resinous or spicy compounds.

It has been argued that, while some of these deterrents may be derived from plant waste products, the great majority, including spines, are produced only at the expenditure of considerable energy on the part of the plant, with a consequent drain on its water resources. It follows that they need to be successful to justify this risk. It has also been suggested by researchers that so much energy is expended on defence that it is a major factor in the low growth rate of desert plants. Often these taste deterrents or toxins within the leaf only develop with maturity: this may in part account for the low rate of leaf replacement in desert plants. Young leaves are more vulnerable, and while in temperate climates those that are eaten or damaged would quickly be replaced, the water and energy economies of desert plants are already so stressed that this additional burden could not readily be borne.

The Israeli botanist Professor Zohary identified moisture as the most important factor in desert plant

The extraordinary flowers of Calliandra houstoniana, *a member of the Leguminosae or pea family, feature in Sonoran Desert scrub.*

survival. He distinguished six types of desert plant. First were those evergreen trees like acacias and tamarisks, which shed old leaves and sometimes branches in summer after the formation of new ones, but never lose their leaves entirely. Second, he grouped evergreen succulents like *Haloxylon* (including the salt-tolerant salicornia) which produce new sections of photosynthesizing stem in winter, while older stems die back in summer. Third, he identified evergreens like *Retama*, which shed some leaves in winter.

The fourth group, the 'wintergreens' like *Lycium*, do the opposite: they lose all their leaves in midsummer. Fifth were *Reaumaria* types, probably the most important group of shrubby perennials in desert habitats. They include *Sueda*, *Artemesia* and *Zygophyllum*, which shed some twigs, leaves or leaflets to reduce their transpiring surfaces at the start of a dry season, leaving buds, or the latest-emerged fresh leaves, in position for the next wet spell. In the last of his groupings, he placed the desert annuals – productive, spectacular and finishing their life-cycles soon after the end of the wet season that prompted their germination.

Within his categories fall a variety of leaf-shedding options, all evidently successful as the plants favouring each particular strategy continue to flourish in desert circumstances: clearly there is no 'best solution' to the problem of water conservation. Some of the plants in his classification have green stems, with stomata carrying out the functions of photosynthesis perfectly effectively. These may or may not (*Anabasis*, and *Haloxylon* respectively) have leaves, and if there are leaves, they may be much reduced (*Reaumaria*). If it is physiologically possible, 'doing without' leaves is clearly an evolutionary approach well worth following in arid habitats. The photosynthetic burden can, it seems, be carried successfully by stems, and the problems of heat absorption and water loss through the leaf surface are avoided at source. It is within the Cactaceae, the two thousand-odd members of the cactus family, that the plant stem reaches its zenith as a survival feature for desert plants.

All the cactus family are endemic to southern North America, Central America and northern South America – or they were in origin. All use their stems both for photosynthesis and for water storage. In the great majority of cactus species the leaves are reduced to spines – and throughout the family there is an infinite variety of spine form, from fine soft 'wool' to the most savage spike. Some are borne singly, others in clusters like a pincushion.

This must be one of the most frequently 'domesticated' of all plant families – perhaps not surprising given their intriguing shapes and beautiful flowers, but astonishing given the painful injuries their spines can inflict on casual handlers. So as house and garden plants, and as accidental or deliberate introductions (the prickly pear is the classic example), various cactus plants are to be found almost everywhere. They range in size from the smooth, tiny pebble cactus that looks just like its name and is perfectly camouflaged against the rounded stones of the desert, to the giant saguaro, which is the biggest – and perhaps the most amazing – of all desert plants.

Giant saguaros can grow to about 15 m in height – around 50 ft. As they develop the initial single column develops side branches, so the mature cactus looks like a monstrous thorny candelabra rising out of the desert. At this stage it may weigh getting on for 10 tonnes, of which 9 tonnes is water. A tree of similar size would have its heartwood of thickened reinforcing cells, the skeleton necessary to support its weight and so robust that from its timber we build our homes and furniture. Not so the saguaro. Most of the interior is composed of thin-walled pith cells called parenchyma – devoted simply to water storage. Running through this soft pith is an extensive and elaborate network of food- and fluid-transporting vessels (the phloem and xylem respectively) with their accompanying fibrous strengthening cells, the whole forming a vascular bundle. These bundles twist and snake through the cactus tissue, branching and rejoining. In a dead saguaro, once the soft flesh has rotted away this giant 'skeleton' of tough tissue remains, reminiscent of a gigantic bathroom loofah.

Saguaros are not deep-rooted. Rather they have an extensive network of fibrous roots quite close to the soil surface. This mat of roots provides a secure anchorage for the towering cactus above, and functions best following the intermittent but often torrential rains that occur in the North American Great Basin. Although these roots may have encountered little, if any, water for many months, they respond so effectively to rainfall that a big saguaro can take up as much as a tonne of water within one day. Structurally, its stem is also well designed to take this load. Viewed from afar, one of the saguaro's aesthetically pleasing aspects is the orderly vertical linearity of its tufts of spines. Neatly and evenly spaced, the rows of spine cushions sit on ridges in the stem, separated by grooves. The grooves deepen, and the girth of the saguaro shrinks, as the drought deepens and more and more of the plant's fluid reserves are used up. When the drought breaks, the grooves expand like gussets, allowing the massive stem to swell.

The stems of the saguaro are green within the waterproof epidermis, which contains plenty of chlorophyll for photosynthesis. As in many plants, the stomata are specially modified to allow them to open during the cool hours of darkness, taking in carbon dioxide and expelling oxygen to the surrounding environment. This carbon dioxide is held in storage until daylight; then, with the stored water and under the action of sunlight, aided by chlorophyll, it is processed into food. The stomata are placed deep at the bottom of the pleats or grooves in the stem, shielded from the sun and to an extent from the wind. Further wind insulation is provided by the spines, which hold a layer of still air in place around the entire surface of the

Largest cactus of all, the giant saguaro towers into the Arizona desert sky.

cactus. The spines, as in many other cactus plants, also defend the saguaro from grazing animals. Additional protection to this enormous and highly desirable water store is afforded by the plant's cellular biochemistry, for saguaro sap is one of the most toxic of all. Few animals can eat much saguaro flesh with impunity.

The flowers of many members of the cactus family are among the most spectacular sights of the natural world. Often they are large, composed of a great many slender petals, sometimes subtle, sometimes brilliantly coloured. The petals are usually arranged in an elongated tuft rather like a feather duster, ending in prominent, protruding anthers and stamens which are often in contrasting colours, particularly golds. The tragedy of these blooms is that almost invariably they are short-lived, bursting during the late afternoon, opening through the night and withering next morning.

In the desert, pollination for all plants, not just the cactus family, can be a problem. Wind pollination to distribute pollen from one flower to another is reasonably commonplace, but many plants are so thinly spread that self-pollination is the practical route for them to follow, regardless of any problems that may result from inbreeding. Insect pollination, widespread in temperate climates and in other largely tropical habitats such as jungles, is also rare. This is partly because there are fewer insects, and partly because in many circumstances the plants are so widely scattered that effective pollination in this way could be difficult.

In the deserts of the Americas cacti tend to form a reasonable plant cover, and insect pollination, particularly by some nocturnal moths, is thought to be widespread. Cactus flowers protrude well beyond the protective armoury of spines, and recent research has shown that pollination may depend on most unexpected agencies. Saguaro flowers are large, and therefore carry an appreciable stock of nectar. It has long been known that not only insects but also birds like the white-winged dove visit the flowers to take nectar, which is valued both for its fluid content and for its high-energy sucrose. The birds occasionally, no doubt, assist with pollination.

The latest exploiter of the rich nectar source, and an effective pollinator, has been shown to be the long-nosed bat. Long-nosed as its name suggests, the bat feeds in flight. It plunges its face into the flower, often literally up to the ears, and in the process gets smothered in pollen grains. If it cannot reach the nectar this way, it extends its very long tongue deep into the nectaries and

Nicknamed 'Indian paint brush', Castilleja curomosa *is found in the deserts of southern North America.*

licks up a meal. Then it backs off, hovers a moment, and flies on to another flower, transferring the pollen to the stigma as it plunges in. The shape of the bat's head, and the contours of the flower, match almost perfectly – certainly so closely that this would seem to be more than a casual association. It has most likely evolved to this degree, benefiting both bat and cactus, over a long period of time.

It appears that the saguaro is not alone in exploiting the assistance of bats. Saguaro flowers are open for much of the night and most of the next day, allowing a variety of pollinators to try their hand at reaching the nectar. Other cacti, like the organ-pipe and cardon, have a much shorter flower-opening period and may be more heavily dependent on the bats for pollination. The organ-pipe also provides food supplies for long-nosed bats later in the year, as they prepare for migration. The mushy, sugar-rich fruits break open and the contents are lapped up, again in flight, by bats anxious to 'fuel-up' before migration. It may be that this process assists in cactus seed dispersal. Agave flowers also provide a late-season nectar source for bats, especially those migrating south to avoid winter hardship.

Among the agave's relatives are the yuccas, splendid desert plants with their tall spikes of bell-like white or creamy flowers. Yuccas exhibit a novel approach to obtaining those small but vital quantities of nutrients that are either lacking or present only in negligible amounts in impoverished desert soils. Many large desert plants achieve substantial bulk – for their height, they probably have greater weight than many temperate species. So their demands, particularly for essential

The spectacular flowers of Trichocereus acanthoplegma, *a South American cactus.*

EVOLUTIONARY ROUTES TO SURVIVAL: ANNUALS AND EPHEMERALS

Desert perennials show what in human terms would be called dogged persistence or true grit, slowly establishing themselves in their desert habitat and set for a long life if they survive the early stages. They have evolved a great range of moisture- and energy-conserving strategies, all highly adapted to the desert environment. But the desert annuals show a marked constrast.

For these plants life is short and colourful. The term 'annual' is only appropriate in those deserts where the seasonal rains are indeed once-yearly, falling at the same predictable time each year. It is more common for rains to be irregular, with many months or even years between periods of rainfall. Plants that flourish under the conditions of both annual and spasmodic rains are

A yucca in flower, about to be engulfed by a shifting sand dune.

nitrogen, may create as critical a situation as shortage of water. In the Great Basin deserts the yuccas have evolved an extraordinary solution: they flourish in areas where desert animals congregate – perhaps to feed, perhaps to shelter, perhaps to chew the cud. It is here that those animals excrete waste products rich in nitrogen. In temperate climates, the flourishing dark green growth of herbaceous perennials around sheep and cattle feeding stations is evidence of a similar situation, as is the growth of a rich plant life on the otherwise unpromising cliff ledges where seabird colonies congregate. Similar, but not the same, for round the byres and water troughs, and on the seabird ledges, the rich nitrogen uptake is through the plant roots.

The yucca, on the other hand, is apparently able to extract from the air, through its stomata, the ammonia given off in gaseous form as urine in particular is exposed to the heat of the sun. Desert animals, as explained earlier, produce highly concentrated urine as part of their evolutionary survival strategy – on this the yucca flourishes. Recent researches by Professor Headon indicate that other desert plants – for example *Quillaia* from the Atacama and Patagonian deserts – may use the same tactic. Yucca plants grown adjacent to stock yards or pig houses dramatically reduce the environmental problems caused by the smell. More than that, stock fed with yucca leaves produce much less obnoxious excretions: the yucca tissue apparently has the capacity to bind ammonia and eliminate its volatility, toxicity and smell even when severed from the parent plant and effectively dying. In the current environmentally conscious era, with effluent emissions one of agriculture's major problems, desert plants may have a major part to play.

better termed ephemerals, which indicates the speed with which they come – and go – after the rains.

The ephemerals cope with the worst elements of the desert environment – prolonged heat, overnight cold and prolonged drought – by avoiding them almost entirely. They do so by remaining in an extremely well-protected inactive resting stage – their seeds – until conditions for growth are favourable. In some ways this parallels the aestivation of small mammals. Even the wind, a major hazard particularly to plant life in deserts, can be turned to advantage. It may act as a means of seed dispersal, allowing colonization of new ground when dust- or sandstorms sweep over the desert. During the brief active lives of these plants wind can be an important pollinating agent, spreading pollen from plant to plant.

Enormous numbers of plants follow this avoidance strategy, shortening their life-cycles so that seed germination follows adequate rains – though just how the adequacy of the rainfall is assessed is not yet fully understood. Certainly too fast a germination after what could be just a single brief shower, however heavy, would be disastrous. Shoots, leaves and flowers are produced in quick succession in ideal growing conditions, and seed formation and ripening are well under way by the time that soil moisture levels begin to fall towards the wilting point for plants.

Amazingly swiftly after the first steady rain begins to fall the seeds spring into life. Some literally spring, in that their hard dry cases suddenly split open, explosively propelling over a large area the seeds within. In other seed cases, coverings of bristles or hairs, brittle-dry for months, take in water and swell, pushing the seed itself erect so that as the fresh rootlet emerges it penetrates directly downward into moist soil. Shortly after the root has taken a hold, growing on food resources within the seed, the first leaves appear – small, but green and ready to contribute their photosynthetic input to accelerating the seedlings' growth.

Opposite   *Also following the rains, a sheet of ephemeral California poppies (*Eschscholzia) *splash colour across the Arizona desert.*

Like colourful palm trees in miniature, Brunswigia *lilies burst into flower soon after the end of the drought.*

Nowhere is the flowering of the desert ephemerals more spectacular than in Australia. Here, the blooming of the desert is far from an annual feature – a decade or more may elapse in some parts between these fabulous events. The 'red centre' of Australia becomes its green heart in these occasional years of rains. There is even a liverwort, which for years has lain shrivelled and brown, that fleshes out and turns gradually greener and greener as the moister environment persists – this is the aptly named resurrection plant.

Among the flowering plants the Compositae – the daisies – often seem to predominate. Purple swathes of parakeelyas stretch for miles, punctuated by yellow daisies and crucifers, the white poached-egg plant (another daisy) and the paper-thin, almost dry flowers and foliage of the everlasting daisies. While most ephemerals shoot upwards from their roothold, sometimes branching, sometimes not, others expand laterally. By far the most spectacular of these is Sturt's desert pea, which pushes creeping shoots out across even the most inhospitably rocky terrain, often advancing by 20–30 cm (about 12 in.) in a single day. At the base of each typically pea-like leaf, which has a central stem with pairs of small oval leaflets along it, is a stalk which bears a lantern-like circular cluster of scarlet and black flowers, each 3–4 cm ($1-1\frac{1}{2}$ in.) high.

Pink rather than purple, and rather bulkier, is the 'wild hop' – more properly the red dock, related to the *Rumex* species of temperate climates. The story goes that wild hop, which can reach pestilential quantities, originated in Australia only a century or so ago when it was accidentally brought in from Asia in the packing of camel saddles. Yet another invader, probably introduced from Eurasia, is the bright blue salvation Jane, sometimes called Paterson's curse by stockmen – appropriately enough as it makes poor grazing.

Photosynthesis for these plants may be limited to just a few weeks each year, and in some years they may not photosynthesize at all. But their productivity is enormous, the colour that they spread over normally stark desert landscapes unbelievably spectacular, and the long-term food supply for other creatures that their seeds provide is absolutely vital to the functioning of the desert ecosystem as a whole.

The parched heartland of Australia is transformed into a rainbow profusion of colour after the spasmodic rains. No floral component is more striking than the fast-growing Sturt's desert pea (inset).

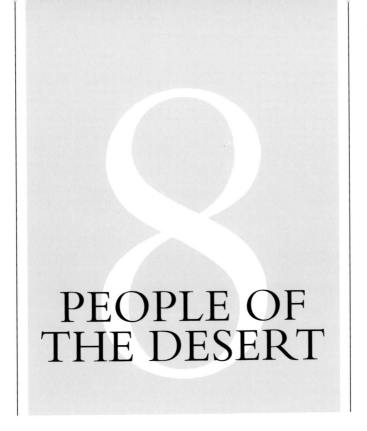

PEOPLE OF THE DESERT

Professor Knut Schmidt-Nielsen, in his treatise entitled *Desert Animals: Physiological Problems of Heat and Water*, wrote of the world's deserts and compared their impact on man and wildlife:

The deserts of the world are hostile to man but have a richer animal life than we usually imagine. It is estimated that between one-fifth and two-fifths of the earth surface is desert. Over vast areas of these arid lands there is no permanent water, and years may go by between rains. Although man can penetrate and sometimes prosper in deserts, he does so only because of cultural adaptations – he depends on water that he brings with him or obtains by digging or drilling. It is our technological culture, not our physiology, that permits us to live there. Without a water supply, man can live for a day, or at most two, in a hot desert. Even the most primitive of living men, the Stone Age aborigine of Central Australia, depends on water. He has no agriculture and lives off the arid land as a hunter and gatherer. Occasionally he obtains some water by digging out a water-filled frog from the hardened mud in a dried-out depression but permanent springs and pools control the range of his extensive travels.

Yet in these same deserts, and in all the deserts of the world, we find a variety of animals that seem to get along well under conditions too adverse for man.

Compared with many animals, humans have an excellent ability to regulate their own temperature with precision. In the heat of the desert this is achieved by sweating. The amount of sweat produced can be staggeringly profuse, at 3 litres (5 pints) or more an hour for short periods and at up to 12 litres (21 pints) per day. Whilst it may effectively lower the body temperature, unless the traveller has access to almost unlimited drinking water this reduction is accomplished at a price that can be ill afforded. The lost fluid needs to be replenished. But normally, even if adequate water is available, the intake falls short of the real need. As a result slow dehydration – perhaps around 5 per cent of the body weight each day – begins. Clearly, this steady loss of tissue moisture cannot be tolerated for many days.

There are problems, too, with the loss of salt, essential to the human metabolism in small quantities day and night. Usually the loss of salt through sweat is appreciable – even in temperate climates, sweat is markedly salt to taste. Salt deficiency is made worse by

Tuareg tribesman, dressed for his environment.

drinking copious quantities of fresh water, as this further reduces the concentration of salt in the body and causes severe and painfully disabling muscle cramps and headaches. So in the desert we must be provided not only with water, but also with a source of salt. In the past, this led to salt being one of the most valuable of commodities, as indicated by the comment in the Gospel according to St Matthew: 'ye are the salt of the earth'; and by the colloquial term 'worth his salt', implying that a labourer is worth his daily salt ration.

The problem for people in the desert seems to be that, despite water stress and inadequate replacement of body fluid, the temperature regulatory mechanism keeps going and so profuse sweating continues. Human kidneys are not particularly efficient, nor are they specially adapted or pre-adapted as are those of some other animals to emit concentrated urine – though in hot conditions the volume of urine produced is appreciably reduced. Thus if no compensatory or alleviating measures are taken, dehydration progresses quite swiftly to the point where water is extracted from the blood plasma, thickening the blood and reducing both its flow and cooling capacity. Death follows an explosive temperature rise past the lethal limit at about 41° or 42°C (105–107°F).

The rate of heat flow from the environment into an animal is proportional to the difference between the body temperature and the environment. The camel is physiologically adapted to allow its body temperature to rise close to its lethal limit, so heat input from outside is minimized, as is the effort to keep cool. Humans, on the other hand, labour physiologically to maintain their temperature at about 38°C (100°F) regardless, and so must tolerate a faster intake of heat from their environment, as well as expending precious water in the attempt to keep cool.

CLOTHING AS INSULATION

Much as hair or fur are of benefit to desert animals, clothing is of great advantage to us in hot surroundings, no matter how paradoxical this may seem at first. Insulation in the form of a layer of trapped air is very valuable. Experimental evidence supports the view that, clad in typical lightweight khaki bush clothing, the human body absorbs only half the heat that it would do if naked. Perhaps even more important, the water loss through sweating is reduced by two-thirds, an often invaluable saving. Clothing that interferes with some evaporative cooling of sweat from the skin would be a disadvantage, so loose-fitting, flowing garments are far more effective than tailored western-style clothes.

The long white burnouse worn by Arabian bedouins is ideal, doubtless derived from centuries of adaptation. Made of fine wool, the burnouse is worn summer and winter, often over a long-sleeved woollen 'nightshirt'. Besides offering protection from daytime heat, it provides warmth during the bitterly cold desert nights.

But the popular belief that white clothing carries additional benefits in reflecting heat is misplaced. Though white may reflect the visible spectrum more effectively than other colours, the really important radiation – including that reflected from the sand or rock – is in the infra-red wavebands, and to infra-red radiation all kinds of fabric or hair surfaces appear black. Thus the black robes worn by many of the Tuareg in the Sahara are by no means as impractical as at first sight they may seem.

THE VALUE OF A NOMADIC LIFESTYLE

The most important element in the successful adaptation of an animal to life in the desert may well be a readiness and freedom to migrate when necessary. Applying this principle to ourselves, the inference is that nomadism is the only way of life that allows human tribes to live permanently in the desert. Strong arguments have been advanced that, as nomadism is based on sound biological principles, it should be supported and 'modernized', rather than discouraged as a political nuisance which is all too often the case today. In North Africa, the human tribe has come to terms with the environment most effectively, and so too in Australia, although the native peoples concerned are immensely different in culture and in their approaches to their nomadic lives.

Nomadism as a way of life for people implies periodic or cyclic movements, with no permanent place of residence. It does not imply a total change of habitat (as migration usually does), nor does it indicate random and unrestricted wanderings. Most nomadic peoples are highly focused in their movement, as not just their success but their survival depends on finding fresh water sources and a food supply that their technology allows them to exploit. Three classes of nomadism are recognized: hunter-gatherers, pastoralists and traders.

Nomadic hunter-gatherers, like the bushmen of the Kalahari, may have daily, monthly or semi-annual shifts of terrain. Their populations tend to be reasonably stable, and they move as small, independent bands through what amounts to a territory. Within that area they know every waterhole, every important tree, the locations of patches of smaller food plants and the habits and movements of potential food animals.

Pastoral nomads are governed by the needs of their domesticated stock, be it sheep, goats, or camels. They too move about within a vast established territory, where they know every waterhole and have an almost instinctive understanding of every seasonal quirk of the plant life. Their movements are dictated by the need to find the best possible pasture, but almost always they will have a focal point, an area where the grass supply is more prolonged and predictable. Some of these groups may also hunt for part of the year, and others may, in their most settled phase, cultivate an area near their base and where they grow a primitive cereal crop. Pastoral tribes, perhaps more than hunter-gatherers will also trade if they get half a chance.

The travelling traders conduct trains of pack animals, usually camels but occasionally asses, mules and in Tibet even yaks, across the desert regions. They act as mobile merchants to the other desert peoples, as well as supplying goods produced on one side of the desert to the townspeople on the other. In temperate climates these people would be called tinkers, or maybe gypsies, and would offer their services as labour or do minor mechanical repair work. Most desert tribes, however, have little need for such additional services: the nature of their habitat and long folk experience has taught them to be self-sufficient.

Overall, a surprising range of peoples have adapted with success to overcome this harsh desert environment and to exploit such richness that deserts have to offer. The deserts of northern Africa and western Asia are peopled by Caucasian stock, and many authorities think that the Aborigines of Australia are more closely related to the Caucasian people than to other major racial groups, despite the fact that the latter are nearer at hand. Central and southern African deserts are peopled by Negroid races. Central and eastern Asian deserts are inhabited by Mongoloid peoples; so are those of the Americas: their ancestors migrated over the Ice Age land-bridge from Asia across what is now the Bering Strait.

It is fair to say that the human adaptations to desert life have been behavioural and cultural, rather than physiological as they have been in so many other animals. Irrigation of desert soils is as old as the oldest chapters of the Bible's Old Testament in the valley of the Tigris and Euphrates rivers, and as old as the cradle of Egyptian civilization in the Nile valley. Irrigation allowed regular cropping where previously the only way of life was nomadic. It led to the building of more permanent settlements, with the practicalities of deep-storage cisterns for water and thick-walled homes with small windows to minimize the problems of the heat and the night-time cold. But this altered lifestyle removed these settlers from the true desert existence as experienced by wildlife.

Today, far less than 1 per cent of the world's population survives in a desert habitat, but the number and variety of peoples involved indicates the capacity of mankind to withstand the rigours of this harsh environment. Just how, in their various ways, do they accomplish it?

THE BUSHMEN OF THE KALAHARI

Current estimates put the number of bushmen in the Kalahari Desert at fewer than twenty thousand, probably less than half of them still following their traditional hunter-gatherer lifestyle. Though not, as often depicted, pygmies, they are short in stature, the men averaging little over 150 cm (5 ft). There are three major tribes, the !Kong, !Xung and !Gwi, all speaking dialects that to western ears are quite extraordinary and frequently punctuated with clicks and other noises produced in the throat by the glottis.

Bushmen travel in groups of several families, linked by either relationship or simple friendship, ranging a territory of about 1000 sq km (400 sq miles). This they know like the proverbial 'back of their hand' – particularly the seasonal distribution of their food plants (the most important component of their diet) and their prey animals (which provide valuable protein supplements). And, of course, the location of good waterholes is well known to them. Their overnight shelters are little more than a flimsy grass-and-branch windbreak.

The women do most of the gathering of plant shoots, roots and tuber, normally close to their camp site. The men range further, hunting all forms of animal – some caught by hand or run down, others secured with poisoned arrows fired from lightweight bows. Their bows and arrows are flimsy and inaccurate, and the bushmen rely on their expert stalking skills to get close enough (perhaps 20 m or 65 ft) to their prey. Animal skins provide elementary but effective clothing.

During the Kalahari winter these groups may fragment, each family living in a more substantial hut made of branches with a grass-and-leaf waterproof thatch, and relying on stored food and plant foods available locally. But as the wet season approaches fruit and tuber supplies become richer, and the family parties again coalesce into larger groupings.

A Tuareg tented camp in the northern Sahara. Commodious, but easily erected or dismantled, and made from animal skins, their tents are low-pitched to minimize wind resistance.

TRIBESMEN OF THE SAHARA

Far to the north, the characteristic people of the Sahara are the Tuareg. They are a Berber-speaking nomadic people, partly pastoralists, partly traders, who traverse the Sahara, largely on well-established routes, from north to south and east to west. Twentieth-century national boundaries, and conflicts, render the making of an accurate census of such a mobile people almost impossible. It is, however, thought that there may be between a quarter and half a million of them, mostly now Muslims. Their name derives from the Arabic for

'God-forsaken' and is thought to reflect not just their lives as travellers across the ultimate in God-forsaken terrain, but also their bloodthirsty habits of raiding both alien and neighbouring tribes. Such feuds may persist for decades, with regular bloodshed followed by equally regular reprisals.

Most Tuareg are fair-skinned and the men are usually veiled, a practical strategy for keeping out both heat and flying sand and dust. The blue cotton strip called a teguelmoust serves as a combined veil and turban.

Southern tribes tend to be more settled and pastoralist, raising camels and zebu cattle, many of which are

stolen in raids by, or sold in commerce to, their northern true desert-dwelling kinsfolk. These people are totally dependent on the camel for their existence as both nomads and traders – they run camel trains, carrying everything from metal ingots to dates and cloth, all over the Sahara. In former times they had a strictly hierarchical society, components of which still persist. There are noble, vassal and craftsmen classes or castes, and even the lower orders may keep Negro 'slaves' who act as herdsmen.

In the past elaborate swords and daggers, with leather shields, were their major weapons. Today, however, much of their feuding and raiding is carried out with the aid of high-powered rifles, and the Tuareg are excellent shots even off camel-back at full and ungainly gallop.

Their homes, mobile in the proper sense, are low, wide tents of animal skins, normally dyed red, but more makeshift frames covered in matting are used by some groups that are frequently on the move. Family or tribal groups merge into shifting confederations, normally with a geographical bias. They include the Ahaggar (or Hoggar), the Azjer (or Ajjer) in the north and the Asben (or Air Tuareg) in the south. Few Tuareg now hunt, and although food gathering is still carried out, most depend more heavily on grain crops grown in the favourable season and stored in primitive but effective silos. Otherwise, they depend on their herds.

The Bedouin derive the name by which the rest of the world knows them from the Arabic for 'people of the desert', but call themselves the Ahl-el-beit: the 'people of the tent'. Arabic-speaking, by tradition they are Mustarabs, naturalized Arabs descended from Ishmeel, in constrast to the true Arabs who trace their lineage to Noah's son Shem. The Bedouin are the wandering people, and from their origins in Arabia have spread over all the arid regions of the Middle East. There may be as many as 10 million of them. It is said that, although they constitute only one-tenth of the population of the Middle East, they use about nine-tenths of the land.

Bedouin hierarchy depends on the beasts that form the basis of their living. Prime among them are the camel raisers and drivers. Below them in order fall the sheep and goat nomads, then the cattle-driving nomads. There are also various merchant, artisan and

Overleaf A camel train about to depart on a desert crossing. Loaded with carefully balanced pannier bags while couched, camels even now have no equal as desert transport.

even entertainer castes. Their social organization is on the basis of tribes, each led by a sheik chosen for his qualities of leadership, or sometimes for his wealth or his courage in battle. Feuds are commonplace between tribes, and today many Bedouin tribes are active in jihads, the 'holy wars' that feature daily in the international press as a major aspect of Middle East politics, often almost incomprehensible to western eyes.

Though in general the Bedouin despise agriculture and manual labour, several tribes do settle in fertile areas close to oases to raise a cereal crop in the dry season. For fuel, they use camel dung. This, thanks to the superb desert adaptation of the camel's physiology, arrives almost dry and within hours is ready for burning.

Fiercely independent, despite their incessant blood feuds the Bedouin maintain a strict sense of honour and have a well-developed sense of hospitality towards travellers that is almost a law in itself. There is always a courteous welcome, ritual tea, and space in the typical black tent, pitched with its back to the wind on the sand, for the tired traveller. But things are changing. In Arabia roads (some excellent) and four-wheel-drive vehicles are displacing the shuttle of camel trains across the desert, and their nomadic Bedouin drivers are under pressure to settle in fixed communities. Although a sedentary life is far from their spiritual, physical and maybe physiological ideal, the settled population is growing.

THE AUSTRALIAN ABORIGINES

Amongst all desert peoples, those with least in the way of material possessions, and with a nomadic way of life closest to nature, are the Australian Aborigines. At the time of Captain James Cook's landing in 1770 near what is today Sydney, most estimates put the Aborigine population at about three hundred thousand, divided into something of the order of five hundred tribes or clans. Today the numbers are very much smaller, perhaps less than one-third of this figure, though the position is confused by mixed marriages with members of settler nations. Not surprisingly, the Aboriginal population density was highest in coastal and other areas with permanent water, but, given the appropriate season, Aborigines were once seen everywhere on the continent. The Aborigines of the desert interior were truly nomadic, each clan wandering, but with a purpose, over a territory whose size was determined by what nature provided in the way of food.

They were – and a very limited number still may be – hunter-gatherers. The circumstances of their harsh environment dictated that food-gathering groups were small and well spread-out. Cooperating in hunting or plant seeking was automatic, as was sharing the product of the collective endeavour. The Aborigines were sustained (and in some cases caused inexplicably to die) by a religious mysticism – the 'dreaming' or 'dreamtime' where mythical and actual beings and animals blended, as did the natural and the supernatural. This is difficult to interpret and to compare with modern western beliefs or those of Asiatic cultures. But when an Aborigine elder went 'walkabout' in the outback, communing with nature and the spirit world, he probably did little that differs, spiritually or physically, from the lives of hermits and mystics. Nor was he significantly different from a member of a Christian religion undertaking a formal 'retreat' and isolating himself from the tumult of the everyday world. As with most religious beliefs, the Aborigine saw himself as a simple component of a much larger spiritual whole.

Out in the bush, large Aborigine groups came together for gatherings called corroborees, but did not camp together for long. Effective hunter-gatherer teams operated out of stable camps in favourable seasons or habitats; when conditions were poorer, forays were far longer, often involving several days' absence from camp, particularly for the hunters. Usually a series of waterholes would be visited, following well-worn pathways and a well-proven calendar.

Rarely did base camps last for more than a couple of weeks. The normal pattern was for the men to be the hunters, the women the gatherers or food collectors. In both cases the location of animals or plants suitable for food seemed to be achieved almost by instinct, quite unnerving in its accuracy and in the minuteness of the signs that had to be interpreted before food was located. In the more advanced areas of the world, with settled communities and the development in parallel of agriculture and industry, a level of civilization has been reached which has resulted in the deadening of many of the 'animal' senses doubtless once possessed by all humans.

Such little property as the Aborigines possessed had to be easily carried as they moved about. Heavier items like grinding and pounding stones (just appropriately shaped local rocks) were left at camp sites, with cooking stones and flat 'platters', ready for use on their eventual return and in the certain knowledge that pilfering would not occur.

The men would carry with them their most important hunting weapons – a varied collection of spears, a

throwing stick for greater range and accuracy, and boomerangs. In areas where tribal fights occurred, clubs and bull-roarers, whirled overhead on a leather thong to strike terror into the opposition, would also be carried.

The women would carry a few stone and bone tools, together with their all-important digging stick, strong and sharp-pointed, which would double as a weapon if fighting broke out. Some groups would have hollowed-out wooden bowls, or bark or plaited-leaf baskets and bags to carry food – and sometimes babies.

On the face of it, the Aborigine lifestyle could be classed as a bare subsistence ecomony, an unending struggle for survival against nature. Certainly skills in tracking both animals and plants were paramount, and life was often tough and demanded tenacity of purpose. The Aborigines possessed enough of this quality to allow art, music and a wide variety of social functions like corroborees to feature in their lives, and still had ample time for their mystical religion.

Somewhere in the tribe would be a musician-storyteller, who would take with him various apparently primitive but evocatively effective musical instru-

The Australian Aborigine, best adapted of all humans to life in the desert.

ments. The stories would be passed on in an oral tradition, with nothing written down, but most groups would also indulge in the visual arts. Cave-painting techniques and drawings on bark were surprisingly well developed, using earth and fire pigments with water, sap or simply spit. This artistry persists to the present day, with clearly recognizable animals and hand imprints ranged amongst mythical objects. Sometimes the knowledge of animal anatomy was surprisingly precise: Aborigine drawings of the barramundi fish show the stomach stones that they commonly swallow to reduce their buoyancy in the creeks.

Interestingly, and in marked contrast to all the other desert-dwelling peoples of the world, almost all Aborigines went naked. Some tribes would have cloaks or blankets of bark for protection at night from the cold, but most relied on the warmth of the camp fire. The heat in central Australia is no less intense than in the other major 'hot' deserts, and clothing would certainly have served the same valuable function as it does for the Tuareg and Bedouin peoples. But until the coming of 'white men' and their sheep, though there were kangaroo and wallaby skins no Australian animal possessed hair or wool suitable for weaving. And in any case the technology of weaving had simply not developed in what could be called, though not disparagingly, a Stone Age relic culture. Skins, or alternatively eucalyptus tree bark, would become rigidly inflexible in the heat and thus impractical as clothing. Hence the Aborigines went without, relying on their instinctive nomadic capabilities for survival.

The more recent history of the Aborigines has been tragic, perhaps paralleled only by that of the American Indians. Their culture and traditions were starkly alien to those of the western colonists who invaded their land. Conflict was inevitable since the early settlers considered the Aborigines as troublesome competitors, who fought back with primitive weapons but advanced

guerilla warfare skills. The kangaroos competed for grazing with the imported sheep and cattle and were consequently slaughtered in millions. Tribal lands were swept into the new Australia with no consideration for their native inhabitants or their highly adapted lifestyle. Aborigine mysticism, with the open spaces and sacred pathways their cathedrals, the wild animals and plants the equivalent of their religious texts, had no part to play in the opening up of a new country and its establishment to nationhood on a world stage. Less than fifty years ago, the Australian government just did not count Aborigines as part of the Australian nation – both metaphorically and literally, as they had no civil rights and were not even counted in population censuses.

Aborigine cave painting of barramundi fish: mystic meaning coupled with unexpected anatomical accuracy.

Massive tracts of former Aborigine land were devoted not just to ranching, but to altogether more destructive operations like the testing of nuclear weapons.

The tide has now turned dramatically, but surely too late. Though much of their traditional land can be reclaimed, vast tracts have been despoiled – effectively for ever in the case of the nuclear test regions. The other facets of the imposition of western-style civilization have made perhaps a fatal impact on the Aborgines themselves, particularly in their contact with a range of diseases including alcohol addiction. Can the Aborigines' unique mystical religion recover from the onslaught of missionary-taught Christianity? Can the old, natural, ways of life recover, and be acceptable, once the trappings, survival strategies and creature comforts of modern civilization – motor vehicles, medicines, prepared food, rifles, radio and television, the list is endless – have taken hold? The most difficult question of all to answer is 'Should they?'

The origins of the Australian Aborigine people are shrouded in mystery. Though they are not Negroid, Polynesian or Mongoloid, their racial ancestry too is obscure. How, and when, they reached Australia – from wherever they set out – remains the subject of speculation. The most popular theories involve an overland trek from the 'cradles of civilization' in Africa and Asia, followed by boat or raft crossings of the inter-island straits along the Malay–Indonesian archipelago. Certainly they were not cast adrift, as it were, like the marsupials when Australia parted company with Gondwanaland.

THE AMERICAN INDIANS

The origins of the American Indians are far better understood, though their recent history shows sharply tragic similarities to that of the Aborigine. There is general agreement that North America, and subsequently South America, was first invaded by peoples of Mongoloid stock during the last great glaciation or ice age. At this time so much of the earth's surface water was locked up in the production of ice sheets that sea levels fell, establishing land-bridges between previously isolated countries. They even linked continents, as in the case of North America, where what is now Alaska was linked to present-day Siberia by a land-bridge across the Bering Strait. That journey could certainly have been accomplished, even by peoples with primitive skills and equipment. It is difficult to imagine the climate at the time being other than extremely cold in such northerly latitudes. This cannot have made the

journey easy, but the facial and other anatomical features, together with language and cultural structures, offer clear and widely accepted evidence of the relationships between the American Indians and the Mongol peoples.

Climatology, geography and history (through radio-carbon dating technology) combine to place this invasion at nine to ten thousand years ago. There is ample evidence that at about this time desert Indian cultures existed in the Great Basin. So the spread of the colonizing tribes across the Americas, and their separation into distinct and identifiable cultures, must have been rapid.

On the vast central plains, the prairie lands, huge herds of buffalo, deer and antelope provided a major food source for hunting Indians. But game animals were comparatively scarce in the desert of the Great Basin, placing greater emphasis on the gatherer than on the hunter in the hunter-gatherer societies that became established. As elsewhere in the world's desert areas, groups were small and wandered seasonally from one area to another as various plants and seeds became available. Obviously any animals that could be caught were eaten, but even in the earliest-known tribes apparatus for grinding plant seeds into flour had been developed.

The earliest of the peoples probably used caves as shelters where they could, and made makeshift camps elsewhere. Probably they knew their territories well, and could readily locate shelter, water and food plants within them. They would have carried out their nomadic migrations instinctively, rather than on a pre-planned basis. Both plant and animal fibres were available to them, and there is plentiful evidence that they wove or plaited baskets, mats and clothing, and even made sandals that must have been invaluable in cactus country. Like the Australian Aborigines the men were hunters, armed with spears and, interestingly, a throwing stick for greater range. The women, again in parallel with Australia, found and ground roots and seeds, and fleshy fruits like gourds and squashes in season. They carried a pointed digging stick as their main tool. Some hunters used spearheads of knapped flint or obsidian, and stone axes. Though constructed in a primitive way, these were skilfully and effectively produced.

This pattern of life continued in the northern parts of the Great Basin until comparatively recently, when many of the tribes or families took to hunting on horseback in the style of the Plains Indians. Then came the destruction of civilization as they knew it when European settlers pressed westward in search of new ground from their established bases in what is now New England.

Further to the south, in the 'hot' desert area of the Great Basin in what are now Arizona, New Mexico, Utah, Texas, Colorado and Mexico, the Indians lived differently. Rather than shifting the bias of their lifestyle towards hunting, where possible they turned to more settled, village-style permanent farming. This was Pueblo Indian territory, within which the two best-known groups are the Hopi and the Zuni. Though their ancestors had roamed the Great Basin regions for thousands of year, it was at about the time of the birth of Christ that their development reached a peak.

The Hopi, from the high, dry Colorado plateau, endured more difficult physical conditions than the Zuni. They coped with their major problem, lack of water for stable crop systems, in two interdependent ways – one technological, the other social. Technologically, they harnessed flood-waters to form crude irrigation systems, and farmed cereals that had evolved to cope with dry conditions. Socially, they relied on a high degree of cooperation between families in sharing resources such as labour and food; each Hopi played a full part in the success of the tribe. Though capable, again collectively, in self-defence, they were never aggressive, but put their energy and resources to better, self-sufficient, use. The Hopi were the prototype of an almost utopian society, sober, peaceful and well organized. Their social framework included the forerunners of parliaments and committees, the basis of today's democratic decision-making machinery.

The Zuni people had access to more predictable waterholes and river courses, and therefore to a more stable food supply. This allowed the development of a considerably more elaborate lifestyle, with heavy emphasis on ceremonials and dancing. This emphasis was if anything increased as the first European 'invaders', the Spanish conquistadores, started to press in on Zuni territory – the reason was partly to distract the foreigners from the more materially valuable elements of Zuni culture.

But the Pueblo tribes are best known for their extraordinarily competent and effective desert architecture. Few houses have been built since with such a comparatively cool interior atmosphere. They were made of stone or adobe mud, with thick walls and small windows to maximize both shade and insulation. The stonework was crafted to an exceptional degree of skill, with faultless close-fitting joints. In their most famous sites, the Pueblo built homes by facing cliff-side caves and ledges, reached by a network of ladders. They had inbuilt water-storage cisterns and grain-storage silos, and once the ladders had been drawn up the occupants were safe from attack and could survive extended sieges.

In about AD 1000, two other major Indian groups swept into the southern Great Basin, in all probability reasonably fresh invaders originating in the far north of what is now Canada. These were the Navajo and the Apache. The Navajo took over the Pueblo culture and adapted, modified and improved it, especially in agriculture, weaving and the various art forms. The Apaches earned their reputation here, retaining a life heavily dependent on hunting and on raiding other, more peaceful tribes, killing and stealing food and livestock. This lifestyle brought them, perhaps more than any other tribe, into armed conflict with European settlers.

Conflict between the Indian tribes, both those living peacefully and militant groups like the Apaches, began with the Spanish incursions in 1540. From then on, though fluctuating, the pressure of the better-organized, better-armed and far more numerous colonialists was relentless. Inexorably the Indian tribes were driven from their territories, often with great loss of life. After a couple of centuries of running warfare the survivors were defeated, disenfranchised and disheartened. They were removed from most of their cultural and spiritual homeland to be corralled in official Indian Reservations. As with the Australian Aborigines, European diseases, alcohol and the lack of a recognizable lifestyle to call their own brought these once-proud peoples close to extinction. Attitudes have now changed, and are continuing to do so, but as with the Aborigines it is surely too late to redress the balance, even if it were today appropriate to try to put the clock back.

PEOPLES OF THE DESERT CORRIDOR OF ASIA

Since the central Asian Desert Corridor was the point of origin for the American Indians, traversing through what are now Mongolia, Manchuria and Siberia to cross the ice age land-bridge into North America, it is

The 'White House', one of the most striking examples of Pueblo Indian building skills, set in a cave high in an Arizonan cliff face in the southern United States.

perhaps not surprising to find cultural as well as facial similarities between the two groups of peoples. As in the Great Basin, the topography of the Desert Corridor allowed both settled farmers and pastoral nomads to develop.

Again as in America, the settled farmers lived in villages of sun-dried mud-brick houses, close to the more fertile soils. With care and skill, and an amazing understanding of the ways of water, they conserved such rainfall as they could, cultivating fast-growing cereals and using irrigation canals to widen the area of land suitable for cropping. As with the Hopi Pueblos, community feeling was strong and cooperation essential for survival. In the turbulent times of the Mongol Empire in the thirteenth and fourteenth centuries, under rulers like the notorious Genghis Khan, these fragile enclaves were quickly destroyed; but they were equally quickly recreated.

The herding peoples lived very different lives, out on the open, windswept desert and steppe. For them, home was a felt tent stretched over a portable wooden frame. As their stock needed to move on to fresh pasture, so did they, following ancient tracks established by their ancestors perhaps centuries earlier, and defended against other groups. Many almost lived on horseback as they tended their animals, which ranged from horses, asses and camels to sheep, goats and cattle. The upland Mongols also domesticated the yak. These grazing peoples traded stock with the village farmers and with people in neighbouring countries like China, where no land could be spared for grazing. In return, the farmers provided the pastoralists with cereal foods like flour. Whereas the settled farmers were densely packed into their communities and vulnerable to attack, the nomadic herdsmen were thinly spread and mobile – if they had not been, the poor desert soil could not have supported their herds, and they would have suffered more at the hands of marauding bands.

Such systems were probably in existence some hundreds of years before the birth of Christ, and persisted, with fluctuating fortunes, almost unchanged until the early twentieth century. Then the Russian Revolution made its mark, and the new Soviet Union began to enforce communist thinking on the further-flung outposts of its territories.

A CRUEL ADVERSARY FOR EXPLORERS

Trading was always an implicit part of life here, and many centuries ago the Desert Corridor became a corridor in another sense. It led from the growth points of civilization in the Near and Middle East across to the Orient, the fabulous source of silks, spices and other precious goods. In the absence of an established sea route from one to the other, it had to be in the Desert Corridor, despite its hazards, that trade routes became established. Further to the south ran the impenetrable ranges of the Himalayas, to the north the impassable summer swamps and winter snows of central Russia.

So exploration of the apparently hostile and unknown lands between the two became a necessity for the major trading powers of Europe. The best-known of these early 'commercial travellers' was the Venetian Marco Polo, who in 1271 set out with his father and uncle to cross the desert wastes of central Asia and meet the Mongol Emperor Kublai Khan. It was twenty-four years before he saw Venice again.

Genuine exploration is essentially a journey into the unknown, and therefore the unpredictable. The potentially lethal nature of this unpredictability is brought home with some regularity even now, in the days of four-wheel-drive vehicles and sophisticated communications; but there are few accounts more graphic than that of Burke and Wills and their attempt to cross the 'red centre' of Australia in 1860. Six centuries after the Venetian embassy deserts were still harsh and unremitting places, and not all those who attempted to unravel their mysteries returned, like Marco Polo, to tell their tales.

Before Burke and Wills traversed this huge continent for the first time other explorers, equally intrepid, had laid the groundwork. The opening up of the Australian heartland demonstrates the particular rigours of desert exploration, which are just as applicable today as they were a hundred years ago and more.

In the early nineteenth century, the pressures to explore the vast unknown centre were extreme. In less than half a century the state of Victoria had expanded from a few isolated and remote homesteads surrounded by enormous ranch-like farms, through the frenetic drama of the gold rushes and the accompanying social upheaval and lawlessness, to become one of the most prosperous parts of Australia. Its adventurous population could raise ample financial backing to expand the boundaries of their territory.

Explorers set out not just to find yet more grazing land, but because of the popular theory that beyond the arid northern borders of Victoria lay an inland sea like the Mediterranean or Caspian. Australians based this belief on the fact that the major rivers, later named the Murray, Darling and Murrumbidgee, all rose in the mountains behind the east coast but flowed westwards, towards the *terra incognita* of the interior. Finding this inland sea, combined with the achievement of being first to cross the continent from coast to coast, became the goal of many an intrepid adventurer.

Among the earliest was Charles Sturt (1795–1869), a British army officer who was posted to Australia to take charge of a penal settlement. After a severe drought in the settled coastal regions in 1828, Sturt and a party of fellow explorers set off literally in search of pastures new. They followed the Macquarie River to its confluence with a large west-flowing river which he named after the Governor of Victoria, Darling. On a later expedition Sturt actually took a boat into the desert with him, so convinced was he of the existence of the mythical inland sea. Instead, he came across and named the Murray River.

A colleague, Edward Eyre, ventured into the interior in 1840. Ill-health – the result of privations endured on his previous expeditions – prevented Sturt from accompanying Eyre into the salt deserts around the aptly named Mount Hopeless. But four years later Sturt felt strong enough to travel north from Adelaide, despite the fact that the weather was against him – it was one of the hottest summers ever recorded. The temperature rose to over 130°F (55°C) in the shade and close on 160°F (72°C) in the sun. Screws popped out of their holes in wooden boxes, and the men's hair and fingernails stopped growing. Disease affected the team – in particular scurvy, because they had nothing in their diet to prevent it. One man died.

After rain eventually came, Sturt sent some of the men back to Adelaide and then pressed on north with the others to Fort Grey. Here he and a companion, Harris-Browne, found and named the infamous Stony Desert, where the stones cut their boots and the horses' hooves to shreds. Although Sturt still felt that good land lay ahead, they continued to encounter nothing but rock, stones and sand. At last he had to concede defeat, commenting in his journal on how unbelievably awful the rigours of the region and its climate were. The journey on horseback from Fort Grey and back had covered some 900 miles (1450 km), and they had penetrated almost halfway across the 'red centre', appreciably further than anyone before them.

The next attempt – the ill-fated, eighteen-strong expedition led by Robert O'Hara Burke, with W. J. Wills as second-in-command – left Melbourne in August 1860. They planned to cross the continent, now the most eagerly sought ambition of all Australian explorers. Because of the hot competition Burke and Wills's plans probably received more publicity than preparation.

The caravan of men and animals was soon in minor trouble, as the heavily loaded supply horses could not keep up the necessary pace. As a result, when the exploration party arrived at their base camp at Cooper's Creek their food stores were still some way behind. At his backers' insistence Burke, Wills and two companions, George Grey and John King, set out alone to continue their journey. Despite the customary appalling hazards and climatic conditions they reached the north of Australia in February 1861, and only impenetrable bush and mangrove swamps prevented them actually standing on the shore of the Gulf of Carpentaria.

The real horrors were to occur on the homeward journey. First Grey died, primarily of exhaustion, on the way back to Cooper's Creek. Before they left, Burke had ordered the back-up party to wait there with reserve stores until they returned – or at least for three months. But by the most terrible twist of fate, having waited for four months the base camp party departed only hours before the three half-starved survivors, with Wills too now near to death, arrived.

In their exhausted, weakened state errors of judgement were made. Wills, too far gone to travel, was left behind with food and water while Burke and King inadvisedly decided to head south for Adelaide rather than wait in reasonable security for a rescue expedition. Within two days Burke was dead from exhaustion. King then returned to Cooper's Creek – to find Wills had also died. For some months King, now the sole survivor of the little party that had achieved so much, wandered around the Cooper's Creek area, cared for and fed by Aborigines.

Meanwhile, complacency in Melbourne had been gingered into acute anxiety by Wills's father, and soon after the return of the back-up party a rescue mission was sent. In due course they encountered the almost unrecognizable King. They buried Wills and collected his diary, meticulously kept up until his dying hours.

Today there is a statue of Burke and Wills in Melbourne, commemorating the first crossing of Australia. In its way, this is a memorial also to the tragically misguided enthusiasm and mismanagement that dogged the expedition from beginning to end, and to the fact that, in pitting their wits, skills and endurance against the desert, human beings should never underestimate their opponent.

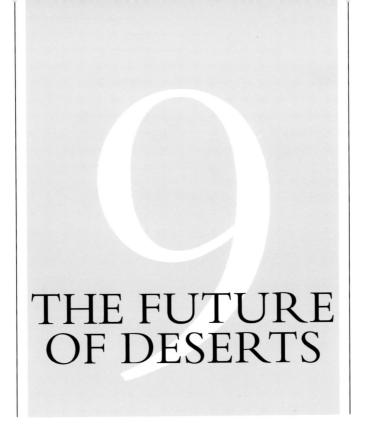

THE FUTURE
OF DESERTS

Over the centuries human beings have explored their planet in different ways for different reasons. The commercial challenge of opening up new regions for exploitation persists. Nationalistic and commercial enthusiasm of the kind that initiated the colonial expansion of the British, Dutch, French, Portuguese and Spanish several hundred years ago may have passed, but its equivalent can still be detected in the international politics which enmesh the future of Antarctica. Enthusiasm for exploration has been fired more powerfully by the increasing sophistication of modern communications. News travels phenomenally fast today compared with even a century ago, and entrepreneurs are demanding that the remaining 'hidden quarters' of the globe be opened up.

More than any other habitat on earth except the polar ice caps, the desert has remained largely unmarked by human activity. The tracks by which Marco Polo crossed the Gobi in the thirteenth century are still used today, and they are not metalled roads. The Sahara, in the heart of civilization, is still traversed by only a handful of hard-standing routes: here and there tarmac roads exist, but there are no proper highways. In America, highways do cross some of the deserts, but they are desolate places which travellers hasten along, and lack the ribbons of urban and industrial development so typical of other highways in the United States. In Africa, it is true that four-wheel-drive vehicles have frequently taken over the role of the camel, but we still shun desert travel, preferring to overfly the hazard in modern aircraft.

Fascinating comparisons can still be drawn. To cross the Sahara, modern jet aircraft need a maintained network of radio beacons, coupled with in-flight navigational equipment. The systems and computers involved occupy the space of a small room and demand the attention of highly trained crew. But a willow warbler, *en route* from its breeding grounds in northern Europe to winter quarters in the tropical African bush, finds both locations with pinpoint navigational precision – overflying the Sahara non-stop in the process. It weighs about 10 g ($\frac{1}{3}$ oz) and its brain is smaller than a pea. Yet in that brain are contained the equivalents of the chronometer, the maps, the compass and the sextant necessary to accomplish the journey with such accuracy. Clearly nature has the edge.

Our greatest need to penetrate into the inhospitable fastnesses of the desert centre is in the search for fossil fuel in the form of oil. Currently the developed world's major energy source, oil exists beneath the Arabian desert in enormous quantities not yet fully explored and assessed. The revenue from oil has revolutionized life in

A drilling rig in the desert.

the Gulf States of the Middle East, leading to the development of, amongst other things, some of the most advanced architecture in the world.

Yet although oil exploration and extraction has led to the building of roads in some desert areas, the vast majority of the old 'Arabia Deserta' remains just that. Oil wells and their adjacent buildings are essentially functional, and have taken no trappings of social civilization into the heart of the desert. Each well houses its staff, often in air-conditioned comfort, in the minimum of space, and the staff itself are limited to those necessary for the oil to be extracted, and for wells, pumps and pipelines to function efficiently. The population growth, and the spread of sophisticated civilization that accompanies oil riches, is concentrated almost entirely on the coasts.

In the past, many desert tribespeople were war-like. Perhaps they had to be in order to defend their living space and food needs in such a harsh environment, but their bellicose nature has become firmly embedded in their way of life and even in their culture. Skirmishes between tribes, between sheikdoms or between small nation states are routine; what has changed is the way these essentially tribal wars are fought. The weaponry has advanced so far from the dagger, sword and rifle of the Bedouin that major damage can be caused and massive casualties accrue. Such is the speed of international communications, and such are international politics, that any such skirmish can easily explode into a major conflict involving troops from far-distant countries.

Resilient though the desert is, as the tactics of such

warfare enlarge it is inevitable that the ecosystem will be seriously harmed. The Gulf War of 1990–91 signals more than the toll in human lives, human misery and pollution. The desert ecosystem cannot tolerate oil wells burning for months, nor the litter of carcasses of destroyed aircraft, military vehicles and weaponry. Much was made of the tragic spectacle of oil pollution in the shallow waters of the Persian Gulf; but we know little of the immediate or, more important, the ultimate impact of even greater oil spillages on the desert sands. Politically, and sadly also ecologically, the fate of the desert ecosystem in the Middle East has been largely ignored.

Deserts are among the world's few remaining unmolested wild places. They contain fascinating wildlife, adapted to survival in some of the harshest conditions imaginable. Fears are growing by the day over the potentially disastrous middle- to long-term impact of global warming, and of more land turning to desert not just in the subtropics but further afield. As temperatures rise and rainfall diminishes, never has it been more important for us to understand how deserts function and to conserve the genetic material that exists within them. We simply cannot afford to contribute to the wanton destruction of desert lands and the plants and creatures that dwell in them. The human race ignores desert ecosystems at its peril.

An astonishing array of plants and creatures have successfully colonized the world's deserts. Understanding just how they survive must become a major research priority. This desert scene is in South Australia.

FURTHER READING

The research for a book of this nature leads the author far and wide in a search to augment his own experience. Over the last century our understanding of plant and animal ecology has expanded enormously, no less in the desert habitat than in any other. A huge number of research workers have contributed to the store of published knowledge on deserts. Over this time others have analysed, condensed and summarized the information available on the topics of prime interest to themselves, and in so doing have compiled valuable catalogues of detailed references that substantially assist the more general researcher.

The list that follows is far from comprehensive. It contains those works that have been of major interest and assistance to me in writing this book. The titles of some may imply that a dauntingly unreadable text lies between the covers – it does not. Others may seem to be directed at a popular readership and therefore perhaps low on science – again, they are not: all contain valid and valuable scientific information, presented in an easily assimilable format. All, through their own comprehensive lists of references, allow as deep a search of the literature as is likely to be achieved, and all offer further insights into that most hostile yet fascinating environment, the desert.

Abbey, E., *Cactus Country*, Time-Life Books, 1973

Buxton, P. A., *Animal Life in Deserts*, Edward Arnold, 1923

Cloudesley-Thompson, J. L. (ed.), *Symposium on the Biology of Hot and Cold Deserts*, Institute of Biology, London, 1954

Cloudesley-Thompson, J. L. and Chadwick, M. J., *Life in Deserts*, Foulis, 1964

Colwell, M., *The Journey of Burke and Wills*, Paul Hamlyn, 1971

Esau, K., *Plant Anatomy*, John Wiley and Sons, 1953

Esau, K., *Anatomy of Seed Plants*, John Wiley and Sons, 1960

Grime, J. P., *Plant Strategies and Vegetation Processes*, John Wiley and Sons, 1979

Hollom, P. A. D., Porter, R. F., Christensen, S. and Willis, I., *Birds of the Middle East and North Africa*, T. and A. D. Poyser, 1989

Jaeger, E. C., *The North American Deserts*, Stanford University Press, 1957

Jaeger, E. C., *Desert Wildlife*, Stanford University Press, 1961

Jaeger, E. C., *Desert Wild Flowers*, Stanford University Press, 1967

Leakey, R. E., *The Making of Mankind*, Michael Joseph, 1981

McGinnies, W. G. and Goldman, B. J., *Deserts of the World*, University of Arizona Press, 1968

McKinnon, M., *Arabia – Sand, Sea, Sky*, BBC, 1990

Monod, T., *Méharées-Explorations au Vrai Sahara*, Editions Je Sers, 1937

Monod, T., *Les Déserts*, Horizons de France, 1973

Paine, B., *The Green Centre*, BBC/André Deutsch, 1976

Schmidt-Nielson, K., *Desert Animals. Physiological Problems of Heat and Water*, Oxford University Press, 1964

Serventy, D., 'Biology of Desert Birds' in *Avian Biology*, ed. D. S. Farner and J. R. King, Vol. 1, Academic Press, 1971

Swift, J., *The Sahara*, Time-Life Books, 1975

Vandenbeld, J., *The Nature of Australia*. BBC/ABC/William Collins Pty, 1988

INDEX

Page numbers in *italic* refer to illustrations.

574.5
FLE

Flegg, Jim.

Deserts.

$29.95

574.5
FLE

Flegg, Jim.

Deserts.